JAACOV

[Pronounced Yah-cove]

Ancient Hebrew – Ya'aqov

Modern English – Jacob

Author

Lynn Zack Wardlaw

For more about the Author: www.lynnzwardlaw.com

DEDICATION

This book is dedicated to the members of ISLE of HOPE BAPTIST CHURCH. The encouragement, patience and love of these fine Christians inspired the writing of "JAACOV." Particular thanks go to Daphne Chestnut for her editing of the book. The character "Jaacov" was inspired by a dramatic performance of Michael V. Dant as "Nicodemus."

Copyright 2014 Wardlaw Publishing CO.

Savannah Georgia

PREFACE

The author had some acting experience, playing parts in Church plays and even had a couple of plays he directed for the Christian Spectrum, an acting group in Savannah, Georgia.

His numerous grandchildren and great grands enjoyed his portrayal of an old shepherd telling of witnessing the night Jesus was born.

He often wondered how the great story of the shepherd's encounter with the Heavenly Host the night Jesus was born made it into the Bible. Thus was born young Jaacov, an orphaned sheep herder, who was chosen by God to live a selfless life. Jaacov went about the tasks appointed by God and never knew why, until he faced his final day on earth. He never questioned his calls, this simple man that only wanted to tend his sheep, but always answered and never knew to what heights he rose in his simple life.

Jaacov is a revealing story of the realism of knowing God and accepting Jesus. Jaacov is a fictional person, but as you read of his life and see how it entwines with the lives of Jesus and the Roman Centurion, Cornelius, he will come to life and you will love him as the author loves him.

The idea of Jaacov was the authors, but the story was inspired by the Holy Spirit. He would read what he had written the day before and often wondered where he was going with this. It may sound foolish, but the words on these pages and the wisdom of the author are worlds apart.

Who knows? There may be more truth to this story than reads the eye.

INDEX

CHAPTER I

The Star

"The cold is early tonight." I spoke not really caring if Malisch even heard or not. The heat of the day had not been bad, as our winter was really just beginning. The sheep huddled together, not for warmth, their full coats kept them warm, even on the coldest nights. It would be at least three months before they would be ready for the shear. It was not the chill that brought them together, it was the scent of the wolves that always lurked about at the hour after the sun had vanished over the hills to our west.

The wolves were there every night. If there were no wolves, it was a sign a lion was near. We much preferred the wolves. I tossed my flints to Malisch as he prepared the brush and scrub wood we had accumulated for our supper fire. I caught sight of the lone wolf as he broached a low ridge. He was beginning his stealthy approach to the flock at a point farthest away from our now blazing fire.

Sheep are not the wisest of creatures and much prefer the calm of a huddle as opposed to the scramble of a chase. If the wolf approaches with reasonable caution, it can take a lamb or weak adult with little problem. A reasonably sized sheep will feed a pack of a half dozen wolves for a few days. We sometimes would sacrifice a sickly sheep just for a couple of, somewhat, peaceful nights.

Tonight was not to be that case. I am Jaacov and at age twelve could not remember anything other than tending sheep. My master would come to our flock sometimes and bring our supply of grain and dried fruits along with the skins of wine that kept us going through the brilliant days and crisp starry nights. He would look over the flock and voice his approval and give instruction as to where we should be in a few days. He would always know if we had lost too many sheep to the wildlife in the country side around Bethlehem. I did not relish his displeasure. He was a just man, but his staff would embellish his mood and I preferred not to excite his anger.

I caught Malisch's attention and with a head nod indicated I was going for the wolf. His body movements indicated "why bother," but my mind was made up. No wolf was going to take one of my flock this night.

On rare occasions I heard some of the older shepherds ask for help from someone named Elohim. No one ever claimed ownership of this Elohim and all seemed to have great respect and expectation from him. There were times that men even called out for this Elohim to damn someone or something and from their actions they seemed fully confident this Elohim would answer their pleas. I called upon his name for help. I felt no reassurance.

I never had a wolf attack me, but heard terrible stories how they could main or kill a human, especially a youth. I picked a stone from my tunic and placed it in the small leather pouch of my sling. I quickly circled the flock and approached the far side of the now somewhat nervous sheep. I was on the down side of the wind so the wolf did not smell me. The animal was now fully focused on a fairly small ewe standing tensely on the outskirts of the flock. The now fully dark night did little to illuminate the wolf, but I could see the dark shadowy figure as it rapidly approached the hapless ewe.

My heart beat wildly in my chest. I felt sure the wild beast would hear my heart. Apparently the wolf had never heard the whir of a swinging sling before and as the mighty creature launched its lunge at the startled sheep the missile struck the creature somewhere on the side of its head. The addled beast stumbled to the side and stopped in a confused state. I was on him in an instant. My staff fell across the top of his head with all the strength my young limbs could muster. The creature yelped with pain and confusion. My staff was now a weapon of death. The sharpened point, kept that way by delicate sharpening and tempered by fire stoking was finding its way to the heart of the now convulsing beast It lay silent. I thanked Elohim. I felt, as if, whoever this great man was had somehow helped me. I lugged the animal's carcass to a nearby jujube tree and draped it across a lower limb. I hoped it would be a sign to other wolves in the pack to stay clear of Jaacov's sheep.

Malisch and I shared a great bustard we had snared the day before at the base of the western hills. The roasted bird was relished as we munched away our meal of bird and grain, washed down by draughts of weak wine from the skin. We slept in shifts as we shared the watch over our entrusted flock.

Tomorrow would be a long day as we had to make the trek to the oasis near the road from Jerusalem to Bethlehem. We had to make our arrival before the caravans arrived. Sheep are not very bright and make quite a mess when they water. We must get our flock watered and away from the oasis so the water can settle before the caravans arrive or we would be in much trouble.

Malisch was a little older than me, but had no advantage in size or knowledge of sheep. He was the youngest son of the Master's head farmer. He was shepherding only as a trainee for some job higher on the Master's list of responsible positions.

Malisch had some tutoring in ciphering and some nights after a meal he would explain the process to me. It was not difficult to understand. The reasoning behind the giving and taking of numbers was only common sense, but the names given to the process was necessary in order to communicate with another the significance of the number.

The moon had risen only a few days since it was full. The days equaled the number of fingers on my hand. To me, this was sensible, but the Master wanted to hear the word five, instead of me indicating the fingers on my hand.

We had lost a sickly ewe and a lamb since the Master visited us seven days ago. Seven was a hand and two fingers of the other hand. The ewe and lamb were two fingers and two was the word I would use to indicate the loss, he would not be happy. He never punished us for a loss, but his ire was enough to make us feel responsible. We wanted him to be happy.

The passage to the oasis was easterly as we herded the sheep through the rocky terrain and then to the gleaned fields near Bethlehem. The harvest had been plentiful that year and the poor had finished the gleaning, so the farmers allowed the flocks to take the remaining stalks of grain for their meals. We shepherds had to keep the animals moving, because a sheep in its limited intelligence would eat the shoot right down to the ground and then pull the roots from the earth. An unattended flock will make a field go fallow and leave a dusty plain, if allowed to stay too long.

There were numerous flocks in the fields and some of the shepherds had dogs. It made a shepherd's job easy if he had a dog. Our dog had died last spring as he attacked a young lion that was laying waste to our flock. The lion was just into his adult years and was making sport of the easy kills. We admired the courage of the dog as he never hesitated in his attack on the beast. Our dog could probably have driven the great cat away by harassment, but chose, instead, to go for a frontal attack and was no match for the giant jaws of the young lion.

The beast killed six of our sheep before retreating with a ewe to feast. The Master took some hunters and tracked the lion to its lair and dispatched the beast with their lances. The lances then had to be hidden as the Romans, strictly forbid such a formidable weapon. The only weapon a Hebrew could have was a knife or short sword. The only exceptions were the Temple and Palace guards. They could have shields, but still no lances

Most of the other flocks had drunk their fill at the oasis, but our sheep were very thirsty, so we proceeded to move them into the palms for water. There were only a few travelers on the far side of the oasis so our sheep was not a hindrance to them. We kept the sheep from moving around too much as they would muddy the water very quickly.

We shepherds are fairly used to the heavy smell of sheep, but when its wool gets wet, there is no getting used to the pungent scent.

Malisch and I were sloshing in the water's edge when a small caravan topped the low rise from Jerusalem.   The caravan consisted of a mixed group on foot along with a half dozen camels and a single Roman guard. At the end of the entourage was a woman seated on a donkey and escorted by a tall man of obvious Hebrew origin. As the small band approached, it was obvious the smell was affecting them. Some of the women in the group spoke to the guard and he immediately spurred his mount to a trot and advanced on Malisch and me with a scowl on his face.

Romans were always a curiosity to us. They seldom attempted to socialize with Hebrews and hardly ever paid any attention to shepherds, but this guard was on a mission. His clean shaven face clearly read discontent. He was probably planning on a nice quite respite at the oasis, but the smell and water, now seemingly fouled by our sheep, had brought complaints.   He probably felt his gratuity would be affected.

I understood little of the harsh rhetoric that the soldier rained down on us. He forced his mount into the water and with his lance began to prod a lamb that was too slow in exiting the water to suite him. I shouted. "Leave my lamb alone!" The soldier's attention was immediately focused on me as I waded out to retrieve the confused lamb.

He leered at me as he spurred his horse between me and the lamb, now stumbling in the water due to the lance prodding. I quickly ducked under the massive steed and swept the bleating lamb up in my arms. The soldier turned in the saddle and thrust his lance in an attempt to block my path. I don't think he intended to harm me, but the sharp edge of the lance sliced into the upper part of my right arm. The pain was not intense and I continued my retreat out of the water and placed the little lamb on the ground. It immediately dashed to the flock, bleating for its mother. I turned my attention back to the Roman soldier as he sat astride his mighty mount and gazed at me with an intensity that made my knees weak.

He spoke lowly in halting Arabic as the caravan began to partake of the oasis' bounty. "I shall never understand you Hebrews – you are so independent!"

I noticed the tall Hebrew man was leading the woman on the donkey to a spot near where the Roman sat upon his mount.

The soldier continued. "You placed the safety of that little sheep above your own and defied a soldier of the mighty Caesar Augustus!"

The Hebrew man was dusty from the trail but was dressed in a fashion indicating he was successful. His wife rode a donkey, but was not in a wagon and to me; this indicated he was a working man but not wealthy.

The soldier appeared to be in his early adult years as his closely shaven face had no shadow on this clear mid afternoon. The slight breeze had a nip to it indicating winter was on the way.

The Hebrew spoke. "Salaam! – the lad was only performing his appointed task – surely a man of your stature can admire that!"

The soldier urged his horse from the water and dismounted. As he stepped away from his mount, the steed immediately relaxed and began to quench his thirst. I could only admire the beast and his training. It seemed as if the rider and mount were one. It was time for them both to rest.

The proud Roman removed his dusty helmet and kneeling, began to splash the cool liquid on his face. He rose and removing a cloth from his belt pouch began to wipe the water from his face and then the helmet. It was easy to see the pride the man took in his position as a Roman in command. He looked at the tall Hebrew and remarked. "Yes my friend – I admire the boy's actions. – I see grit in this boy that I see in all you Hebrews – I don't understand it – but I definitely see it. – You are a vanquished people – yet you still move about as if your future is yours – You refrain from accepting the proven ways of the Roman Empire and refuse to bow to the will of the mighty Caesar. - You bend under our rule, yet you do not break! – It is most unusual and I find it very interesting!"

The Hebrew helped the woman from the donkey and it was quite clear she was heavy with child. The woman took no notice of the soldier and made her way straight to my side. As she drew close, I could see she was quite young, I suppose she was only a few years older than me.

"You poor boy!" She whispered as she pulled the sleeve of my tunic aside and examined the wound on my upper arm. Her hand was cool to the touch and I felt a comforting surge of compassion as she dampened a cloth and began to wash the cut. I felt an exhilarating closeness to this young woman. In most cases, I would shy away from strangers. It was not usual for anyone to get close to me, as people would be offended by my ragged attire and foul smell. I felt my first sensation of being loved. It was spellbinding. My body began to buzz from deep within and a feeling of euphoria and well being was enveloping me. I was transfixed.

The tall Hebrew approached the Roman and his voice took a mellow tone as he softy spoke. "We are the children of God and bow to the will of no earthly power - we accept only the will of Elohim and need not bow to it - for we willingly embrace it."

The Roman slowly shook his head in disbelief. "There's that God thing again!" He almost whispered. "I will never understand how a people can find it sensible to worship a God that you cannot see and especially a God that would allow you to become a conquered people!" The Roman soldier seemed to take a great deal of satisfaction in this bit of logic as his stance took on an air of authority.

"I am Joseph of Nazareth and we journey to Bethlehem for the census tally." The Hebrew said as he began to prepare a pallet for his wife to rest.

"Oh! – Looks like rest must wait a bit! – my friend" – the Roman loosened his belt and dropped his sword to the ground. "Your young wife has found a poor soul to mother! – I did not want to harm the lad – but he knows nothing of discipline and brought it upon himself!"

The feeble effort to dismiss the action did little to remove his obvious feeling of guilt. "Here! – Perhaps this will help the boy!" He removed a small clay container with an aromatic ointment and casually tossed it on the ground next to the young woman.

The Hebrew looked lovingly at the beautiful young lass, bursting with the glow of pending motherhood as she knelt by my side, dressing my now soothed wound.

He addressed the soldier. "This is my wife – Mary - I could not leave her at home in this condition – I waited much too late to answer the census and fear she may give birth before we can arrive in Bethlehem."

"Ahh! – exclaimed the Roman with raised eyebrows. "So – you are a descendent of your great King David!" He had a definite expression of respect in his voice.

"It is so!" - replied Joseph – "Come Mary - you must rest a bit." Joseph motioned to the pallet.

Mary smiled as she gently patted my bandaged arm. She rose with a sigh of effort and proceeded to lie upon the pallet. Joseph fetched some water and as the lady drank, I could not help but see a glow about her face. Her skin was like the cool alabaster that was on the Temple walls and her eyes shined with an innocent glow that words cannot describe.

The Roman soldier seemed transfixed as he gazed upon the scene. Again he spoke slowly in his halting Arabic. "I am Cornelius - from Rome - I am the grandson of Senator Faustus Cornelius Sulla who was an officer with the great Emperor Pompey when Jerusalem was conquered - My grandfather escorted the fallen King Aristobulus to Rome."

The Roman grew wistful as he continued. "I have listened to many stories of how brave and mighty the Hebrew warriors are - My grandfather could never understand why the Hebrews would not join the mighty Roman Legions and share in the glories of Roman conquest."

Suddenly the Roman, Cornelius, regained his poise and called in a loud voice, this time in Hebrew. "PREPARE TO TRAVEL!"

"Joseph" – The Roman spoke. – "We will be in Bethlehem shortly after dark – perhaps you will teach me more of this Hebrew language – I think I will be in your country quite a while." Joseph nodded approval as they prepared to leave. The Roman helped Joseph pack his pallet and belongings and as Mary mounted the donkey, she gave me a smile and I felt warm all over.

As the caravan began to move away I could hear Joseph explaining to Cornelius how an invisible God could indeed talk to you. The Roman apparently was very skeptical as I could barely hear Joseph say. "Let me tell you what Elohim spoke to me."

The voices faded in the din of hooves, bells and creaking leather as the caravan moved away. As the end of the group crested a small hill, Cornelius, the mighty Roman soldier stopped his horse briefly and looked back at me. He raised his lance in what seemed to be a salute. I simply raised my head in acknowledgement. I held no grudge. There was no pain in my arm and my sheep were calling.

The night was quite crisp. Malisch and I had moved the flock further south and bedded down for the night. We were to share a nice fire and roasted mutton with four of the neighboring shepherds. We separated our flock with enough space so the occasional wandering lamb would not wander into a different flock and settled down to enjoy our meal. The mutton was some of the meat from a ewe that was carried off by a wolf. Baliue, a much older shepherd, had tracked the wolf and killed it with his swift arrow. Baliue would thrill us with his stories of when he was a mighty Hebrew warrior and fought the Romans.

An eerie stillness fell upon the countryside. We could see the faint glow of distant Bethlehem as the torches lit the streets to accommodate the many people there to register for the census.

Baliue began to tell us once again, the Hebrews did not fight for the Assyrians that ruled Judea at the time of the Roman invasion. The Hebrew's fought for Judea and the land God gave them. Baliue's eyes grew moist as he told of the thousands that died that day. He sat as his legs began to quiver from the day's journey. "I was but a lad - no older than you - Jaacov – I was placed on a low hill and told to discharge my arrows into the steadily advancing line of Roman shoulders. I had no arrows left - but I did not run! – No! – Not Baliue! – I did not run! – I stood there, bow in my hand, as the mass of Romans with their giant red shields forming a moving wall marched right over me. No lance! – No sword! – No arrow found Baliue's heart that day. The Will of Elohim was done!"

In the silence that followed I felt a sense of serenity, knowing this old man had such faith in this Elohim. I often wondered – "who was this Elohim?" - Why did he never come to the countryside around Bethlehem?

Suddenly the wind blew a gust as cold as the deepest of winter's gales and then utter stillness. It was so still we began to strain our ears for a sound of any kind. Through the silence came the faraway strains of music and voices singing.

Caleb, one of the other shepherds, boldly stated. "There must be quite a celebration in Bethlehem this night! – We have never heard sounds from the village like this before!"

Baliue slowly rose and turned his face upwards toward the heavens. "The light! – Look my boys! – do you see the light? His face almost glowed.

We raised our eyes to the sky and were amazed to see the heavens as bright as early dawn, yet it was not quite midnight.

Suddenly the heavens flashed with a light so bright that we could see nothing else. The sky began to part and bright brilliant clouds were billowing as if a giant storm was about to descend on us. There was a great rush as from a powerful gale but we felt no wind. The ground began to shake with such force we could hardly stand. Baliue shrieked in terror and fell to the ground as if in agony.

I don't know what the other boys did, but I too fell to the ground. I was terrified. No words can describe the terror that one feels when confronted with something they know nothing of, but can feel its intensity and power. In my confused and petrified mind, I suppose I felt, whatever it was, might pass over me, if I made myself small enough. I cringed into as small a knot as I could make.

Instantly there was complete silence. I became aware of Baliue's whimpering and the other boys seemed to be pleading with some unknown entity. In an instant I knew the answer, it was Elohim, he heard me question him and he was seeking me out to vent his wrath. My spirit sank in desperation.

From the Heavens came another brilliant flash and I knew the end must be near. Suddenly the feeling of desperation left me. I was no longer afraid, yet I still could not bring myself to look up.

From the Heavens came the most beautiful voice I had ever heard. It had the ring of a giant bell, the tone of a great horn and the thunder of a magnificent drum.

The voice spoke. "DO NOT BE AFRAID – I BRING TO YOU GOOD NEWS OF GREAT JOY THAT WILL BE FOR ALL PEOPLE!

I wanted to look up, but was sore afraid.

The voice continued. "TODAY IN THE TOWN OF DAVID A SAVIOR IS BORN TO YOU - HE IS CHRIST THE LORD! - THIS WILL BE A SIGN TO YOU - YOU WILL FIND THE BABE WRAPPED IN SWADDLING CLOTH AND LYING IN A MANGER!" I could hear Baliue mumbling something about a Prophesy, as he continued to cringe.

The heavens were suddenly filled with countless voices as heavenly beings began to sing and give praises. I had never been to the Synagogue, but had heard the praises that people would sing to Elohim. I suddenly realized that this Elohim was not a mere human like us. He was by far a greater power and I should not treat him lightly.

The heavenly voices sang. "GLORY TO GOD IN THE HIGHEST AND ON EARTH - PEACE TO ALL MEN."

My mind repeated the words of the heavenly beings. I realized with a start that this Elohim was a Hebrew name for God and God was the greatest of all. I was determined to find out more about this God and now he had sent a Savior named Christ and he was born this very night in Bethlehem.

Instantly, all was quiet again, the darkness returned and all felt normal but the air of exuberance remained.

I was startled when Baliue jumped to his feet with a vigor I think even surprised him. "A Savior!" he shouted. "A Savior! – Now we will cast the Romans back into the sea and the Assyrians will scurry away like the rats they are! – God's chosen people will once again rule the Promised Land!" The old man danced, but only briefly as he huffed a breath of exhaustion and sat with a deep sigh. "Ahh! – My Lord – You have blessed me with the greatest gift you can bestow on an old man - I have seen the glory of Heaven!"

He grew quiet as we began to lowly discuss what we had seen. Each of us was concerned that perhaps we had dreamed it all. We soon agreed that we all saw and heard the same spectacular display and exclaimed great wonder at it all.

As we sat around the fire, Shadiech slowly rose and began to mumble. "Shadiech – my friend – are you ill? I asked. He only pointed toward Bethlehem.

I could not believe my eyes. Would the wonders never cease? There, high in the heavens above Bethlehem, hung a brilliant, blazing star. It looked like a star, but was not like the other stars in the sky, where some are small, some are dim, others are bright, some will flicker and some will shine with a steady light. This star seemed to burn with a light that pulsed as if it had a heart. There was no radiant light that lit the country side, but a shaft of light came down directly over the little town of Bethlehem.

"Boys – you must go!" It was Baliue that spoke, his voice weak and quivering with emotion. "I cannot make it to Bethlehem and back by morning - the sheep cannot be left alone – God sent us this great message for a reason! – You must go! – Quickly now – go and see this Savior and remember what God told us!

"Malisch, Caleb, Shadiech and I quickly gathered some grain and a piece of mutton each. We were not really concerned about Baliue, he was capable of handling bedded down sheep, aided by the other remaining shepherd. We had a special feeling about this night. It was a midnight clear and all was well with the world. Surely nothing bad would happen this night.

We departed with a brisk pace and were much aware of the exceptionally clear sky with more stars than we had ever noticed before. It was evident at first glance the new star was very high in the sky, but was much closer than the plain of twinkling stars that covered the broad expanse of the heavens.

The trip, by foot, to Bethlehem took us only about an hour, as our young legs were quite accustomed to the rocky terrain that was the landscape between the mountains near the Great Sea on our west and the mountains near the Salt Sea to our east. The land did have sparse growths of trees, but no great forest at all.

The air in the town was heavy with the pitch of burning torches and even at this late hour, people still milled about in small groups.

I had only been into Bethlehem a few times in my young life and only once to Jerusalem, to see the Temple. I really did not care for the close confines of a town. It seemed as if everything must be shared. I liked having all of nature to myself and my sheep.

The shaft of light from the wondrous star was quite easy to follow. I remarked to my friends that the many people around us seemed to pay no attention to it. My shepherd friends took little notice as they were focused on the light and probably were as frightened as I.

There ahead was a fair size group of people gathered at a lane that led behind an Inn. The Inn was near the outskirts on the eastern side of town. Some of the woman and youths in the crowd would stand on tiptoes and crane their necks attempting to see over the cluster of people.

As we approached, a small group emerged from the lane, exclaiming they saw nothing spectacular about a baby in a stable, and lying in a manger was, by far, better than lying on the ground. What were the parents to do, there was no room at the Inn and this was the only place available.

The voice from Heaven rang in my ears. "This shall be a sign to you. "You shall find the Babe lying in a manger!"

I lost all concern for my friends as I wormed my way through the people crowded in the narrow lane to the stable at the rear of the Inn. The smell of a stable was thick in the air, but it did little to dampen the intense smell of the sheep I tended. As I picked my way closer to the stable, people would look at me and cover their noses with their hands in an effort to lessen the awful scent. I knew I should withdraw but my curiosity drove me on. The crowd parted and in my anxiety I almost fell right at the feet of a woman sitting by a manger in the dim light of the torches in the stable.

I rose to run when a soft voice spoke. "Somehow I knew you would be here." I was astonished as I looked into the beautiful young face of Mary, my benefactor from yesterday. Her face definitely had a glow about it. A halo seemed to encircle her head. I slowly began to survey the scene and found Joseph standing across from the manger. His face was chiseled as he gazed intently into the crib. My gaze now focused on the small Babe that was wrapped in swaddling cloth and lying on the straw. The child seemed to shine with a light that came from within and I was instantly drawn to him. I suppose my body reflected my desire to reach out to the child and I felt the compulsion to withdraw.

Mary placed her hand on my shoulder and asked. "No! - don't leave - What are you called boy?"

I found it difficult to speak through the emotion that flashed through my body. I was not accustomed to being around people and personal contact had been limited to other shepherds and the Master. I fumbled for words. "I am called Jaacov."

"Ah! – A follower!" Mary stated, as she motioned me closer to the child. "Touch him – feel how soft and yet how strong he is. "

I shifted my crouched position and extended my right hand toward the infant's cheek. I was instantly aware of how soiled my hand and arm were. It didn't matter. The Babe reached up and touched my arm. A sensation flashed through my body that almost knocked me to the ground and I withdrew my arm in a flash. Mary issued a low laugh. "He affects people like that!" I was dumbfounded and began to rub my arm. There was no pain but the arm definitely felt differently.

Mary leaned forward and whispered. "Let me see your arm, Jaacov." I swung around partially and she pulled my tunic up to expose the wound from yesterday, I instinctively knew, deep inside, what she would find as she gently un-wrapped the wound. All that remained of the gash was a small pink scar. The touch of the Babe had a marvelous power.

I proceeded to tell Mary of the most wondrous experience we had witness in the fields that night. She was silent as I recanted the heavenly voice speaking of a Savior and he was for all people. I told her the voice told us exactly how we would find the child.

She was silent with a faraway look in her eyes. I sat and watch her glowing face and noticed tears began to well in her eyes. I thought perhaps I had said something to hurt her. "Lady Mary! – I am sorry – did I----?" She stopped me.

"No – No! – Jaacov – It's so –so much has happened and Joseph and I have also heard the voice of God! – Jaacov – this is the beginning of a most wonderful thing and I feel so small and humble. – I hear and see all this and ponder it in my heart!"

The hand that grasped the scruff of my tunic was hard and course. The force that pulled me from Mary's side all but took away my breath. I was dragged through the crowd and thrust upon the ground in the lane. From the corner of my eye I could see the giant foot of my assailant as he drew back to deliver a mighty kick. I tensed for the impact.

A lance pierced the ground and the swing of the assailant's foot caught the shaft of the lance just above his ankle. The booming voice sounded a series of obscenities and called for damnation by gods that I had never heard of. My assailant was really angry.

Suddenly there was another voice, this time the voice was softer, but no less powerful. The voice spoke in a stern tone. "Now! Now! – Why would a great man like you want to punish a little brother?" It was Cornelius, the Roman soldier from the oasis.

My benefactor was staring into the face of a heavily bearded man that had been intent on giving me quite a kick. The man was definitely not Hebrew. Even I knew, from my limited exposure to people, that Hebrew's wore their long hair and beards in a fashion that reflected centuries of custom.

The man spoke, almost frothing at the mouth. "This foul smelling son of a dung beetle is no little brother of mine. - My family was abandoned in this stinking country when you Romans took it from we Assyrians - I now must live among this rabble and deal with you Romans as well!"

Cornelius casually pulled his lance from the ground and slowly began to wipe away the dirt from the finely honed edge. He turned to the Assyrian and spoke with great concern. "It seems you are in great misery due to us Romans taking away your Hebrews – I have added to your misery by your foot striking my lance – and this seems such a wonderful peaceful night – I feel as I owe you some relief from your misery!"

Cornelius deftly lifted the lance into a thrusting stance. "I think this lance through you heart will definitely end all your misery!" The Roman made a thrusting motion with the lance and the Assyrian fled with a scream, only to stop a short distance away to cry, yet another insult. Cornelius took a quick step his way and the man disappeared into the dim light.

The Roman soldier turned back to me and with a snicking sound of his tongue spoke. "Boy! – you have a knack for getting into trouble!" He stooped and with a mighty grasp swept me to my feet. "Are you hurt – Boy?"

"No - but look here - at my arm!" – I answered. I pulled up my tunic at the arm and his eyes widened. He immediately spun me around and examined the other arm. Turning me back, his look was far beyond belief. "How! – How could this be? – It was only yesterday and now it's almost as if it didn't happen!" I could tell he was visibly shaken.

"It was the Babe – He touched me and it was as if I was struck by lightning! – I don't understand it but as you see - it is real!" I was greatly relieved that someone else knew of the occurrence.

Cornelius stooped and asked. "Is there more?"

I nodded.

"Follow me!" He ordered. I balked.

"Trust me – boy – no harm will befall you as long as I'm around!" Somehow, I believed him.

We moved swiftly through the narrow streets and in a short time arrived at the Roman post near Jerusalem Road. Bethlehem, being a peaceful town only had a small detachment from the Jerusalem Centuriae. Cornelius fixed a portion of fresh fruits and placed it before me.

He leaned close and asked. "Did you see the star?" I nodded. "Did you see a light shining down on the stable?" I nodded again. "Tell me! – Boy – did you hear anything?" Again I nodded. "Your name – Boy – What is your name?"

"Jaacov – I am called Jaacov!" I answered as boldly as I could without alarming the nearby sleeping soldiers.

"Ohhh! – Jaacov!" I could sense the Roman was struggling with a great burden he could not comprehend. His face grew soft and he looked at me with a longing expression. This man needed to know what we heard.

He continued with a quivering voice. "I heard the thunder as the great voice spoke - but the words were not to my understanding – I heard the beautiful voices from on high as they sang - but again I could not understand the words – Ohhh! - Jaacov - my new young friend – I beseech you – please tell to me the words from the heavens!"

As I recounted the words of the great voice from Heaven, I saw the agony in Cornelius's face slowly change into an expression of revelation. As I softly whispered the phrases of the song from the Heavenly Host he fell to his knees and began to sob.

The man began to babble lowly about, how so many people could be so wrong about different gods and goddesses. He began to thank this Elohim for including him in this most wondrous night of revelation.

As I silently made my way from the Roman post, I heard the mighty Roman soldier, through his sobs, thanking God for sending this Savior for all men.

I could not find Malisch, Caleb or Shadiech anywhere, so I made my decision to return to my sheep. As I drew away from the town I could see the shaft of light still descending on the little town of Bethlehem.

The weeks that followed were just as before, full of chasing wolves, caracals and lions. The sheep were getting fat from the fields around Bethlehem and to the western hills before the great sea. The wool on our sheep was full and rich.

Once again the Master made me separate the lambs that had been born with black or spotted coats. In the past he would bring some men and they would load the animals into a wagon and cart them off. This year he simply slaughtered two and took the choice cuts of meat and told me to get rid of the rest. There were seven bleating little black and spotted lambs tethered together as the Master road away. The master left me with instructions to be near Capra at the base of the hills before the Salt Sea when the new moon rose.

I occasionally would cross paths with the other shepherds and Baliue was obsessed with recounting the night we saw the light. He was growing frail as the weeks went by and soon I realized I saw Baliue no more. Rumor came to me that his swift arrow was not true to the mark and a wounded lion sent Baliue to join his mighty Hebrew Warriors in Heaven.

I could not bring myself to kill the blemished lambs. I kept them separated but still with the flock. Malisch had returned to the Master and was now part of the staff that would shear the wool. I would only see him now at the spring shearing. I had never felt the sensation of loneliness before. I had always had another shepherd with me, but I suppose the Master felt I was old enough to handle the flock by myself.

Moving the flock was not a great task as sheep are not very smart. Sheep have a natural tendency to pick a leader. It may be a male or in many cases the leader may be a female. I have witnessed the process and I truly do not believe the leader ever aspires to be a leader. In my mind, I think, one of the sheep is a little brighter than the rest and is quicker to sense danger and follows directions better. The other sheep sense this and just naturally follow the smart one. We quite often attach a bell or anything that will clatter around the neck of the lead sheep, so when movement is necessary we simply get the lead sheep moving and the rest usually follow.

I don't know how true it is, but I heard the tale of a wolf killing a lead sheep and as the wolf dragged the sheep away the rest of the flock followed.

I arrived at the plain near Capra a full day ahead of the New Moon and herded my flock into a freshly blooming field of wild flowers. The grass and tender shoots were soft and succulent. I felt the sheep had a good day of grazing before they would start hazing the land. I wanted to explore the low hills that separated us from the Salt Sea. I knew that wildlife was not prevalent here due to extreme shortage of fresh water. I needed a place to dispose of the blemished sheep. I never understood the thinking of the Master when he disposed of the black or spotted sheep. I had cut some of the wool and used it for bedding and warmth. It was as strong and useful as the white wool. I had eaten of the flesh of the blemished sheep and it, too, was as tasty and tender as the white sheep. I did not understand, but I obeyed.

As I made my way into the hills, I found what seemed to be a wide trail. The trail was not visible from the plain because of a giant rock that stood before the trail opening. I would not have found it, had I not been searching for a place to hide the sheep's corpses.   I also needed soft earth to cover the bodies.   It is not wise to leave great quantities of meat for scavengers.   They will begin to expect it and will make shepherding a nightmare.

Instantly I knew the sound. It was the all too familiar whir of a sling. I dove for the ground and as the wiz of the missile zipped by I rolled behind a rock. A terrifying silence engulfed the rocky terrain as I crouched behind my small rock. I had no idea from where the sling was launched.

I called in Arabic. "Sadegi! – Sadegi!" The silence that followed gave no indication that anyone heard. It seemed an eternity before a faint scuffling in the rocks resulted in a loose rock cascading down the hillside. A male voice called out. "Show yourself – Boy!"

"I think not – Sadigi – for your sling may find its mark this time!" I answered.

The sound of a muffled laugh ensued and the voice stated. "I don't think I need to kill a boy this day – I only need to know why such a ragged lad is wandering in this forsaken place where no one ever comes!"

I slowly rose from my sanctuary and there above me was an apparition as terrifying as any horror story we shepherds had ever told. The man was clothed in a ragged skin of some mottled colored animal. His hair was thinning and the bones protruded from his body everywhere. His eyes were sunk deep in his head and he seemed to shake as he stood pensively on the rock above me.

Why are you here boy?" His voice now had lost all sense of lightheartedness. The man stood above me and his demeanor was sinister. "I see no threat in you – Boy – but you have stumbled on something that may end your life here this very day!"

He pulled a horn from his tattered skin tunic and blew a blast that wafted with echoes through the hills. Presently the sound of scurrying feet and the huffs and puffs of labored breathing were heard as sliding rocks began to evidence the advance of people from everywhere. There were squat figures completely covered in ragged cloaks. Others were as gaunt and hideous as the man that spoke. High above, the now visible apparitions stood a tall man dressed in what was once a robe of great finery. It was a dark crimson with gold brocade embossing the sleeves and hem.

The figure raised his arm and the shocking white of his skin told his story. He was a leper. "What have you caught for our dinner – great hunter?" He addressed the living skeleton that stood above me.

My brave heart crumbled at these words. I was only seeking a place to dispose of my poor blemished lambs and now was apparently on the menu for the supper of these poor wretched souls.

My mind raced with the thought to escape. I was fleet of foot and none of these men seemed capable of running at any speed at all. My eye caught the outline of a bow in the hands of a robed figure on the rock to the right of the path entrance. I slowly glanced to the left and there too was a bowman. It was clear to me I could not evade the two bowman.

I slowly raised my head to the heavens and softly asked my new found friend, Elohim, to accept my spirit. I truly believed that he would hear me. It did not occur to me to ask to live, only to be with him.

The booming voice of the robed man rang out. "Who are you praying to – young ragged one? – It is not me – for I hear no petition - It is not the hunter - for he hears no plea! - I ask – to whom do you pray for life?" His voice echoed in crescendos as it trailed off into the hills.

I cried. "I do not plead for my life – only that God will accept my spirit!" The figures in the hills stood transfixed.

"Is this God the same God that spoke to Abraham?" The tall figure asked.

I searched my mind. I knew nothing of God, only that he was called Elohim and he had sent a Savior and He touched me and I knew that my life was different and He answered prayer.

Suddenly a thought flashed in my mind. I answered. "I don't know about Abraham - but he was the God of the great King David!" A murmur went through the group and all heads turned toward the robed man.

"Aha! – Little one!" – we have heard how our people hid this King David in our caves many years ago and when he was restored to power, he sent food and clothing and balm for our sores!"

There was a pause. "You may go – however - if you tell of this place we shall seek you out and feast upon your flesh!" I heard sighs of disappointment as the figures obediently faded into the rocks.

I made my way back to my flock and suddenly I knew this occurrence was not just accidental. I gathered my small flock of black and spotted sheep and slowly began to move them away from the flock. I retraced my steps and placed the sheep at the head of the trail behind the huge rock at the entrance. I felt the eyes of the hunters on me, but heard neither whir of the sling nor twang of the bow. I bid a farewell to the blemished few and felt a tinge of sorry for them. I remembered when each was born, yet I knew this was their destiny. I left hastily.

My fire had burned to a base of glowing coals. The night chill had urged me to pull my wool cover over my shoulders as I lay on my side.

The soft clanking sound of a leather pouch hitting the ground by my fire woke me and abruptly I sat up. I saw nothing in the dim glow of the fire; however, I was aware of a presence. The presence was close and I could sense the heat from its body. I could smell a faint aromatic fragrance in the air.

The presence spoke. It was the distinct voice of the tall robed man from the hills. "I suspect your presence here today is not just a chance event."

There was a pause as he drew a labored breath and then continued. "The sheep you brought were proof of that - I know of the Hebrews desire for only the pure white sheep and they will destroy the blemished - This task was entrusted to you, but the sheep did not get blemished overnight - You tended them and cared for them and brought them across this vast plain right to our hills - You did not know of us - nor did we know of you - The God of Abraham and King David knows of you and he knows of us - You are his emissary young shepherd - Now! – What are you called my son?"

"With quivering voice I answered. "I am called Jaacov. "

"And your parents – who are they?" The tall man questioned.

"I have no parents. – I remember only the sheep and the Master." I answered.

"'And your Master's name – who is he?" Again the tall man questioned.

I paused and hesitantly spoke. "His name is Master – that is all I have ever known – only Master.

I heard the rustle of the tall man's robe as he moved in the shadows. "If ever you need sanctuary - come to us - as you pass the big rock - call out in a loud voice. I AM JAACOV - JAACOV OF THE SHEEP - and you will be safe! - Your name shall be known in the hills!"

The breathing of the tall robed man grew more labored. With great effort, he said. "Sleep well - my boy – for your Elohim will require much of you over the years – that pouch lying by your fire contains the stones my people find in the hills - your people place great treasure in them - they mean nothing to us as they bring no solace to our misery - use them wisely!" The silence told me he was gone.

The master seemed pleased as he looked over the flock. "Come sit with me Jaacov." He spoke with a tone I had never heard from him before. The Master never spent much time with the flocks and seldom talked with the shepherds longer than necessary to give brief instructions.

He had his servants pitch a tent that gave some shade and provided a shabby pillow on which he motioned for me to sit. "Jaacov – you have been a good shepherd over my flocks these past years - You grew up here in these rocky plains and you have always given great care to my sheep - You could find grazing and protection for them when others would complain - Ahh! - Your mother would have been proud of you – young shepherd." I had never heard the Master speak of my mother or anything about parents.

"My Mother – you speak of my mother – Master?" I was suddenly aware that this was not an everyday conversation for my Master.

The Master looked at me and asked lowly. "Do you remember anything of your mother, Jaacov?" I shook my head. "Speak! – Jaacov! – you are not dumb!"

"No Master - all I remember is sheep!" I answered, hoping not to incur his wrath.

He looked intently at me and spoke again. "Jaacov – Your Mother and Father came to me many years ago with a small flock of sheep - They offered their services to me if I would allow them to keep their small flock with my sheep and provide them the same sustenance as my other shepherds - You were born in these rocky fields Jaacov." I moved my pillow closer to the Master, eager to hear more.

The Master continued. "I agreed and they lived up to the bargain – One day I came to the flock seeking your Father - Your Mother simply told me he was not here - I asked where he was and she told me he was near - I left it at that and found much later that your Father was a victim of a rogue lioness - Your mother was in fear that I would take her sheep and cast her out - She continued to shepherd the flock and nursed you as well."

I suddenly felt a sensation that was entirely new to me. My heart began to ache and my eyes started burning. The feeling was similar to how I felt when our dog died in the jaws of the young lion. I had a vague recollection of the sensation when I heard of Baliue's death. This feeling, however, was much more intense.

"Jaacov - my boy - you are so much like your Mother." The Master voice quivered a bit as he spoke. "I came to find the flock one day and they were nowhere in sight – so I began to backtrack to the last meeting with your Mother." He continued to gaze into my face.

The Master placed his hand on my shoulder as he spoke. "I topped a small hill and was surprised to see a lad scarcely over three years of age standing face to face with a lone caracal - the lad was you Jaacov – You stood between that giant cat and a small lamb - I chased the Caracal away and asked for your

Mother - You simply pointed to a distant wisp of smoke where I found your Mother dead on her pallet."

The ache in my heart grew unbearable and the burning in my eyes was replaced with tears. It was the first time that my young body had felt the full torment of sorrow. I had never thought much about my parents. I had never witnessed any type of parent - child relationship. My mind flashed to the night I saw Mary looking down at the Babe and immediately knew what I had lost. The tears continued as the Master waited in silence.

I knew that this new feeling was self centered and was not going to change anything. I pushed the feeling aside and rose. "Might I return to my flock now – Master?"

The Master also rose and spoke. "Jaacov - you will take the sheep to my khah-vah – along the way you will join with my other flocks – much is about to happen and it will affect you greatly - I will see you in a week."

As he rode away his attendants began to store his tent and gear on the camels and donkeys and soon departed. The master left two young boys with me, both were Nubians and knew little of moving sheep, but were quite agile and willing. A small donkey was left as well and we were blessed with ample and succulent stores.

The rest of the afternoon was spent in festive manner as the Nubian boys were away from the care of elders and masters, I suppose, for the first time. We had ample stores and when they finally drifted off to sleep, I realized the boys would be no help standing any night watch. I slept well but was always alert for the slightest sound of danger.

We made good time as we headed north of Bethlehem, stopping at the oasis on the road from Jerusalem. We had many hundreds of sheep now and quite a few shepherds. The Nubian boys and I stayed away from the others as they were somewhat older and took great delight in their wine and gaiety at night.

It was easy to move about at night now with the star above Bethlehem shining as a beacon for which we could take our bearings. The Nubian boys could easily see the star, but, somehow could not see the shaft of light that shone down on Bethlehem.

The oasis was really a shady spread of palms and cedars that grew around one of the springs that was so prevalent from north of Bethlehem to al-Walabe.

The spring created a large pool as the cool water was captured by the rocky soil and provided a small refreshing rest in the day's journey from Jerusalem.

I began to tell the boys, once again, of that most marvelous night when the star first appeared and the voices came from heaven. I could see them roll their eyes and lift their hands in exasperation as I realized I had told the story many times in the last few days. It had been over a year since the miracle had occurred and the boys were the only ones I had been with long enough to feel comfortable in telling.

Baliue, before his death, had not been timid in the least. He would shout out to strangers in the distance and dance as he told of the new King and how He would lead the Hebrews back to the days of glory. My friend Malisch, being much educated, had no problem in relating the night in great detail.

I was still uneasy around crowds of people and stayed far back from groups when at the springs, yet that night was still fresh in my mind.

We bedded the sheep far enough from the spring that none could wander into the water and cause any problem. The wooly creatures had drunk their fill and had no desire to lounge in the water so we began to relax and build a small fire to ward off the nights chill.

The piercing sound of a bugle broke the late afternoon silence and our attention was turned to the small hill coming from Jerusalem. The clattering of many horses gave notice that a detachment of mounted Roman soldiers was coming. The bugle was a signal to clear the way. Romans always called attention to themselves and were very gruff in their association with the common people.

We knew they were Romans, for only very wealthy people could afford horses to ride, and also the horses were shod with metal shoes. The common man on horseback would normally ride an unshod horse.

We could see the banners streaming from the lances as the rider approached the hill. It was a detachment of ten Roman foot soldiers and a mounted officer in the lead. I strained my eyes to see if, perhaps my friend Cornelius was among the soldiers. I could not see any soldier that looked familiar. It had been over a year and I felt sure he had probably returned to Rome.

The Nubian boys had stolen some meat from an Ibex that was the victim of a predator the day we left the eastern ills. We had placed the meat in strips on a slender line and it had cured as we made the journey west. The meat was tender and very nourishing. It went well with the grain and wine the master had provided.

The sound of a horse, as it blew through its nostrils, startled us and we were instantly on our feet. The hardy laugh of the Roman Officer turned into Hebrew as he laughingly shouted. "Well! – So much for being alert! – what if I had been a wolf?"

The boys fell on the ground in obvious terror and prostrated themselves in respect.

It was Cornelius. He was clad in the obvious finery of a Roman Officer. Gone were the lance and shield. His helmet was of fine silver and lined with a bright gold bodice and sported a magnificent furry, crimson crest across the top. His chest plate was of fine bronze and his tunic was of the finest crimson cloth. He flashed a broad smile as his crimson cape flared in the breeze.

Cornelius spoke. "Speak! - brave Jaacov! – what if I had been a wolf?"

I gathered my courage and composure. "Sire Cornelius! – A wolf would not have approached me from the back where brave Roman soldiers are - He would have approached me from where I faced and I would have seen him and slain him with my staff!"

"Well stated my fine young friend and I can see our Elohim has watched over you!" Cornelius's voice softened as he dismounted and called for one of his soldiers to come care for his horse. The soldier that came had an obvious scowl on his face. It was evident he cared little for a stinky shepherd boy and two Nubians that somehow drew the attention of his commander.

Cornelius sat by our fire and told me of all that had transpired over the last many months. He called for the soldier to bring some sweet cakes for our meal as he began to share the dried Ibex we were eating. The Nubians sat wide eyed and pensive as Cornelius spoke with me.

"It seems that only a very few people can see the light - from the star - shinning down on Bethlehem - They all seem to be most intelligent and very close to Elohim." Cornelius spoke of the wonder as to why he could see it also. The Officer stated, with a subdued tone, he no longer believed there were many gods. "Jaacov! - There is only one God and that Baby in Bethlehem is his son!"

Cornelius continued to unfold the happenings of the many months that had passed. It seems he had become friends with

Joseph and Mary, the Childs parents. He told me that Joseph had found work building the addition to the Roman post and had become a much admired carpenter in Bethlehem. He moved the family to a house in town and they are quite comfortable.

The Nubians were transfixed at the scene of a mighty Roman officer sitting and talking with a shepherd boy as if they were brothers.

Cornelius talked on. "Joseph has told me many wonderful things about God and his promises to the Hebrew people - he has taught me much of the Hebrew and Arabic language - it is the reason for my promotion! - I have a much better incite in dealing with the people now."

"He looked directly at me and said. "Now! – brave Jaacov – let's hear your tale of the last year or so!"

I recounted the many months and when I spoke of the encounter with the robed man in the eastern hills he asked to see the small bag of stones. I had only looked at them briefly from time to time and had never shown them to anyone.

An involuntary 'HUFF!" issued from his lips and he jumped to his feet when the bag of stones poured into the palm of his hand. The late afternoon sun danced through the stones in emerald and ruby hues. There were some as clear as rainwater and other as blue as the salt sea. The stones made a melodious clatter as he moved them about in his hand. Suddenly he clinched his hand and with great haste placed the stones back in the bag.

"Jaacov!" He drew me to the side where the Nubians could not hear. "You must never show these stones to anyone you do not trust or have the utmost confidence in! – Do you understand me?"

I did not understand him. I only knew he was upset and I instantly felt guilty for his distress.

"I will throw them away and it will be better!" I cried. He immediately grabbed my hand as I clutched the bag.

"NO! NO! – Jaacov! – do not throw them away! - Do you not understand – Jaacov? - You are a very rich young man!" He stopped and looked around to be sure we were not overheard. The Nubian boys were completely engrossed with the sweet cakes and were of no concern.

I did not know what being rich meant. "What is rich – Sire – I don't understand?" I turned my face toward the Roman and he suddenly pulled me close and held me with a mighty grip. I could hear a distant murmur as his troops witnessed this display of manly affection.

Cornelius offered no explanation; he simply held me close and began to mumble in that strange language the Romans spoke. In a moment he released me and spoke. "So where are you off to with your beautiful sheep young shepherd?"

"The Master gave me these Nubians and told me to be at his khah–vah in al-Walabe by tomorrow night." My answer drew a frown from Cornelius. He grew quiet and withdrew in deep thought.

With his hand at his chin in deep thought, he appeared to be quite wise. He lifted a finger on his hand at his chin and asked. "Jaacov – is your master a Hebrew – that area is mostly Assyrian!"

The question of who my Master was never entered my mind. All I ever knew was Master. I pictured him in my mind and answered. "Cornelius – Sire – I am quite sure he is Hebrew for he wears his hair in Hebrew fashion."

The Roman shook his head and with an air of understanding, turned to me and said. "Jaacov – I am sure your master is the great Hebrew business man that Caesar Augustus has commissioned to handle all of Rome's sheep in northern Gaul - I hear your master will acquire a great deal of land and wealth to make sure that Rome's wool and mutton stays plentiful - I also hear that your master will be helpful in dealing with the troublesome Britons on the Island to the north of Gaul called Britannia."

I knew nothing of these places and to tell the truth, it was quite difficult for me to simply try and keep my sheep from ravaging the land, as we moved about.

Cornelius knelt on one knee and pulled me close to his side. He spoke with a tone I never heard before.

"Jaacov – I am pledged to uphold the agreement between Rome and this Judean land. - We are not to get involved in the political or religious matters and only intervene if Rome's interest is at stake!"   He paused as if to measure his words. "If your master wants to take you with him to Gaul – there is little I can do to stop him! – As a slave – you are his to do with as he sees fit!"

The great Roman officer looked up, as if asking for Elohim's help. He spoke hastily. "Jaacov! - If a slave were to run away and found his way to Joseph in Bethlehem! – it would be quite easy for him to remain hidden until some foolish Roman officer could come to his aid!"

With that being said, Cornelius rose and in a loud voice called out. "Mount up you noblest of Rome! – We make for Bethlehem to seek out this rebel king that plagues the great Hebrew King Herod!"

CHAPTER II

THEY MUST DIE

I lay in mental anguish as Cornelius words rang through my head. He left me with so many questions. I lay by the fire and one of the Nubian boys was standing the first watch near me in the shadows. I called to him.

The boy came close and crouched near the embers of the fire. "What is a slave? I asked him. I could see the outline of his face against the starry night sky and his brow knit in deep thought.

"That would be us - young Master!" The youth replied.

"I am not a master – boy – I am but a shepherd!" I answered with what I thought was reason.

The boy replied. "The Master ordered us to do as you bid – that makes you our Master - You do as the Master bids and that makes you his slave - There are masters and there are slaves - we are slaves and you are both master and slave!" He rose and his expression was one of great satisfaction as he felt he had surely sorted this situation out. I was still confused. As I tried to sleep, I suddenly remembered the Roman's words about King Herod fearing a rebel king. I slept fitfully.

The following day brought great downpours of rain. We pressed our sheep on in the deluge in order to reach the master's khah-vah by late afternoon. I had never been to the giant estate, but the Nubian boys and other shepherds knew the way quite well.

The rain subsided late in the afternoon and as we started down a long sloping hill, I noticed the fields turned to beautiful grassy plains. In the distance I saw a sprawling complex of buildings that were by far nicer than any town I had seen. To the west of the khah-vah was a vast expanse of olive trees bordered to the north by date palms as far as the eye could see. The countryside was teeming with workers going about the business of working this great khah-vah. This was the home of my Master.

The sheep were herded into a massive area surrounded be a cross pike fence. I saw long troughs full of grain and the sheep needed no urging as they made their way to the fragrant fare.

A voice came through the din of bleating and men shouting orders. Again I heard the voice. The voice was calling my name. It was Malisch.

I turned and stood on my toes to see him waving from across the pen. Again he called. "Jaacoc! – Over here – Jaacov – do you hear me?"

A pang of emotion pounded in my chest. I was amazed at all these new sensations that were coming alive in me. I raised my hand and shouted back. I was stunned, for I had never shouted before. It felt good, so I shouted again, this time even louder. I felt a feeling of pride and thought to myself. "I think I may become a great shouter!"

The sheep were safe and apparently I was not needed at present. I made my way through the mass of sheep and raced to greet my old friend, Malisch.

It had been well over a year since I had last seen Malisch, and he was much different than when we were with the sheep. I was now a little taller than he and my skin was much darker. Malisch was dressed in a fine cloth tunic and wore a shoe that completely covered his foot. He smelled of flowers and his hair was in the familiar Hebrew style with the locks hanging down his cheeks. He carried a slate and a small stick of chalk. He called it his tally slate.

I was now nearly fourteen years of age and Malisch was close to fifteen. "Ahh! – Jaacov – I looked for you everyday – my friend! – I envisioned you coming over the hill riding on the back of a great lion and a young wolf for a wife!" He laughed heartily at his humor and with a sweep of his arm he embraced me. It felt good to know that someone was feeling joy at seeing me

I stepped back from his embrace and made a noticeable sniffing gesture. "Malisch you smell like the women that giggle in the tents at the oasis. I laughed heartily at my humor.

Malisch pinched his nose and said with a gag. "Uck! – I need not tell you what you smell like! – Come my friend – we will make a new man of you!"

It was my first bath. I had been in the water of many springs and had rubbed my hands with wet leaves to cleanse away soil, but had never considered or witnessed what Malisch called a bath.

The Nubian girls that attended us giggled as I threw off my tunic. Malisch said to ignore them as they would giggle at a dead bug as it lay upon its back. I stored my tunic and possessions in a basket provided for me.

Water was poured from giant pitchers and I was rubbed with a creamy mixture that wafted of jasmine. The water that ran from my body was the color of the water that ran in the clay gullies of the hills.

"Now! – Follow me – Jaacov!" shouted Malisch as he pulled a great curtain aside revealing a small pool of the clearest water I had ever seen. At the far end of the pool was the figure of a beast's head with water gushing from its mouth. I drew back in alarm. Malisch laughed at my caution and urged me in.

My first bath was most memorable and Malisch taught me the proper way to bath. I noticed the marked difference in my skin color that was covered by my tunic. I never thought of how white I was. I also noticed that hair was beginning to grow in the most unusual places.

I didn't want the bath to end as Malisch insisted we withdraw to the court of the sah-Pahr. I was given a tunic of fine cloth the color of the sunset. I was rubbed with a lotion that made me also smell of flowers. My entire body had a sensation of newness.

I mentioned this to Malisch and he told me it was probably the first time I had been bathed since my Mother died. I felt that twinge again, the one that I now knew to be sorrow.

I was placed in a chair and a man began to pull a toothed stick of some type through my hair. It was not a pleasant thing and I pulled away. Malisch calmed me and stated he was instructed to make me presentable for a meal at the Master's table this evening. I reluctantly allowed the man called the sah-Pahr to continue.

A mixture was rubbed in my hair and the toothed stick, called a comb, was not as annoying now as it passed through my tangled mass. I was amazed at the length of my hair as the bush of tangles began to straighten. I could feel the ends touch the lower part of my back as the sah-Pahr began to use his shears.

I was not at all happy about losing my hair, after all, I had spent many years growing it and it was a part of me, but I trusted Malisch and he was doing the bidding of the Master.

I noticed that quite a group of young girls had gathered at the curtain hung at the entrance to the room. They whispered among themselves and would cast glances my way. The sah-Pahr ordered me up and led me to a highly polished piece of metal that stood at the wall. I was shocked to see a young man looking at me from inside this large polished metal plate.

I suddenly felt a little angry because this young man appeared to mock my every move. I said nothing. He said nothing. I leaned closer. He leaned closer. The laughter from my observers burst forth at the instant I realized I was looking at myself. The polished plate was called a mirror. The only reflection, of myself, I had ever seen was in the rippling waters of a spring. I stared in amazement.

The laughter subsided and the group became engrossed watching a young man discovering himself for the first time in his life. I began to have strange thoughts. If I had seen a reflection of myself, for the first time, along with other people, I would not know which one was me. I did not know myself.

The youth I saw was darkly tanned with hair not nearly as dark as most Hebrews. His eyes were dark and glistened with the innocence of living alone. His physique was lean and muscular due to the harsh life he had led. The now properly groomed hair was typical of Hebrew custom, being shoulder length with a long ringlet down each cheek. The scar on the right arm was not even visible.

The observing girls whispered approval and cast sly smiles as my eyes darted their way. I did not understand why I felt flattered. It was another strange sensation, but it felt good. I looked really hard at my reflection. I wanted to make sure I knew myself should we ever meet again.

I knew, by this time, to observe those around me. I had never sat at a table for a meal and there were disks of copper for the food as we ate. I observed how the other people sat upon low stools or curled their legs as they sat upon cushions. I choose a stool and immediately noticed the metal tools by which the food was cut. The table was covered with bowls of fresh fruit and servant girls stood about with pitchers of wine and water. I noticed that only the fruit was being sampled and by hand. I was used to that method and choose to eat a slice of yellow fruit that was soft and sweet with a mellow taste. I also sampled a green piece that looked to be the same fruit, only a different color. It was easy to tell it was the same type fruit, but a different flavor.

The master entered and everyone rose. The master waved his hand and all sat, once again. I had never seen the Master in such finery. His robe was deep blue and flowed to the floor. It was embossed with silver brocades. His hair fairly glistened and his hand flashed many rings on his fingers.

He made a motion to the heavens and a robed man with a staff lifted his hand to heaven and proceeded with a prayer of thanksgiving to God for the bounty we were receiving. The robed man was a Priest and continued to give thanks for our health, the crops, the rain and sun. His voice was melodious and as I raised an eye, I noticed the Master was fidgeting. He made a slight, curt motion with his hand and the Priest ended the prayer.

I thought how busy this God must be, for the Hebrews were constantly calling on him for help and giving thanks. Surely he must grow weary. I had much to learn.

Malisch explained that this was a feast to celebrate Rosh Hashanah and we would have to do no work for a few days. He pointed to the servants and noted that they were all gentiles and would do all the work. He told me the Master wanted to talk with me in the morning.

I had much to learn about food. The servants brought foods I did not know existed. I suppose the meats were from the same animals, but prepared in different ways. The vegetables were varied and unfamiliar. As a shepherd I had passed many vegetable gardens but knew to keep my sheep far away. I had never sought to explore what grew in these gardens and laughed to myself as I thought of the danger the gardens were now in, due to my new knowledge.

I felt uncomfortable as I knew that eyes were upon me. This was an acute sense I had developed as a shepherd. I could feel the eyes of the wolf, caracal or lion as they would scout our flock and make plans for a kill. I slowly scanned the room and my gaze became fixed on the dark flashing eyes of a beautiful young girl sitting beside one of the Masters guest. I leaned to Malisch and slyly asked who this maid might be.

Malisch looked up and laughed haughtily. I was immediately embarrassed and again noted a new sensation to my growing list of new feelings. I had not yet identified the feeling I had as I looked into the eyes of this young woman that sat across from me.

"Stop your howling! – Malisch – or I'll stuff this fruit down your throat!" I threatened him with a handful of dates.

"That girl – my dear friend – is my treacherous sister and she will tell my father of any and everything I do that might cause me grief! – Please – Jaacov – throw the dates at her! - She is called Rachel - but I call her Rascal – Believe me – she is trouble – don't even look her way!"

How could I help but look her way. She was beautiful and her eyes were always fixed on me. I had that feeling again. I didn't know what it was and it frightened me. I was not in control.

The next day dawned with great bursts of wind and the rain came in squalls. The thunder and lightning was horrendous. The animals around the farm were very frightened and confused. I ran to the giant enclosure to help with the sheep. Malisch called for me to stop. He informed me that I could not work this day as it was Holy.

"Malisch – the sheep don't know about a holy day and God must not either or he would not have sent this storm!" I tore from his grasp and dashed on. The sheep now numbered in the hundreds and were quite uneasy.

I ran back to my basket that contained my meager belongings and fetched my crude flute. It was one of my few possessions. I could never remember where it came from, it was just always there. You simply placed it between your lips and gently blew. It made a musical note. There were a number of small holes down the slender length of the tube. You could place your fingers on the hole and as you uncovered each one or a series of holes the flute made different notes.

In my mind were melodies that somehow I knew. At night when it grew stormy in the fields, I would play these melodies and the sheep took on a much subdued attitude. I rushed to the sheep and finding a dry place under a thatched shed I lay back and began to play. The lilting melody pierced the wind and the sheep, did indeed, begin to calm.

My mind drifted back and I vaguely remembered a warm embrace. The sound of the flute, in my memory, seemed much more beautiful than any sound I could make. I wondered if the warm embrace was my mother as she held me close and was the melody from the flute my father played. My eyes began to burn. The tears soon followed. I now played my flute to sooth my tormented spirit. The tears and rain fell in equal torrents.

The rain had subsided considerably and suddenly I was again aware of eyes upon me. Surely a wolf or lion would not come this close to people for a kill. I instantly sat up and began to search the distant horizon for the tell-tale outline of a wolf. I scanned the rocks and brush clumps for a lion as it crouched.

I reached and grasped a pike that lay against the post of the shed. I slowly rose to gain some height in my scanning and heard a slight movement behind me. I whirled with the pike ready to thrust and was startled by a weak gasp of fear.

It was Rachel. Her eyes were wide with fear as the somber young man, playing a flute, she had been spying on, was now at her throat with a pike. Again she gasped and placed her hands to her throat and began to slump.

I instantly dropped the pike and grabbed the young beauty before she fell. I scooped her into my arms and gently lay her on the hay beneath the thatched shed. That feeling came again, what was that feeling? I felt weak but I had picked up this girl. I felt confused, but had presence of mind to not let her fall.

I wanted to run, yet I stood looking down at this lovely creature. Words cannot describe the sensations going through my mind and body. I called upon Elohim for help.

Rachel's eyes fluttered and she immediately fled the shed. I called after her. "Rachel! – Rachel! – I meant you no harm – I thought you were a wolf!" She slowed and stopped some distance away.

I must have looked menacing as I could tell she wanted to return but could not make her feet move. I took a pensive step her way. She did not move. I took a second step, still she did not move. As I drew near she turned her head as if fearing a blow.

"Rachel!" – I reached and gently took her hand. "Please come sit with me and teach me to talk to a woman."

She froze as if terrified. "I really thought you were a wolf." I said. "You see, I was dreaming of when I was in the fields guarding my sheep.

Rachel raised her eyes to mine and her hand relaxed a bit. She took a halting step my way and asked. "Why were you crying – wild Jaacov?" She took another step my way.

"Rachel –I do not know why the tears come – you see – they only started the other day at the oasis. - I had never cried in my life - not even when the Roman sliced me with his lance." Her eyes widened and she proceeded with me to sit upon the hay in the thatched shed.

"Please show me the scar – brave Jaacov! She was excited and the fear seemed to have passed. I lifted the tunic sleeve and pointed to the faint pink line across the upper part of my arm. "It doesn't appear to have been very serious to have left so faint a line." She almost pouted.

"Aha! – that is another story altogether! - I don't think you would understand!" I felt I had said too much.

"No! No! – Jaacov – Please tell me - I want to hear all you have to say." She took my hand and moved closer on the hay.

Once again that strange feeling came over me and I simply did not know what it was. This time I noticed I became quite warm all over.

"Oh! – Jaacov!" She exclaimed. "My pesky brother has told me so much about you and the Master says you are, by far, the best shepherd he has ever had."

I looked into those blazing eyes that resembled fire shinning through the deep black water of a well.

She continued. "Malisch has told me of how you killed a wolf with your sling and staff and the Master tells how you stood down a caracal when you were a mere baby.

I interrupted. "I feel maybe your brother talks too much!"

"Oh! – I suppose the Master talks too much when he says you have the fattest and woolliest sheep of all his flocks and you lose fewer sheep that any other shepherd and you roam the outlands and you are never late for a rendezvous! – Wait until I tell the Master you think he talks too much!" My blood ran cold at this threat.

"Rachel – What I meant to say was -----!" She stopped me.

She leaned close and whispered. "Brave Jaacov – I would never say anything to hurt you." Her hand felt like a blazing coal. That warm feeling turned to a deep heat in my chest and sweat began to run down my back. I wanted to run and throw myself into the midst of my sheep. I would be safe there. This woman was making me dizzy.

I stood with all intentions to run, but I did not. I simply stood there with my back to Rachel. The silence was overpowering.

Even the sheep could sense the intensity as they stood transfixed.

"Jaacov! – Jaacov!" It was Malisch calling, his voice had alarm in it.

"Here ! – Malisch! - Here in the shed! – Rachel is here also!" I called back.

"The Master seeks you! – He seeks you now!" I ran toward the great house with Rachel close on my heels. Malisch was visibly upset. "I told you last night that the Master wanted to see you this morning! – don't you remember – I told you?"

"Malisch – It will be alright – I will take the blame if the Master is angry!" I followed Malisch as Rachel stopped at the gate and as I looked back she had her hands clutched over her heart. I wondered if she suffered the same pain as I had felt.

Malisch ushered me into a great hall with columns that reached a domed ceiling. The tiles on the floor were so polished I could see my feet as I stepped toward the Master sitting in a great chair in front of an open window. The view from the window covered the vast expanse of his estate toward Jerusalem.

The Master spoke. "Well! – Jaacov! - for the first time you are late."

For a boy, who had spoken to only a few people in his nearly fourteen years, it would seem difficult to speak with such a great man as the Master. I really felt no fear as I spoke. I simply spoke the truth.

"Master – last night, Malisch told me you wished to see me this morning - As the dawn came - so came a great storm - with Elohim creating great thunder and fire from the sky - The sheep do not understand this and were frightened! - Your slave – Jaacov - went to his sheep and calmed them with his flute - I am distressed that I angered you – Master!"   I fell prostrate at his feet.

The Master was silent and after a moment he drew a long breath and spoke.   "Jaacov – you are truly a wonder - Somehow I feel God has placed his hand on you and has a part you must play in his great plan – RISE! – Young Jaacov – and hear this! – You are not a slave – Your parents came to me with a business proposition and died living that proposition and you fulfilled it. He raised his voice.   "HEAR THIS - MY PEOPLE - JAACOV IS NO SLAVE – HE IS HIS OWN MAN AND ANSWERS ONLY TO GOD!"

The words sent a great surge of well being through my body. I did not understand why, for I had only considered myself a slave since the Nubian boy had referred to me that way only a week ago.   The term slave had no bad meaning to me, yet I felt overjoyed at being my own man.

The Master spoke again.   "Come Jaacov - sit by me – we must talk."   He pushed a cushion to me and I sat at his feet.

"Jaacov – I have been given a great commission and truly feel it is my destiny to accept Caesar Augustus's offer to move to northern Gaul and manage Rome's interest there - He will give me a vast amount of fertile land and the resources to build a great enterprise – Jaacov – I wish you to join me and help with the livestock. – You too will become a great man – young shepherd!"

My mind was awash with doubts.   I could not picture where this country called Gaul was and I remembered Cornelius spoke of an island called Britannia.   All I knew were the rocky sloops and grassy plains around Bethlehem.   Fear began to swell in me. It was another new sensation, but I instinctively knew it was fear.

"You are the only Master I have ever known."   I spoke in a hushed voice.   "I will do as you wish!"

"Excellent – my boy – it is well we leave Judea - for I fear bad times are upon us!" His face turned to a look of gloom as he spoke these words.

The look gave me concern and I asked. "Bad times – Master?"

"Yes – Jaacov – It seems as our King Herod has suspicions of a new movement and a new king! – He senses a revolution - He has asked the Romans to help seek out this new king - If there is a revolution – there will be much bloodshed - It is best that we are not here."

I don't know why, but this made my heart heavy. I remembered Baliue telling of the massacre he witnessed as a young archer for the Hebrews. I pictured the Hebrew soldiers dying as they fought the mighty wall of Roman shields and great Roman warhorses. The Master's words stayed in my mind as I left the great room.

Malisch and Rachel were waiting in the hall. Malisch was all smiles and Rachel threw her arms around me and cried with great relief that I was a free man. I really felt no different; for I had never aspired to anything except tending my sheep. I don't think I wanted anything else. I wanted to rest.

The following weeks were hectic as the household prepared to leave for a ship to take them to Gaul. The Master gave me fifty shekels for the sheep that my parents put into the flock years ago. I knew nothing of the value of money, so I simply placed it in my bag with the stones and hid them away in my old wooly tunic.

One afternoon, the Master sent for me. As I entered the great room I was much surprised to see a group of men that were definitely not from around Bethlehem or Jerusalem. Their dress was richly adorned with fine gold and silver brocades and they wore crowns of brilliant jewels much like those hidden in my pouch.

The Master spoke. "Jaacov - I know you have not been around people much - but these men come seeking a new king that they have heard of in a prophesy - Have you anything you can tell them that may help in their search?" My heart felt a chill.

One of the richly adorned men looked at me and said. "Young man the three of us here are Magi in our lands from the east - we have seen the great star in the east and our scholars tell us it is a sign of a great king sent to save the world - We journey to Jerusalem to ask permission of your King Herod to go and honor this new King – We heard one of the shepherds - there that night - may be here - Can you help us? – Your Master here tells us you witnessed the night the great star appeared." My blood ran cold.

I did not want to lie. I had never had to lie. I really did not know how to lie, but I knew I had to choose my words carefully. I stammered in my answer. "Sire – I was in the fields that night and I heard great sounds and bright lights and it was terrifying. – I followed the beam from the star into Bethlehem, but found only a milling crowd of people and a new baby born in a stable and an Assyrian tried to kick me. I am sorry - Sire - I found no king –I can be of no help."

My Master waved me away and as I left, I heard the Magi say they would continue on to Herod and seek his permission to find this new king.

The day of departure had arrived. I had my meager belonging packed neatly in my pack and was helping to load the last cart. The sound of marching men came from the road to Jerusalem. A detachment of Hebrew guards approached at fast march. We seldom saw Hebrew guards unless they were escorting royalty or staff from King Herod. The Temple also had guards, but required special permission to venture from the Temple grounds. The Romans did not allow any army to exist in a country unless it was enlisted under Roman command. The Hebrews refused to serve under any command that was not ordained by God.

I stood at the rear of the heavily burdened cart and peered around its corner at the guards in their dusty black tunics, helmets and shields. The shields were affixed with the beautiful Star of David.

The guard in charge called for the Master. Malisch ran to the great house calling the Master. Rachel stood to the side and watched with teary eyes.

Rachel's and Malisch's family was not going to Gaul with us. Their father was being left in charge of the vast estate and should something happen to the Master it would become theirs. Rachel had begged me not to go. I knew nothing else except to do the Master's will.

The Master emerged from the great house and was clearly upset by the guard's demands. It was not a popular thing to associate and boldly co-operate with the Romans and the Master felt that King Herod may be upset that he was going to Gaul to aid them. The Master knew he had the support of Rome and with an attitude of superiority asked for the purpose of this visit.

The guard appeared ominous with his full Hebrew beard and was not the least intimidated by the Master's attitude.

"We have come for the shepherd boy that may have knowledge of this new rebel king we search for!" The guard puffed his chest as he exerted his authority. A hush fell over the yard as all activity ceased.

The Master furrowed his brow and I saw Rachel's head jerk my way. The Master slowly shook his head, and said, as if it was of no importance. "I think perhaps the boy you speak of has already gone to the coast to help load the ship for our journey."

He looked around and purposely avoided looking at me as I was almost fully hidden from the view of the guards. "I don't see him here - so he has surely departed! - What purpose would a wild story from a shepherd boy serve our great King Herod?" The Master asked.

The guard answered. "The King's court is hosting some visiting Magi from the east. - These great men have come to honor this new king that is prophesized to save all mankind. - King Herod has ordered these men to return to him with the location and identity of this new king, so he too may honor him!"

The guard continued. "King Herod feels the shepherd boy may assist the visitors in finding the new king." My heart froze with terror. It was another sensation that I had felt in times of danger, only this time it was most intense.

The Master spoke. "Well! I'm sure the boy is gone! – However, if he were here and saw such a mighty force seeking him, he would surely flee!" As the Master uttered these words he turned his head and looked directly into my peeping eyes.

I needed no further instructions. I reached into the cart and pulled my pack to my chest and disappeared into the rocks across the road. My heart was filled with dread, another new sensation. My last glance at the magnificent Khah-vah of the Master was centered on Rachel as she clutched her heart with both hands and watched me depart through her tears.

I ran through the olive groove until I was sure I was not seen. I circled around the estate and proceeded east. I was heading for the oasis on the road from Jerusalem to Bethlehem. My mind raced, filled with the dilemma of what to do. Only a few weeks ago, my greatest problem was wolves, lions and caracals. As I ran, I called to Elohim. "Help me! - Oh great Elohim! – I am but a boy – why not give me back my sheep and let me be in peace?"

It was as if I could not tire. I ran at a gait that even surprised me. I felt no thirst nor did I hunger. My mind and heart was set on the oasis and it was as if a voice in my head urged me on. I ran through the morning and into the afternoon.

Suddenly I saw the tawny flash of a giant caracal as it leaped from the rocks on my right. My sling was packed away in my bag strapped on my back. I had no staff. I could not outrun the giant cat.

Again I called on Elohim and the voice is my mind simply said to run on. The beautiful beast with giant bounds drew close and began to keep pace with me on my right. I could see the gleam in the great yellow eyes as the cat matched my stride. The fear left me as two of Elohim's creations ran side by side. Suddenly the great cat was gone.

I stopped to catch my breath and all was quiet. Behind me in the distance I could hear the calls of a wolf pack. I had passed through the pack unharmed, escorted by a caracal simply out for a relaxing run with an advisory. Elohim was indeed a wise God. The oasis lay only an hour away. I was beginning to grow weary.

I pushed on even though my every muscle cried for rest. I had a driving urge to reach the spring by mid afternoon. I fell upon the grassy slope that led to the pond and feel into an exhausted sleep.

The rush of a cool breeze woke me. It was near sunset and the oasis was quiet. Had any caravans or travelers passed, I would have heard.

I began to reason in my mind the significance of what had transpired that day. I had awakened early and ate with Malisch and Rachel. It was disappointing to find they were not going to Gaul with the Master and me. But the estate would be left in good hands. Rachel was distraught at my leaving. She said she would never find another wild beast as nice as me. Malisch teased her and said she was in love. I didn't fully understand but I did feel a great attraction for this raven haired beauty with the flashing black eyes.

The night chill was approaching. I spread my robe of wool on the ground and unfolded my tattered tunic. The tunic had been cleaned by the Nubians at the Khah-vah, but the smell of the shepherd was still there. The faint fragrance brought back the memories of those simple days and my eyes began to burn. I fought back the tears that would follow and again began to think of why was I here.

I opened my leather pouch and poured the stones and shekels upon the robe. They made a comforting clinking sound. I knew nothing of the great riches in my possession, but they gave me a strange feeling of power. I quickly placed them back in the pouch. I did not care for anything that gave me a new sensation. I had enough of this newness these past weeks.

I was hungry. A quick search found some over ripe dates. They would suffice and along with a long cool drink of water, I was content, at least until morning.

The afternoon sleep, was from exhaustion, and had no effect on me falling to sleep quickly. I was in the cool night breeze, lying on my familiar robe with my old tunic as a pillow. I was home.

The creak of leather and the plop of camel's hooves brought me from my slumber. It was quite dark with a starry sky, but no moon yet. This told me it was still early night. The dark figures of a small caravan were silhouetted on the road from Jerusalem. It was evident; they planned to camp the night at the oasis.

I always stayed on the westside of the oasis, away from the road and near the rocky fields where I could bed my sheep. The caravan had no idea I was there. I had built no fire, so I sat on my robe and watched as the camp was organized.

A large tent of obvious nomadic design and a smaller version was all that was set up. A fire was started, but not the kind that would prepare a meal. The fire simply was for the purpose of human consolation. I had found this out years ago. We shepherds would build a fire, simply to set and watch it burn to coals. It brought comfort and was a source from which we drew security.

I began to hear voices from within the large tent. They spoke an Arabic dialect that I understood little of. One voice sounded familiar. I rose and stealthily moved closer. I found a spot in the deep shadows at the rear of the large tent and made myself as small as I could, to listen.

The familiar voice was distressed at being forced to do something. The others seemed in agreement, but it seemed there was nothing they could do.

"We are in a foreign land and at the mercy of, I think, a villainous king!" The familiar voice proclaimed.

At this the other voices urged him to lower his voice and take care of what he says. "This king must have spies everywhere – he even ordered us to spy for him!" A man proceeded from the tent and looked about, he even came to the edge of the tent where I lay and looked down the dark road toward Jerusalem. He never looked my way. I thanked Elohim.

The three men walked into the night air and gazed at the bright star over Bethlehem. The familiar voice whispered. "I will never understand why no one can see that star's radiance coming down on Bethlehem - Everyone sees the star - but the beam is only seen by few!"

Another voice whispered. "I do not trust this King Herod – he says he wants to also honor this new king -but he doesn't want to hear about the Prophesy of his own people!"

"Perhaps we should abandon our search!" Another voice urged - "We can just slip away and go home."

The familiar voice spoke in a chiding tone. "Slip away home? – Are you an explorer - do you know this wild country – do you know that a giant chasm does not block our way home or if some band of thieves will let us pass? – I am sure that every road is watched! - No! – My friend – I am afraid this King Herod has us trapped - tomorrow we must find this new king! – God's will be done!"

I quietly returned to my pallet and lay there with the words of the visitors pounding through my head.

The call of the morning bird brought me to my feet. I stood and looked toward the tents of the visitors. The Magi that spoke to me at the Master's Khah-vah was looking straight at me across the pond. I did not panic. I simply stood motionless, hoping he would simply think I was a lone shepherd.

Slowly he began to thrust his head forward as if studying me. He took a small step closer as if that would help him to focus. Suddenly he raised his face to the heavens and placed his hands together and began to cry out in his native tongue. I had no idea what he was shouting, but it was clearly a prayer of thanksgiving. I looked over my shoulder to see if the heavens had opened and he too was seeing a miracle.

The other Magi dashed from the tent, all were still dressed in their long sleeping garments. The first Magi began to excitedly babble and pointed at me. The excitement must have been contagious as the other men began to jump and raise their hands in thanksgiving.

Suddenly the Magi gathered their long sleeping gowns up in their hands and began a gangling run around the pond. They were coming my way. I felt no fear and it would have been easy to gather my few belongings and be over the nearest hill and out of their reach. I watched them as they approached. It was evident that they had seldom run in their lives. The slippers they wore did little to cushion the many stones they stepped on and the rush of energy that prompted them to run to me was quickly spent.

It seemed that these great men would have simply commanded me come to them. In my simplicity and respect for others I probably would have gone. I felt honored that they dropped all pretence of importance and came running almost barefooted in their sleeping gowns to talk to a shepherd boy. I felt a new sensation. I don't know what is was, but I put it aside until later.

I stood as the men approached breathless and panting, instinctively looking for a place to sit. I felt remiss in having no stool or cushion to offer.

The Magi that spoke to me placed a hand on my shoulder and gasped. "Young shepherd! – You are a pawn of God! - We prayed and he sent you! - Praises be to God!" The three men spoke, in unison, a prayer in a language and chant I did not understand.

"God is truly good - young shepherd! – Last night we were in such a dilemma and prayed for God's will to be done and he sent you!" This Magi was recovering quickly from his brief run. "Come! – Young man and share our breakfast – we have much to ask you.

I relished the idea of a nice breakfast, but did not want it on a misunderstanding. The words of the Magi troubled me and I needed to clear it up.

"Sire! - A question if you please?" I asked.

He looked at his friends and all nodded approval.

"Sire – You said you prayed for God's will last night and God sent me?" They nodded in agreement. I continued. "That is what confuses me – you see I left my Master's early yesterday morning."

There was a brief moment of utter silence and then all three men broke into that deep genuine laughter that comes from utter surprise. I was more confused than ever.

"Come – my boy – you can teach us much – you pleasure us with such simple honesty!" The Magi placed his arm around my shoulders and we walked to the camp.

The breakfast was wonderful. The Magi introduced themselves as Gaspar, Balthasar and Melchior. Gaspar told me that the sausages contained the meat of the swine and perhaps I should not eat it. I asked what a swine was and found it to be the same as our wild pigs. I knew that some of the shepherds did not eat the flesh of the pig, but I had found it to be quite tasty. This sausage had a seasoning that made my eyes water and required some water to calm the fire. This sausage would require getting used to.

The Magi insisted I tell the story of that night the star appeared. As I retold the story, I would rush by some detail I felt to be personal. Gaspar would stop me and insist on every detail, no matter, how I felt about it. They were totally intent and devoured every word.

The Magi discussed my rendition and all agreed that it fit the Prophesy perfectly.

Gaspar spoke. "Your name – is Jaacov?" I nodded

"Jaacov – we have a dilemma – your King Herod wants us to return to him with the information on the new King - He has made it quite clear – we don't have much choice in this affair – We three do not feel good about giving him the information – God warned us in a dream that no good will come of this situation.

I pleaded. "The new King is a child – surely no King would fear a child!

Balthasar held up a finger.   "Herod does not know the Prophesy – it is only a matter of time before one of his counselors will convince him that the new King is a child and that is what we fear."

The Magi began to tell me of the Prophesy found in all the old writings and scrolls. It was more than I could comprehend. They spoke of the ancient scrolls of Moses – Isaiah – Hosea – Malachi – Jeremiah – and even in the songs of King Solomon and the story of David. The city of Bethlehem was even named in Micah. The Magi were very wise men and had studied the Prophesy all their lives.

Melchior spoke up! "This is not a popular belief – but to me the Prophesy clearly states - this child is the son of God!" I was stunned, and immediately a heated discussion flared between the Magi.

Gaspar raised his voice. "Enough! – We have been through this before and have all agreed that we must see the child to be sure!" Quiet reigned again.

I had a thought. I felt perhaps I shouldn't offer my thoughts to such wise men. I felt sure they had thought all thoughts already.

I asked just the same. "A question Sire?" They nodded. "If it is true that this child is the son of God – then I don't think any man could cause him harm – so why worry in vain?"

The Magi all looked at me with an air of understanding. "That is a wise assumption – young shepherd and we feel the same – however – the Prophesy tells us it will be different and the scrolls of Isaiah even tell of his death - It seems that our Savior will resurrect and then his kingdom will be established.

I had another thought; I feared the wise Magi would tire of my thoughts.   I ask just the same. "A question – Sire?" Again the men nodded.   "You called this Savior your's – this Babe is a Hebrew – you are not Hebrew." The Magi looked at me intently and Melchior spoke. "Wise young shepherd – do you not recall your own words as you repeated the voice from Heaven?"

I thought and it came to me. The voice from heaven said. "FOR ALL PEOPLE!"

The wise men then told me that the knowledge of God was with all men that sought truth. They explained how God was before anything else was. God has always been, God is now and God will be forever. There is nothing that is not of God and nothing made without God. Wise men can see this and seek the knowledge of God.

Melchior stated. "God made a covenant with Abraham – but the scriptures tell us that before this covenant Abraham paid homage to a Gentile Priest of God.

They explained how God had chosen the Hebrew people to exemplify his relationship with man. The Magi continued, but my simple mind could not comprehend it all.   Something deep inside told me to do the bidding of these wise men.

Gaspar leaned close and said. "You have been chosen by God to play a role in the greatest event to unfold before mankind – can you do it Jaacov – can you?"

I simply nodded. My mind was lost in the words of the wise men and I felt very small.

"Then take us to the Christ Child!" The three wise Magi cheered as children and they ordered the camp to pack and proceed to Bethlehem.

I asked the Magi to have the servant gather as many of the fermented dates that had dropped on the ground as they could carry. They wanted to know why and I asked them to simply trust me for the camels would need them.

The plan was to enter Bethlehem and go to the Inn. They would make arrangements to stay the night and simply lounge around the Inn as if refreshing from their long journey.

I was to find Joseph's home near the Inn as Cornelius had told me. I would then see if the visit was convenient. If so, after the visit, the Magi would return to the Inn and pretend to retire for the night. After all were asleep the Magi would slip out and I would show them another way home.

The Magi had decided they must obey God's message in the dream. Returning to Jerusalem and Herod was out of the question. I knew these plains and hills for they were my home.

Joseph did not recognize me, but Mary stood and breathed a sigh of relief as she said, "Jaacov you are safe and well!"

"You know this boy – Mary?" Joseph asked. It was clear he did not recall our meeting almost two years ago.

"Joseph!" Mary chided. "How could you forget the young man that Cornelius struck with his lance at the oasis?"

"Ahhh! – That young man – I would hardly recognize him – seeing how he has grown and wearing such a tunic and his hair all cut and neat – well – almost neat." Joseph gave a genuine smile of approval.

I suppose the long run and two days being out in the open had an effect on my hair. "Lady Mary – where is the Babe?" I asked with baited breath.

Mary smiled and said softly. "He is no longer a Babe – he is quite a runabout now – he is out back with the animals."

"May I see him?" I asked.

"Of course you may see him!" - Mary rose and stepped toward the rear of the house and called sweetly.   "Jesus! – Jesus! – Jaacov is here – come quick! I could hear the patter of small feet as they approached the rear door.

"Yes Mother – I am here." The child stepped into the house holding a small rabbit with a bandaged foot.

He was radiant. He looked just like any child nearly two years old, but he seemed to glow from within. He looked at me as he scratched the bunny's head. I felt a warm ripple flow through my body. The most magnificent feeling of wellbeing swept over me. He raised his hand and pointed at me and softly whispered. "JAACOV" I nearly fainted.

Mary began to speak.   "I have told Jesus all about our encounter at the spring and Cornelius has made you seem like a legend - Have you seen Cornelius since the oasis?"

I told Mary of my meeting Cornelius some weeks past and how proud I was of him being an officer.   Mary told me they worried about Cornelius being a Roman and now believing in Elohim. She also told me that Cornelius was concerned about the personality change in King Herod. It seems he has a growing fixation on finding this rebel king, as he puts it.

I then told Mary and Joseph of the wise Magi that waited at the Inn. They wanted to honor the Christ Child. Joseph said they were told in a dream and had been expecting them. Joseph said it was part of God's plan.   I left and proceeded to the waiting Magi.

As I entered the Inn I saw Gaspar and Melchior at a table in the rear of the room. Gaspar lay a finger to his lips and motioned me to look out the side window.

My heart nearly stopped as I saw two Roman soldiers talking with Balthasar.   I looked frantically at Gaspar and he motioned me to meet them in the stable. I hastily left the Inn and proceeded to the stable, using the far side of the building and scaling a stone fence. My heart was beating wildly in my chest and I shut my eyes. I begged Elohim to let me wake up and be in the field with my sheep.

The three wise men entered the stable and assured me all was well. Balthasar had been informed by their servant that one of the dukhans had broken.

The dukhan was made to carry supplies on a camel's back and needed repair before they could travel. Balthasar had asked the soldiers where he may find a blacksmith or possibly a carpenter.

I could not believe how God went about working his will. I breathlessly told the Magi that the Christ Child's father was a carpenter.

The three men gasped in unison and fell on their knees and once again raised their hands and faces to heaven. The prayers that followed were in tongues I did not understand. I felt very inadequate to be a part of God's Plan.

These most important, wise, wealthy and intelligent men were on their knees giving thanks to an unseen God and all I had done was note my amazement at how God was working his will. I had a lot to learn about this great God called Elohim.

The Magi regained their composure and now had a genuine reason to seek out a carpenter, that just so happened to be the guardian of the Christ Child.

The broken dukhan was cinched on a camel's back and loaded with some packages wrapped in fine silk.

As we proceeded through the street toward Joseph's house the servant made it obvious that he had to hold the broken dukhan to keep the packages from falling.

Frequent request were made for the carpenter's house. All was going well and we reached the home of Joseph and Mary. There should be no reason to suspect this visit to be anything more than to repair a broken dukhan.

The Magi were visibly apprehensive as they each took a package from the camels pack. The rest of the gear was set by the wall of the house as the bearer removed the wooden platform and set it on the ground as well.

The three men stood mute and then with eye and head gesture only, Gaspar was chosen to knock upon the door. The emotion was evident as he raised his hand and stopped momentarily before his hand fell on the door of their lifelong dream's fulfillment. The sound of his rap seemed to echo through the streets and began a crescendo that rose to the heavens.

There was a deafening silence and then the door open and the sweet voice of Mary broke the silence.

Her words were simple. "Welcome – Jesus wants to see you!"

The door closed and I was left outside. I immediately wanted to run to the door and call about the broken dukhan, but in my head a voice said that God's Plan was in progress. It said. "Be still!"

I sat with my back to the wall and there was silence in the house. I could feel a power radiating through the walls, but heard no sound. Presently I heard the small clear voice of Jesus as he named each of the Magi. "GASPAR – BALTHASAR - MELCHIOR" I then heard the astonished gasp of the wise men as the realization came full force. This was, indeed, the Christ Child. Silence again.

Shortly the door opened and Joseph stepped out and picked up the broken dukhan. He looked at me and said. "Well done – young Man – but your night is not yet over!" He turned and proceeded around the house while motioning for the servant to follow him.

I sat alone and listened as the Magi told of the Prophesy and their life's work. The emotion in their voices gave evidence of their conviction.

Mary told them of an old man at the Temple named Simeon that recognized Jesus as the Christ. She related the story of how Simeon thanked God for allowing him to live long enough to see the Savior of the world. She told the Magi that Simeon said that Christ was for the Gentiles as well as the Hebrew people.

Mary continued telling of a woman named Anna that had served the Temple since she was widowed as a young woman. She too, recognized Jesus as the Lord's Christ.

The Magi presented Jesus with gifts of gold, frankincense and myrrh. They then bowed and lifted their voices in praise, worship and thanksgiving for having had their life's work and passion fulfilled this night.

Joseph returned with the mended dukhan and assisted the bearer in cinching it to the camel; he then went into the house.

Presently the Magi emerged with the most glorious expressions on their faces. We returned to the Inn without a word being spoken. As we entered the stable, Melchior called to the servant and gave hushed orders to be packed and ready to leave around midnight. Melchior stressed that no one must know we are leaving. I told the servant to mix all the fermented dates in the feed for the camels. Again I was bombarded with questions as to why.

I explained. "I have seen my sheep eat these over ripened dates and for some reason they have more energy than they can stand! --They will run and cavort and it will last for hours! - They don't think of food and water or even look as if they are tired - this night I will show you a way to escape - but it will require your camels to travel fast and far! - When King Herod realizes you are not returning he will request Roman assistance and they must not be able to overtake you.

Gaspar leaned over to me and said. "You are indeed sent from God!" Come now – we must rest!"

The streets were empty and it was very quiet. It seemed as if the camel's hooves were hammers striking giant drums as they plodded along. The leather creaked louder than I had ever heard. The lone Roman guard simply looked up as we exited the town and started up the lonely road to the oasis. The guard simply thought we were on the way back to Jerusalem. He may not have even known of King Herod's request for the Magi to report to him, but when questioned he would say they departed toward Jerusalem.

We reached the oasis and the Magi voiced great concern for me and pleaded with me to accompany them on the journey home. I told them all I knew was sheep and felt my place was in this land. They departed reluctantly.

I explained to the Magi. "Just over the crest on the road to Jerusalem is a low ridge of hills that run east - There is no trail as it is only used by shepherds - You must turn east and keep the hills on your left until you come to an ancient river bed that runs through the hills - The land in this river bed is dry and very flat."

I explained. "Now! – Great Magi – is the time for your camels to fly - The moon will light your path and there is little for the camels to stumble on - Make great haste north, until the light of dawn - you may now turn east and continue to your eastern homelands with no fear of King Herod."

Nothing further was spoken as the small caravan creaked away. I watched the shadowy figures until they crossed the crest and listened to faint plods of the camel's hooves until the silence overpowered them.

I heard the faint howl of the wolves as I sat by the spring and thought of all that occurred since that night the star first appeared. I lay back to relax and drifted off in cautious slumber.

Something was not the same. I slowly gathered my slumbering thoughts and began to examine them. I heard no sound of wolves or the caracal. I felt for my pack, it was at my side. I noticed the moon was low on the dark horizon ----"That was it!" – Dark! – The star was gone. I look around the sky, I don't know why I looked around, I knew where Bethlehem was and the star had been there almost two years. Yes! – It was definitely gone. A feeling of panic came over me as I jumped to my feet.

Suddenly there was a new sound. It was not the hooves of horses or the plods of camels. It was the sound of feet, many feet. Soldiers were coming at fast march. Why would soldiers be coming so fast as this early hour and if they were Roman where was their commander who was almost always mounted.

I began to hear voices and could tell that the breathing was labored. I grabbed my pack and retreated to the bushes to hide. The soldiers topped the hill and began to shout in relief at the site of the spring running through the oasis. No order was given but the timed step of the soldiers gave way to a flurry of uncontrolled running as the men descended on the cool refreshing pond.

I began to hear heartfelt thanks as numerous prayers were lifted to Yahweh, Elohim, and other names that Hebrews used for God and realized the soldiers were guards from the palace of King Herod. These soldiers hardly ever left the palace without Roman supervision. My mind raced. These men were my kindred and fellow countrymen. Why did I have this feeling of fear and foreboding

I crouched low and listened as two of the soldiers came near and lay upon the ground.

A gruff voice spoke. "I tell you I don't like it – I'm almost tempted to run out into the wilderness!"

The other voice replied. "Shush! – You imbecile! – You will get both our heads chopped off with that talk! - Besides we all know this is no time for a rebellion and surely no King could be better to us than Herod!"

Again the gruff voice whispered "I know! - I know! – But still - I don't like the idea of killing our own people! – Why not get the Romans to do it?" My body froze at these words.

The other voice spoke with a patronizing tone. "Now listen – my friend – the Romans do not share Herod's belief in some new king leading a rebellion and they certainly would not see any threat from a child.

"I still don't like it!" The gruff Roman uttered. "The Romans are going to be very upset by this deed!"

The other Roman replied with confidence. "Herod will explain that it was in Rome's best interest and necessary to quell a rebellion and that will settle it. - Remember the Kings words my friend! – All male children two years and younger – from Bethlehem to the coast! – THEY MUST DIE!"

CHAPTER III

FLIGHT TO EGYPT

I heard the Hebrew guards exclaim surprise as I dashed from my crouched position.

"That has to be an Ibex!" One exclaimed.

The other voice exclaimed. "No! - The foot sounds are much louder and close together – I think it may be a caracal – No matter! – It is no threat to us! – Come we must get back to the others – there is much to do before dawn!"

I felt as if my feet scarcely touched the ground as I fled toward Bethlehem. Joseph and Mary must be warned. My heart pounded in my chest as I thought of that sweet little child at the point of a sword. The voices had said all little boys two years of age and younger in Bethlehem and to the coast.

As I ran, I met others as they began their daily routine. They were masters taking supplies to the shepherds in the fields. A small caravan was making its way along the rocky road and I heard the cry of a small child in the back of a wagon. My eyes began to burn and the tears flowed down my cheek. I stopped and turn back.

I shouted through my tears. "Leave the road! – Take to the rocks! – Soldiers are coming to kill your man-child!" The wagon stopped and the man turned to look at me. He said nothing, he simply looked. A woman's head appeared from under the wagon cover.

Again I shouted. Flee! – Flee to the rocks – The soldiers will kill all boy babies! They were motionless. I could delay no longer and as I turned and dashed down the road, I once again cried. "Flee! – Flee!

I could hear the creak of the wagon as it set out once again. I never knew if it did flee or not.

I ran on and as I entered Bethlehem, the faint glow of dawn was breaking over the horizon where Jerusalem lay. I wondered if that monster, King Herod, was asleep in his bed or was he thinking of the gruesome order he had given to shed the precious young male blood of his own countrymen.

I ran through the dusty streets still damp with the early morning dew. I dared not make a noise for fear that someone would stop me and I could not warn Mary and Joseph.

As I turned at the corner past the Inn, I saw a wagon with a donkey at harness. As I approached, Joseph stepped out with an armload of belonging and placed them in the wagon.

I called with gasping breath. "Sire Joseph! – Soldiers come to kill Jesus – they come now!' I fell to the ground. Exhaustion overwhelmed me.

Mary was instantly at my side. She bathed my face with a cool cloth. "We are packing now – Jaacov! – We are preparing to leave! She smiled, but I could sense the tension in her voice.

"Lady Mary – the Christ Child must not die! I pleaded.

"Joseph's calm voice came to my ears. "We know – Jaacov - God told us in a dream - we must flee to Egypt!"

My mind froze in panic. I felt as if the world would end. The child would surely die. The Prophesy said he would die.

"Not Egypt! - Sire Joseph! - That road will be watched and even if you leave town before the soldiers find you – the wagon will slow your progress and you will be overtaken!"

Mary eyes grew wide with concern and Joseph stood transfixed in thought.

I bowed my head and called on Elohim. I bowed my head only to give my plea full concentration. My mind seemed to go blank and all I could hear was emptiness. The emptiness reminded me of the field and rocks where I tended my sheep and I heard the faint sound of the horn as it wafted through the hills.

I strained my ears and there was another sound! - yes another sound! It was a voice and it was repeating the word "Sanctuary! – Sanctuary!   Suddenly the voice was my own thoughts as I remembered the tall robed man in the hills to the west near Capra.

His voice came to me. "Yaacov! - If you ever need sanctuary – come to these hills!"

I jumped to my feet. "Sire Joseph! – I know a way! – Yes! – There is a way! - They will not find you. - They will not even consider looking this way for the Christ Child!"

Joseph looked at me intently. "God has a plan and Jaacov – you are no doubt a part of his plan – lead us young Jaacov!"

"Sire! – we must carry all the water and wine we can find and much food for the donkey - We must hurry!" I felt honored for neither Mary nor Joseph asked about my plan.

Bethlehem began to fade in the distance as we headed east. It seemed we could hear wails and screams floating in the breeze as we progressed. The day was beautiful and I thought how strange for something so horrible to be going on in the distance.

God had provided a flock of sheep. The shepherd and I had crossed paths in the past. I explained nothing, but told him if we could travel with him, we would all share a nice dinner. This pleased him greatly and Joseph flashed me a knowing smile. If the soldiers even considered we would escape into the badlands toward the salt sea, we would simply look like shepherds fortunate enough to have a donkey and wagon.

As we traveled, I explained my plan to Joseph. I prayed that the tall robed man was still alive and remembered his promise.

We saw no pursuit. The shepherd remained in the grassy plains where we had lunch. I could see the hills of the salt sea ahead. We would have just one night in the open and would be near the big rock late on the morrow. We did not camp that night. We rested a bit and then proceeded.

The donkey being unused to such demand, began to balk. Joseph, in his kindness, was reluctant to press the animal. The young boy, Jesus rose from his little pallet and taking the reins from Mary, gave a gently snap of the leather straps across the back of the donkey and as if refreshed by a night's slumber and a hearty breakfast the animal briskly move along.

The shadows were getting long as I finally located the big rock. We stopped on the other side and I walked to where Joseph stood. "Listen carefully for the whir of the sling on the twang of the bow!" I suggested, as I looked at Joseph.

I said "I prayed to Elohim that this was the right thing to do! – Sire! - I heard no voice like that night in the fields as the Angel spoke of the Babes birth - but we are about to find out if this plan is what God wanted." Joseph nodded approval.

I stepped forth and called as loud as I could. "I AM JAACOV - JAACOV OF THE SHEEP – WE SEEK PASSAGE!"

The silence was deafening. No breeze, no cries of animals. No flutter of birds. We waited and our eyes scanned the rocks.

Again I called. "JAACOV OF THE SHEEP SEEKS A WORD WITH THE ROBED MAN!" Still the silence remained. I wondered if possibly they had all died or been killed by some plague worse than their afflictions.

My mind raced and suddenly that little voice I thought was my own mind said. "King David and the Prophesy!"

I stepped further forward thinking it would help me to be better heard.

"JAACOV OF THE SHEEP BRINGS THE PROPHESY - BORN TO SAVE ALL MEN - THIS CHILD IS THE CHRIST AND COMES FROM THE HOUSE OF KING DAVID – KING HEROD SEEKS HIS LIFE AND HE SEEKS PASSAGE TO EGYPT THROUGH YOUR MOUNTAIN PASS – WE ARE AT YOUR MERCY – WILL YOU GRANT SAFE PASSAGE?"

The silence lasted only a few moments and a horn was sounded and then another horn and another, suddenly the hills were filled with the glorious triumphant blast of horns. There were hundreds, maybe thousands of horns blowing the sounds of welcome to the Christ Child.

-------------------------- --

The wagon and the Holy Family were still faintly visible as they made their way through the trail that led to the salt sea. When the sea was reached they would turn south and follow the river that led to the plush and fertile fields. The family would then turn west and find the main caravan road that led to safe haven in Egypt.

I could not find it in my heart to go with them. Joseph and Mary pleaded with me and pointed out all the bad things that could happen if Herod found I aided in the escape. All I wanted was to go back and tend my sheep. Hopefully I could find a flock that needed a good shepherd. I felt insecure in the roles I had been placed in. Surely Elohim would let me go back to my sheep. I felt I was not suited for God's Plan.

I lay on my wooly robe that night and the vision of the Child pointing at me as the wagon pulled away ran through my mind. He softly said my name and that wonderful feeling of wellbeing surged through me again.

Still, I slept fitfully that night. I would startle at the least sound. It seems silent in the fields and in the mountains when you are listening for a sound, but when you lie and try to relax your senses to sleep, the little beetle rolling a dead wasp along will sound like a camel with six legs, dragging a sled filled with pottery.

I arrived in Bethlehem shortly after mid-day and found the town like a tomb. The people that wandered the streets looked haggard and wistful. I would pass some houses and could see the dried spatter of blood on a wall or door sill.

Paying closer attention to the sounds, I could hear the sobbing and sing song prayers of the distraught parents as they tried to reason why their King would take the life of their baby boy.

There were no signs of any funerals. In Hebrew custom, the dead must be placed in the grave by sunset. I found the house of Mary and Joseph. I entered and found the house a shambles. If the Child had been hidden, the soldiers would surely have found him. In the small stable for the donkey I found some stale bread and grain in the crib. That would suffice for my meal.

I was exhausted and lay on the bed. The furniture was all still in the house, but most of the covering was gone. The straw mattress was very comforting. I fell into a hard sleep that is often the result of exhaustion. This type of sleep can cost a man his life. The little mental alarms that alert you to danger are simply silenced and you can sleep your way to death.

The crash of the door woke me with a start. I was in a momentary daze. Was I in the hills with the robed man, or perhaps at the Khah-vah with the master or by the spring at the oasis? Where were my sheep? The door lay half off the hinges and the silhouette of a giant caped man blocked the sunshine from entering.

I could hear the man wheezing to catch his breath. I could also hear the great heaving sound of a horse's labored breathing.

The air was suddenly filled with the stench of animal and human perspiration

The man issued a gigantic sob and fell to his knees. The light now illuminated his head. He wore the tufted helmet of a Roman officer. The man was Cornelius.

"The Child is safe!" I whispered.

The Roman did not know I was there and was startled at the sound of my voice. He strained his eyes to focus on me as I sat in the bed.

I whispered. "Do not fear – Sire Cornelius – The Christ Child journeys safely to Egypt!

Again the Roman strained his eyes as he leaned forward. "Jaacov – Is it you Jaacov?" He spoke hesitantly.

"I whispered again. "Yes my friend Cornelius! – It is Jaacov." The man rose in a flash and dashed to the bed. He scooped me in his arms as if I were a child and the sobs that came forth were a genuine sign of his relief.

Amid the sobs the man asked. "Is he really safe – Jaacov?

I answered. "Yes Sire!"

He continued. "Mary and Joseph – they too are safe?"

"Yes Sire – they are all safe."

The sobs subsided and the man released his embraced. He held me by the shoulders and looked me up and down. "My Hebrew friend, you are growing like the weeds in my grandfather's abandoned garden in Rome! Come we must talk."

The Roman removed his helmet and loosened his belt as he straightened the table and set the chairs upright. We sat and I unfolded the entire story from the time we had talked at the oasis until he crashed through the door.

It was almost funny to hear the Roman say he wished he was a Hebrew. "We Romans never have miracles happen to us this way! - We have to make our own destiny and most times it is a disaster!"

He never once voiced any doubt about anything I told him. He said that our God was truly the greatest God of all. I interrupted and asked forgiveness for being bold. I told him that our God was the only God so there were no other Gods to be greater than.

He laughed at my saying this and looking at me, he said. "That statement could only come from the wisdom of Godly innocence!"

He grew solemn and with measured words he whispered. "I am now a firm believer in the God of the Hebrew - Being a Roman soldier - I owe my allegiance to Rome - and I still see no evil in the Roman way of governing the provinces."

"Young Jaacov – everywhere I go I see the people under Roman rule are better off than before - the strife that occurs is a result of a rebellious attitude -   Rome always responds to protect its interest."

Cornelius continued. "Rome cares not what anyone believes or what God they worship as long as they continue to serve Rome's interest - I believe I am now a part of God's plan for all mankind and I believe that God wants me to use my position as a Roman officer to serve him.

I had no argument, but I had a question. "Cornelius Sire – Is the murder of these little boys in Rome's best interest?"

"Damn you boy!" The brutal Roman was back. I was shocked and Cornelius's face grew livid.   He rose and pounded his massive fist upon the table as he leaned toward me. I thought I was dead.

He spoke with deliberation. "We Romans knew nothing of this and would have not permitted it - had we known - I was in Caesarea dealing with some Assyrian pirates and returned as soon as I heard - This King Herod broke the agreement he had with Rome and overstepped his authority - His use of a rebellion and uprising is a total lie and comes from his personal fear and insecurity.! - The sad thing – boy - is Rome will do nothing about it - It is an internal religious matter and they will censor Herod and that will end it!"

He turned and walked to the door. He motioned me to follow. He step out and looked at the sky. It was evident he wanted God to hear what he had to say. "Great God in Heaven! - I am Cornelius – an officer in the Judean Centuriae of Rome! - I pledge to you - My God - to do all in my power to never let this King Herod use his influence to harm your people again!"

He paused and then took a deep breath as if air would clear his mind. He turned to me and said. "It looks as if your Master has set sail for Gaul without you – what are your plans – my friend?"

I looked away so he could not see the uncertainty in my eyes and answered. "I will find a flock of sheep and will shepherd them as I have always done – this taking part in God's Plan is dangerous and I am not very good at it."

"Jaacov – you are truly an innocent soul – if you cannot see how God is using you then you need some help – Jaacov! – You will come with me to Jerusalem and will be my aid. I need someone I can trust and someone that can blend and mingle with your Hebrew brothers. I will never ask you to spy because my heart lies with the Hebrews – but you see – Jaacov - I need you and God needs you. – What say you Jaacov?"

I answered with only one reservation. "Sire Cornelius – Do you have any sheep?"

CHAPTER IV

Roman Justice

I had never been astride a horse before and sitting behind Cornelius was drawing attention as we entered Jerusalem. The Roman soldiers we passed simply thought I was a wayward young hoodlum that a Roman officer had apprehended. The Hebrews cast a doubtful eye on me and I felt quite uncomfortable.

I slide from the horse's back and stepped to the ground. Cornelius immediately stopped and spun around. He looked at me and suddenly saw the curious look on the people in the marketplace. It only took him a moment to assess the situation and instinctively sensed the atmosphere.

In a voice of authority he boomed. "There! – Boy! - You have rested enough – now follow me and keep up this time!" He swung his mount around and proceeded along the street. He never looked back.

The crowd instantly went back to their activities. The relationship between a Roman officer and a young Hebrew boy was clarified.

I followed at a comfortable distance and was no longer drawing any attention. I felt more relaxed and began to enjoy the sights of a big city. The streets were not of dirt as in Bethlehem, but stone and very smooth. The houses and shops had awnings of colorful cloth over the fronts of the buildings. People sat around on stools and some even lounged on pillows. We passed the Temple and I vaguely remembered it from a short visit some years before.

It was magnificent and many people were going in and out of the gates. I marveled at the smooth finish on the walls. The Temple guards lounged at the gates, some sat on stools. Their shields of black with the Star of David on the face lay idly against the walls.

As we approached the last gate a Hebrew guard stopped a man dressed in rags and after a very short conversation the tattered man was turned away and not allowed to enter the Temple courtyard. I felt compassion for the ragged man as probably all he wanted was to pray to Elohim.

The smells were appetizing as we passed Inns and places that served food. Some tables were set outside and the patrons were enjoying their evening meal. I was getting hungry.

Cornelius called back to me. "Do not lag - Boy! – These Hebrews will put you to sweeping their steps! – It is not much further – Stay close now!"

I wanted to laugh at his pretense, but he realized that Hebrews would frown upon a friendly relationship with a gentile. I noticed a sly smile as he turned his head. I decided to play this game and picked up my step with a humble bow in my posture.

I thought it strange that in only a few weeks I had learned of the class differences in people. I thought I was a slave and then found I was free. I felt no different. I was beginning to relish the bond I had developed with this Roman. Now he was pretending I was his slave and I was enjoying it. I suddenly missed my sheep. I did not have to pretend anything with them. All they wanted was for me to lead them to food and keep the wild things away.

We turned a corner and at the end of the street was a hill. Atop the hill was a stone fence. A red tiled roof was visible above the fence with a trellised balcony under the gable of the roof.

Cornelius looked at me and nodded toward the site. This was the home of Cornelius.

The guard at the gate snapped to attention as Cornelius approached. "Cornelius returns! – Cornelius returns! The guard shouted in a loud voice.

Immediately there was a stir from within the walls of the complex as we entered the gate. Roman soldiers in various modes of dress came running from all directions. Some were only in their undergarments, others were dressed in the familiar Roman soldier dress but without swords, helmets or the leathered plates that provided armor against the sword and spear. We viewed a large courtyard surround by nine villas all with a balcony under the gable of each red tile roof

All seemed extremely happy to see this Roman officer. One of the Romans spoke. "Cornelius my friend – it is good you are back, I certainly hope your adventure was rewarding– because Flavius wants an audience as soon as possible! This remark caused Cornelius to pull his mount to an abrupt halt.

"Flavius? – Did one of you – my fine friends - tell him I was gone?" Cornelius was very concerned.

The Roman soldier spoke again. "There was no need to tell him – he sought you out!" He was quite upset when word reached him of the massacre in Bethlehem - he came to send you and your men to investigate! - You told no one anything when you stormed out of here! – We told Flavius we thought you had gone to see for yourself!"

The Roman drew close to Cornelius ear and spoke lowly. "Cornelius – No one here told him of your friendship with the Hebrew family in Bethlehem!"

Cornelius and the soldier embraced in a quick manly clank of metal, leather and hard muscle. A cheer went up from the surrounding soldiers. It was evident of the affection and loyalty that bound these men together.

"Gnaeus my friend – I wish you to meet my new – Eh! – servant – Yaacov!" It thrilled me that Cornelius referred me as his servant. All the servants I had seen were well fed and seemed to live a comfortable life.

Cornelius continued. He now spoke much louder so all within earshot could hear. "Harkin my brothers! – This young Hebrew is the one I told you of last year – Yaacov - he has the strength of a young lion - the stealth of a wolf and the cunning of a caracal. He is my servant – but also a free man - He goes as he pleases and is free to leave whenever he wishes!"

A shout went up from the men and I felt good. I cannot explain why, but I simply felt good.

A voice from far in the rear called out. "Cornelius my friend! – He is quite pretty – this Hebrew boy – I thought surly you brought us a new playmate!"

A hush fell over the courtyard. Cornelius slowly stepped out into a clearing among the men. All could tell he was going to speak profoundly. "I - Cornelius – Decanus in the Roman Centurae of Jerusalem has never shed Roman blood! – However – If any harm befalls this Hebrew lad at the hands of one of you – my friends!" There was pause as if Cornelius could not believe he was really saying these words. "My sword shall taste your blood! – Now! – Someone send word to Flavius that Cornelius has a report for him from Bethlehem! - and will be there as soon as he washes the camel dung and donkey guck from his body!" Another resounding cheer went up from the men gathered in the courtyard and they began to disperse.

"Come Yaacov – we must bath – I have some explaining to do!" Cornelius led the way to the last villa at the end of the courtyard. The surrounding villas had once been homes to some of the elite in Jerusalem. The Romans simply had a wall built around nine of the homes and then had a common courtyard built for the assembly of the soldiers.

Cornelius and Gnaeus were the two Decanus housed at this complex. Each had about twenty soldiers under their command. Across Jerusalem was another compound of equal strength which housed the Centurion, Flavius.

Cornelius and I stripped for a bath. I watch Cornelius carefully as I did not want to assume anything in this very strange environment. I was shocked at the massive muscles that Cornelius had. His close shaven face did not match the rest of his body. He had massive chest hair and he noticed my curious glance. He laughed.

"Don't Hebrew men have hair on their chest?" Yaacov. He clearly had a humorous note in his voice.

I answered. "I have never seen a naked Hebrew man – Sire – only naked sheep – there does not seem to be much difference." I did not intend any humor, but Cornelius roared with uncontrollable laughter. He laughed so hard that tears came from his eyes. These Romans were, indeed, a strange lot.

Our bath consisted of a large vase of water that pivoted on a high stand. We would stand naked under the vase and pulled a long cord attached to a lever and the vase would tilt and pour the water over us. There was a clay bowl on a stand that contained a scented paste that we rubbed on our bodies. The dust and dirt was then rinsed away with a second tilt of the vase. Very large and soft linens were folded nearby that we dried our bodies with. It was invigorating to feel the newness that results after a bath. I thought how I might get used to this bath thing.

"Yaacov – I will need you to go with me! – You see – I may be in serious trouble with my Centurion!" Cornelius spoke solemnly. "I left without orders and for personal reasons! – This is a serious offense in the Roman army! - Do you understand – Jaacov?"

I nodded.

"Jaacov – do not speak to anyone!" He was insistent. "Answer only to me and Flavius if I ask you!" Is that clear – my friend.

Again I nodded.

"Yaacov! – it is very important to always be truthful in what you say – If you are not truthful – people will soon loose trust in you!" Cornelius gazed at me intently. "If you are not part of a person's world of value – they will usually have no use for you!"

I began to realize, this Roman was concerned over his visit to Flavius.

Cornelius lowered his head in deep thought. He now spoke lowly and I moved closer to hear.

"Yaacov! – I if I say anything that sounds not to be quite true – Please! – do no react in any way - I do not want my life to end in disgrace!"

This Roman was the most powerful entity I had witnessed on earth. I had seen the magnificent display of Elohim's power on that wonderful night the star appeared. I had felt the power in the touch and look of the Christ Child, but Cornelius was the epitome of a power figure, yet here he stood, clearly fearing an encounter with this man Flavius.

We proceeded to the Roman complex across Jerusalem. We passed the Great Temple again and headed east in Jerusalem. Soon, at the end of the street, the complex loomed into view. It appeared much the same as Cornelius's, having the same type wall, but the roof tops were of varied types and the roof of a much larger villa was visible at the center.

A trumpeter sounded a blast on his horn as we entered the gate and Roman soldiers began to wave and call out to Cornelius. Cornelius simply nodded or raised his hand in a slight wave. The Roman Decanus dismounted at the door of the large villa. He turned to me and handed me the reigns to his mount.

"Tend my horse - Jaacov – stay here and speak to no one - my friend – I will send for you shortly!" He turned and disappeared into the massive door of the villa.

I held the animal as some of the soldiers wandered aimlessly over to where I stood. They eyed me with a sense of curiosity.

Shortly one of the soldiers moved closer and spoke to me in that strange Italian tongue.

I simply looked and acknowledged him with a polite nod. I did not reply in any other form.

The soldier was very young. He didn't appear much older than me but his face and arms showed the scars of battle. I wondered how one so young could have become a soldier.

The youth leaned close and spoke. I had no idea what he wanted. I looked directly at him, thinking perhaps he would indicate what he was seeking. The words of Cornelius rang in my ears. "Do not speak to anyone!" I slowly shook my head, trying to tell him I was ordered not to speak.

The soldier grinned at his friends and struck a pose of authority. Again he spoke, this time the tone was demanding.

I simply looked at him, not knowing what to do. The face of the young soldier became dark with fury. I knew something bad was going to happen. "Oh! Cornelius - my friend - please come now!" My mind called out.

The soldier stepped closer and undoubtedly wanted me to do something. My mind raced as I tried in vain to find some way out of this pending situation.

Suddenly the young Roman reached out his hand as if to place it on my head. I deftly dipped my head to the side and he grew quite insistent with his hand. I finally allowed him to place his hand on my head and he immediately tried to force me to kneel.

I had been given a task by Cornelius to hold his horse. Cornelius had asked me to speak to no one unless he asked me. This young soldier was trying to get me to kneel and becoming quite upset because I refused. I did not understand his intentions, but clearly knew it was not in keeping with Cornelius request.

The young soldier was undoubtedly well trained in combat. I had never fought anyone. I had numerous encounters with wolves and had fended off caracals with my staff. This young Roman soldier was bent on making me kneel. I probably would have knelt had I not been charged with Cornelius's horse, but that was my task and my allegiance lay with Cornelius.

The soldier was becoming infuriated and it was obvious that I had to do something.

I looked at the young Roman and shouted. "DAI!" as loudly as I could.

He did, indeed, stop. A look of surprise crossed his face as he dropped his hand. The look slowly changed to one that I recognized. I had seen that look in the eyes of many a wolf. It was the look of determination, when the mind is made up and the attack is launched.

The hand of the Roman went behind his back and from the folds of his crimson tunic came a dagger. The dagger come in a wide arc aimed at my neck.

I simply did what I would have done had a wolf attacked. I threw my left arm up and it caught his arm as it swung toward my neck. With all my strength, I deflected his swing and the dagger clanked to the ground.

Suddenly my mind flashed a memory. I remembered a time when I jumped over a fallen acacia tree and a limb struck me in my groin. I delivered a kick directly at the Roman soldier's groin. The effects were instantaneous: the youth fell to the ground and let out a cry that could have been heard in Rome. His hands went to his groin and he began to slowly writhe in pain.

The observing Romans roared in laughter and guffaws that startled Cornelius's hose and he started to shy away from the group of Romans. I held the reigns and softly spoke in a consoling tone and the horse began to quieting. Suddenly the soldiers grew deathly quiet.

"HOLD!" The stern command came from the steps of the large villa. I looked to see Cornelius and another imposing Roman figure standing at the door.

"What is this? – The war of Jerusalem again and this time the Hebrews win?" The Roman, Flavius spoke with an air of sarcasm.

The young soldier was recovering and rising from the ground. On his face, through the mask of pain, I could see the eyes of hatred aimed at me. I felt a chill as if a caracal were watching me from the rocks as I shepherded my sheep.

"Come! young Brutus and you too - Hebrew boy!" He motioned to me with his hand and at the same time directed a nearby Roman soldier to take Cornelius's horse to the stable. Cornelius had not spoken a word.

The villa was much plusher than Cornelius's. We made our way to a large room, very similar to the Masters room at the Khah-vah. Flavius sat upon his giant chair and held out his hand. A nearby soldier handed him a handle of thin wooden rods, bound with leather thongs around a small axe. It was ornately designed with small golden leaves and undoubtedly was a significance of authority.

"Now! – Boy! – Explain to me why I find one of my soldiers at the feet of a slave boy and obviously writhing in pain?" The centurion looked somewhat amused at the discomfort of the young Roman, Brutus, as he asked this question.

I felt that strange feeling again. The feeling I felt as I ran to warn Joseph and Mary of the danger to the Christ Child. I had never felt fear and it was not a feeling I relished. I somehow knew that my answer would decide my fate.

I answered. "I am no slave – Sire!"

The young Roman soldier gave a faint gasp as I uttered these words. I turned to look at him and could see a frantic look on his face.

He held up a trembling hand with the palm toward Flavius and slightly bowed his head. Flavius nodded, granting Brutus permission to speak.

He fumbled for words and somehow managed something about apparently startling Cornelius's great warhorse and he must have undoubtedly kicked him.

The centurion tucked his head to hide his obvious smile and then struck a pose of being in great thought. The young Roman began to visibly tremble.

I thought how odd it was for a soldier showing the signs of brave battle could shiver in the presence of another man. I had much to learn of loyalty, honor and patriotism.

Flavius turned to Cornelius and spoke. "Cornelius my trusted Decanus – what punishment would you place upon your magnificent steed for this act of aggression against one of Rome's finest?

Cornelius face took on a tone of righteous indignation as he spoke. "Sire I shall withhold his weekly ration of honey that laces his oats and barley – I will also have his stall window left open at night so the night chill will remind him of his horrible mistake in kicking one of Rome's finest!"

Flavius looked at Brutus and leaned forward. He lowered his voice as if speaking intimately. "Justice is done – young warrior – now depart!"

The young Roman almost dashed from the room as Flavius turned his attention to me. I was confused. I had just heard a series of lies and obviously everyone knew them to be lies, yet all seemed satisfied that justice was done.

"Well! –That bit of trivia is handled! – We now must handle this "New King" thing! - Herod has broken some major rules set upon him by Rome!"

The Roman Centurion face took on a stern look. "Young man! – let not this episode - you witnessed here - influence you to lie to me - I want the truth!"

"Did you see this new King?" His question chilled me to the bone. I cast a quick glance at Cornelius, his eyes were closed and his face was slightly raised toward Heaven. I had no idea what discussion had transpired before I was called in. I said a quick prayer to Elohim and asked for wisdom.

"Yes Sire!" Was my simple answer.

Flavius mouth fell open and he leaned forward as if expecting more. I had answered his question and knew nothing else to tell him.

A moment of silence and Flavius's face began to redden. "Well! – Boy – how many soldiers did you see?"

"None Sire!" Again a simple answer.

The Centurion rolled his eyes and almost shouted. "THEN WHAT MAKES YOU THINK HE IS A KING?"

My reply was instant. "The voice from Heaven told me and the great star pointed him out – Sire!"

Flavius threw his hands up in a sign of exasperation and shouted at Cornelius. "This is the rabble that you find so fascinating – my fine Decanus? – I have no interest in this prophesy mess! - Rome cannot abide Herod killing all these future taxpayers and taking upon himself his personal vendettas under the pretence of a make believe religious rebellion!"

Flavius turned his attention back to me. Elohim had given me the wisdom to answer his question honestly and briefly.

"Describe this king to me – boy!" His question was direct.

My answer was also direct. "He was a child!"

Flavius was now resigned to dealing with my brief answers. "Does the child live?"

"Yes Sire – he lives!" I answered.

The Centurion continued. "How do you know he lives – young shepherd boy?"

I spoke honestly. "I led him and his parents to safe passage!"

"And where is this safe passage?" Flavius asked.

The mountain pass to the east of Bethlehem that leads to the Great Salt Sea. I answered truthfully.

Flavius motion to an elderly Hebrew that had been lurking in the rear doorway. The two spoke in whispers and the Hebrew whispered at length in the Romans ear. Flavius raised his eyebrows in apparent enlightenment.

"What is the boy's name – Cornelius?" Flavius asked.

"He is called Jaacov! – My Lord!" Cornelius replied.

Flavius now seemed much more relaxed. "Jaacov – do you know what lies in that pass?"

I answered simply. "Yes Sire!"

"Well! – Jaacov! – Blast you boy! - Help me out here! – Tell me more!" The Centurion was relaxed but now getting impatient.

"The passage goes through the domain of the unclean – but I know they gave safe passage to the child to Egypt!" That is all I know – Sire!" I truthfully knew no more.

"Tell me! – Jaacov – What is this about some kings coming to offer an alliance to this new King?" He asked with a cocked eye.

"Sire! - I led these men, who called themselves Magi, to the child and they gave him some gifts - I then led them to the ancient river bed to the east of Jerusalem and they fled to their country in fear of Herod.!" Again I answered truthfully. Cornelius was looking at me in mute astonishment.

"And what of these king's armies – young Jaacov?" Flavius moved to the edge of his seat in anticipation.

I answered. "Sire! – I saw no army – only three Magi a servant and four camels – they all fled!"

"AHAA! – Crisis solved – The new King is in Egypt and is no threat to Judea! – There are no armies to threaten Rome or Herod's feeble mind - Cornelius my friend - you have done a great service to Rome! – Your quick response may have saved many lives and has led to a most proper complaint to Rome! – We may now get a Prefect that will deal with this pompous Herod and put him in his place!" Flavius was on the verge of ecstasy.

As we left the villa, I caught sight of the young Roman, Brutus, standing in the doorway of his house. I was not close enough to see his face, but I could feel the intensity of his stare. It is unnerving to know you have an enemy lurking about and can try your nerves at times.

Cornelius stressed to me that I was free. I had no obligation to stay with him. His offer was for me to basically be his servant. I would see to the needs of the household and accompany him on some of his assignments. I would have no horse, but that would really be no problem as I did not know how to ride.

The political situation in Jerusalem was a mystery to me, but as time went by I began to understand some of the currents that ply the waters of a nation under foreign rule.

It seems that Judea was not considered a major asset of the Roman Empire. Rome prized the wool from the sheep and the cedar wood from the northern country near the coast of the great sea. They loved the delicate flavor of the Judean olives and relished the dates from the lush date palms that prevailed in the area.

Rome's occupation was simple. The Empire offered protection from previous enemies and in return they received taxes and goods from the country's economy. The soldiers and young men from the conquered country were offered a place in the mighty Roman army under Roman control. Rome offered citizenship to people of influence that yielded to Rome and could benefit the Roman Empire.

King Herod adopted Judaism and ruled Judea with the approval of Rome. He made sure that Rome received their proper taxes and did all he could to appease the Romans, however he was insecure in his rule. The ancient prophesy of a new king had him in a state of mind that affected his reason.

Judea had no Roman Prefect. It seems Rome was satisfied with their alliance with the Herodians. There was only a Centuriae assigned to Jerusalem, numbering about eighty foot soldiers and no cavalry. Herod knew he was favored in Rome and held the Roman soldiers in disdain.

Flavius, the Centurion, was constantly vexed by Herod taking actions that normally would be the job of the Romans.

Herod's orders to send Palace guards to kill all little boys, two years old and younger would have never been approved by Flavius. Herod knew this and even circumvented the Hebrew clergy to ease his tormented mind.

Flavius challenged King Herod in Rome's name. The King paid little heed to Flavius's accusations. King Herod stated he was Rome's appointed Govenor and the Roman soldiers including Flavius were simply there to police Rome's interest and a religious rebellion was of no concern to Rome.

Flavius was infuriated and from this time on was constantly aware of everything the King did.

A formal letter was sent to Caesar Augustus and the Roman Senate. The letter outlined the details of the mass murders and of many other things that Herod had done over the years. Rome had suspicions that Herod was overtaxing the people to finance his lavish lifestyle. Rome's position, however, was to leave the situation alone as long as Rome's interests were not affected.

Flavius wrote a glowing commendation on Cornelius's quick decision to rush to Bethlehem. I never knew exactly what Cornelius told Flavius.

King Herod was Archelaus, son of "King Herod the Great." His father was, indeed, a remarkable man. He had rebuilt Jerusalem and a beautiful new Temple. The Sanhedrin, Sadducees and Scribes were always upset with him, because he built the Temple as he saw fit and paid little attention to Hebrew custom and advice.

His reputation as a brutal King was well earned as rumors persisted of how he killed some of his own family to protect his thrown.

King Herod also built a massive walled fortress on a mountain plateau named Masado and another fortress at Herodium. The port of Caesarea had been expanded and was a port of great influence, but unfortunately had given way to being a haven for Assyrian pirates.

After King Herod's death, the land was divided between three of his sons. Herod Archelaus had the kingdom of Judea, Herod Antipas ruled over the lands of Galilee and Philip had the lands east of the Jordan River.

The land of Judea, Galilee and east of the Jordan River had many Assyrian inhabitants left from when the Assyrians ruled the land. Rome somehow seemed to favor the Hebrew people and the remaining Assyrians found this to be an undesirable situation. There was always conflict between the Hebrews and the Assyrians. King Herod took great pleasure in referring these problems to Flavius, they were a constant thorn in his side.

I missed my sheep. I would dream of sleeping under the stars and fighting wolves, caracals and lions. I was beginning to feel quite empowered as I grew older. Cornelius would train me in the use of the short Roman sword. Other soldiers in the Roman enclosure would use me as a sparring partner.

The general offensive of the Roman soldier is a close wedge formation with their shields held in front. The soldiers have a lance that is thrust over the tops of their shields and is jabbed at the enemy. The Roman soldier has bronze armor over his chest, shoulders, upper arms, thighs and shins. The armor may sometimes be hardened leather that deflected a lance or sword with much efficiency.

The short sword is used in close combat and is designed to stab rather than slash. The Romans felt that a light stabbing sword was more effective than a heavy long sword that would tire a combatant in short order.

I introduced the Romans to the art of fighting with a staff. Their lances were heavier than the new staff I had fashioned. I had much experience fighting off wolves that threatened my sheep. The staff can be used as a club as well as a lance. The Romans had tipped my staff on either end with a sharpened iron point and it would now make a fine weapon for fending off the wild animals.

Cornelius provided an educator for the Romans. He strongly felt his men should have a working knowledge of the languages that prevailed in the area. I learned much about the Roman way of life and the Italian language.

I admired Cornelius for his nature of tolerance. The Roman soldiers had absolutely no conscience concerning honesty or respect for others. The soldiers would not directly steal anything, but if it was left lying around or unattended, they felt a perfect right to claim it for their own. This attitude led to many fights and arguments among the men. Cornelius would deal out his discipline and then proceed to handle the culprits as if nothing ever happened. The men had great respect for him and would have followed him into a fiery pit if he led them.

I learned to ride a horse as Cornelius would allow me to take his mount for exercise runs. Cornelius was sometimes smothered with duties of settling disturbances between the Hebrews and the Assyrians.

The Assyrians were untiring in their efforts to gain property from the Hebrews. The territory southwest of Jerusalem was particularly plagued with conflict. This is where the Master's Khah-vah was located. I thought of Malisch and Rachel. It had been nearly three years since I had left under threat of Herod's guards.

My heart quickened at the thought of Rachel. She was a raven haired beauty and was the first girl I had ever really noticed. I wondered how she would look after three years had passed.

Cornelius did not try to conceal his belief in Elohim. He never coerced his men to yield to his belief, but was constantly reminding them of Elohim's rules of fair play, honesty and respect for others. He never missed an opportunity to tell his men of the futility of calling on their false Gods for help or guidance. His testimonies were brief and to the point.

One hot afternoon, the soldiers were removing an old acacia tree that had died. A rope had been tied high up the tree trunk and a pit was dug at the base of the tree and the roots protruding into the pit were cut away. The plan was to simply pull the tree toward the pit and it would fall where the roots had been cut away.

All was going well until the tree started to fall where it would not be in the pit. The soldiers pulling on the rope began to scramble to re-align the rope and the soldier nearest the pit lost his footing and fell into the pit.

The earth was very loose and the soldier's efforts to climb out of the pit were defeated by the crumbling earth and he would simply slide back into the hole. The tree was not falling at a fast pace as the roots were slowly releasing the grip. The other soldiers had stopped pulling on the rope but the tree was well on its way to coming down.

No one rushed to the aid of the fallen soldier as it was evident there was no way the tree could be stopped and anyone that went to his aid would be crushed as well.

The soldier could only cower under the shadow of the falling tree as it continued its downward course of pending doom. Fortunately the upper branches of the tree cushioned the impact and the soldier was only pinned under the trunk against the soft crumbling earth. He began to call for the god, Ceres, to aid him in his plight.

Some of the other soldiers immediately jumped into the pit and began to shovel the soft earth away and the soldier was soon released. He only suffered some scratches and sore ribs from the impact of the tree trunk.

Cornelius went to his bedside as the soldier was resting and told him he should have called upon a real God like Elohim for help. Calling upon gods that are simply figments of the imagination could never result in any miracles. The soldier drew a labored breath and stated he would try and remember that next time a tree was falling on him. Both men laughed.

Cornelius would seek Hebrew's to come to his villa and tell him of Elohim. He did not have great success as most Hebrews, though they believed, had insufficient knowledge to be instructive. He had no success in learning from any Sadducee or Scribes. They could not understand any Gentile being interested in Elohim unless it was for devious reasons. It was very perplexing to Cornelius, as he was truly a believer and sometimes felt maybe God didn't want him.

My training in worldly affairs continued and I was now handling all the financial affairs of the complex. It developed, by far, a better working relationship with the populace of Jerusalem. I was a Hebrew and began to understand the way the merchants did business.

A Roman soldier had a menacing air about him as he conducted his business. It may not be intentional, but they were always wary of being taking advantage of and the merchants were always wary of being coerced. Dealing in the Roman's behalf was easy for me, as the merchants felt I would suffer if the deal was not fair and I would not take advantage of the merchants on the Romans behalf.

The sound of Roman soldiers dressed in battle armor is distinctive and can be heard from afar as they approach. This sound came to our ears one early morning as we were practicing our sword skills in the courtyard of the complex.

The Roman platoon marched smartly through our gateway and came to a sharp halt as Gnaeus stepped out to meet the Decanus of the visiting platoon.

The traditional hand thump over the heart and grasping of forearms of the two Decanus's demonstrated the years of tradition and trust that develop while serving in the mighty Roman army.

The platoon dispersed and old friends began to re-unit, as the Decanuses retreated into Cornelius villa to discuss some pending matter of importance.

I looked up to see the young soldier Brutus heading my way. It had been a few years since our brief but violent encounter at Flavius's villa. His face still bore a scowl of hatred. I realized I held a sword in my hand. I prayed to Elohim. "Elohim - my God - I beg you! – Please do not let blood be spilt here today!"

"JAACOV - COME QUICKLY – You are needed!" The call came from one of our soldiers at the doorway to Cornelius villa.

Brutus stopped in his tracks. "Thank you - God!" I thought as I placed the sword in the training rack and without looking at Brutus, ran to the villa.

"Come here Jaacov! – The Assyrians have seized much property in al-Walabe, including the khah-vah where you stayed with your Master!" Cornelius voice had a sinister tone. My heart skipped a beat. I thought of Rachel and Malisch.

"You lived there Jaacov! – will you draw a map we can use to allow us to plan an attack?" Cornelius asked. I could tell he was greatly concerned.

"Cornelius – Sire – do these Assyrians have an army?" I asked out of ignorance. I had never seen any sign of Assyrian forces in all my years of shepherding. All I had ever seen were individuals or small groups that would cause a ruckus or make demands. Most of the disputes were over property that had been confiscated hundreds of years in the past by the Assyrians or Babylonians when they invaded Judea.

In later years when Rome came into power, some of the Hebrews reclaimed their property and thus came the disputes. Both sides felt justified in the conflict and Rome would normally ignore the lesser incidents.

This was, however, a major case, because the Master was so highly favored by Caesar Augustus.

"No – Jaaacov – there is no army. But we cannot allow the people to simply take what they want. We must maintain order and that order must be in Rome's favor.

I thought for a moment. There was no army. The Assyrians that attacked the khah-vah must be from around that area to feel they had a claim to it. The approaching Roman troops would alert the Assyrians and they would probably melt back into the surrounding countryside and wait for the Romans to depart. I saw no way to force an encounter. I voiced this concern to Cornelius and the other Decanuses.

The Romans looked at me with a look of disdain. I realized that it was not out of dislike but out of curiosity that a servant would challenge the proven attack style of the mighty Roman war strategy. I meant no disrespect, but still, how can a victory be achieved if your enemy is not there to fight. I simply told them this. They fell silent and then began to speak lowly so as not to allow me to hear.

After a few moments, Cornelius called for some wine and cheese. "Come let us sit and confer on a strategy for this mission!" He motioned for me to join them. I felt a deep sense of honor. Cornelius treated me as a younger brother, but I really had no bond with any of the other Romans.

The Romans discussed the situation at great length. It was finally agreed that a frontal assault would not achieve any lasting effect. The Assyrians that had perpetrated this seizure of the khah-vah must be punished as an example to the others. The complaint had come from King Herod. The Romans were to keep the peace and protect Judea.

It was announced that King Herod was quite ill and the physicians did not seem to be able to squelch his fever so expediency was important to ease his anxiety.

I drew a map of how I remembered the countryside around the khah-vah, and pointed out some of the concealing attributes of the terrain.

A plan was formed to not fight the traditional Roman frontal attack as the enemy would simply vanish, only to emerge another day to continue the fight. It would be like a wolf attack. The soldiers would surround the khah-vah and take the Assyrians as they closed in, not allowing any to escape.

The decision was made to kill all the people involved in the seizure and simply allow this to be a swift and direct message that Rome would not tolerate any disruption of authority.

The Romans were very adapted at the strategy of combat. The platoon from Flavius compound was under the command of the Decanus, Appias, and consisted of twenty men. Flavius had ordered them to report to Cornelius. Cornelius was to take his platoon and command the entire operation to restore the khah-vah to operation that would benefit Rome.

Appias suggested I could sneak into the khah-vah and provide a scouting report. This seemed to make sense for I had lived there nearly two years after the Christ child was born.

We departed Jerusalem in small parties of six to eight soldiers at the time. The soldiers shed their armor and carried only their short sword and dagger.

I provided directions for the soldiers to take routes that would not alarm the Assyrians. The road to Al-waleba could not be used at all. Assyrian lookout would use the ram's-horn and the khah-vah would be alerted before the troops were clear of the city.

The southern road to Bethlehem was well traveled and would not be suspected. The soldiers would mix in with groups of farmers and shepherds as they left the city. Some would act as guards for caravans going south. They plan was to simply move into the country side and let the group you were with continue on. No effort was made to move west through the rocky plain until the group moved out of site. All ears were to be tuned for the sound of the ram's horn.

The soldiers were to gather at the base of a hill east of the khah-vah. They would not be seen unless an Assyrian lookout had been placed there. This was not thought to be very likely as sneak attacks by Romans were not their normal way of fighting.

The Romans made no secret of their approach. Great fanfare was the order of the day. Drums and trumpets and the marching of men would shake the earth and giant flags and staffs with military figures would grace the skyline. The intimidation of force and magnitude was used to coerce the enemy into submission. The world also knew that to oppose the mighty Roman army usually would prove disastrous.

I left the city well ahead of the soldiers. Cornelius embraced me as I prepared to leave. He did not pull me to the side or try to hide his obvious affection for me.

He pushed me away from his embrace and with his giant hands on my shoulders loudly stated. "Men of Rome! – This young man came to us a shepherd only a few years ago and today he departs to set our stage for battle. I pray to Elohim and I suggest you pray also!" He paused a second and with a frivolous wave of his finger in the air, stated. "Pray to - Eh! – To whatever you pray to – that we will bring Roman justice!"

As I picked up my staff and threw my small pack across my back, I caught a glimpse of Brutus, my Roman nemesis. His leering look of envy and hatred made my blood run cold.

It was no problem making my way out of the city and shortly turned west across the rocky plains and low hills that prevailed to the khah-vah of the Master. I made good progress, and the trip was invigorating as I remembered my days as a carefree shepherd.

Suddenly I heard the faint sound of a ram's horn. I instantly stopped in my tracks and from experience froze in place. If I had been seen, it was only my movement as the ram's horn was very far away. I slowly stooped to the ground and surveyed the surrounding countryside. The only high ground was the distant silhouette of the hill where I was to rendezvous with the Romans. I heard no further sounds. I proceeded with great caution as any quick movement will catch the eye.

It was late afternoon as I approached the low hill that was our rendezvous point

My heart stopped as the silhouette of a man standing atop the hill caught my eye. I instantly dropped behind a rock and held my breath. I knew I was much too far for him to hear me breathing, but still, I instinctively held my breath.

I peered around the rock and saw the man leaning on his lance. Hanging at his side was the clear outline of a ram's horn. The man was a lookout. It was his horn that gave me such a start.

I knew I was at least two hours ahead of my Roman compatriots. I thought how hopeless it would be for me to try and warn each group of soldiers as they approached.

The lookout was definitely Assyrian as his silhouette accentuated the hairstyle and dress. As I observed him, he made a distinctive surveying swing, viewing the country side behind me to the east and pulled his horn to his mouth. A long blast ensued and the lookout again seemed to relax and rest upon his lance. He had given an "all clear" signal. I relaxed.

A sudden chill ran through my body as I realized that if an "all clear" signal was missed, it was as good as an alarm signal. My mind went numb with the thought; a sneak attack was not possible.

I wished I could be high on the hill to see the Romans approaching and my mind told me that I needed to be near that lookout in case he tried to sound the alarm. I began to organize my thoughts.

What if that horns blast was a warning? The lookout made no attempt at leaving. If the blast was a warning and he did not leave, that meant they were coming to him. I calculated the distance to the khah-vah. The average man traveling with purpose could make the trek in about a half hour.

A sudden movement caught my eye and I looked to see the lookout gathering his belongings from the ground. He stood and with his free hand gave a wave to someone on the far side of the hill. The lookout turned and concentrated on a brief search of the countryside again before departing.

I had to know what was happening. The lookout was heading downhill and whoever he was to meet was not near as indicated by the wave.

I left my hiding placed and raced as silently as I could, using my stealth from years of sneaking up on wolves and caracals, to the top of the hill. I crouched behind a boulder and cautiously peered down to the plain below.

The lookout was exchanging greetings with another Assyrian. The newcomer appeared to be much younger than the first man and not nearly as large.

The new lookout took possession of the ram's horn as the greeting was concluded. He began to pick his way up the rocky hill and took his place at the exact same spot as the first lookout. The youth began to survey the land to the east with great scrutiny. I prayed that the Romans had not exceeded my calculations and were much nearer. The diligence the young Assyrian placed in his scanning gave proof that the Romans were not near enough to be detected.

I relaxed. My next thoughts were in avoiding detection. I was only a stone's throw from the lookout, so any noise would give my location away.

The lookout finished his scanning and reached for the ram's horn. He took his time and pulled a bit of cloth from his pouch and proceeded to thoroughly wipe and clean the mouth piece of the horn. It was quite evident, he wanted all traces of the previous lookout gone before he placed his lips on the horn.

The young man raised the horn and the pitiful sound almost made me laugh. He was definitely not adapted at blowing a ram's horn. He wet his lips and taking a giant breath blew into the curved instrument again. The irritating bleat that ensued began to change tones as the youth began to clinch his lips and move the horns pitch to a level that sounded quite loud enough to reach the ears of the khah-vah.

I heard the distant laughter of the relieved lookout as he made his was way home. The young Assyrian cursed in his native tongue and released the horn in disgust. I suddenly realized the "'all clear" horn blasts were done in the time increments it would take to reach the khah-vah. It made sense. The alarm was probably a different series of blast and would allow at least thirty minutes of preparation at the khah-vah. If no blast was heard, the khah-vah still had thirty minutes of preparation time.

The Assyrian relaxed and prepared to eat his supper. He built no fire, nor did I see evidence of any. He simply sat upon a rock and unfolded a packet holding some dried dates and figs. He munched on some bread and drank sparingly from his wine skin. All the while his casual gaze was eastward across the rocky plains and rolling hills. His youthful vigor left little chance that the Romans would arrive undetected.

I realized I was the only chance for the Romans to succeed. My mind turned to my sheep. Every time I was perplexed with a decision or problem, my mind would retreat to thoughts of when I was a young shepherd. The thoughts of nights under the stars with the rancid smell of sheep's wool wafting on the breeze and the cool night air with the sky bright with millions of brilliant stars brought me much comfort.

This life was not nearly as simple. I had to consider this lookout an enemy. He and others like him had seized the property of the Master and what fate had they brought on my friend, Malisch and the sweet beauty, Rachel? In the approaching Roman soldiers, with whom I am aligned, was an enemy. Young Brutus, was a Roman veteran and his hatred for me was evident in his face. Perhaps I had handled his bullying out of instinct rather than diplomacy. That encounter had influenced my association with every new person I encountered.

I lay behind my rock and prayed the young Assyrian would not venture my way when he sought to relieve himself.

Suddenly my senses were alerted and I recognized the smell that wafted in the late evening breeze. The sentry also was alerted as I saw him rise and scan the distant countryside. I could not rise to gain the level of sight the lookout had, but the smell clearly indicated a flock of sheep was on the way. I rose as high as I could without the lookout seeing me and in the distance was a rather large flock of sheep approaching from the distant oasis I had frequented so often.

Something, however, was not right with this picture. The flock was rather large and would require more shepherds, but the number of shepherds was, by far, too great. Suddenly a flash of the familiar crimson of the Roman tunic caught my eye. Some of the shepherds were Roman soldiers. It was a great ploy, but shepherds simply did not have the resources to have such fine attire. I knew the lookout would realize this before the soldiers could stop him from sounding the alarm.

I peered at the lookout. His body language indicated he was not alarmed but his curiosity was aroused. I could tell he was counting the shepherds. Soon he would reason the many crimson clad men were not really shepherds. The alarm was only a ram's horn away. I reached into my pouch and slowly pulled out my sling. I had not used it since bringing down a rabbit on my last shepherding venture before going to my Master's khah-vah.

I reached for a pebble in the mass of rocks at my feet. I placed the stone in the pocket of the sling and positioned it to be brought to swing at the instant I arose.

Suddenly the young lookout realized something was wrong and immediately knew he had allowed too much time to expire before sounding the alarm.

His hand shook with anxiety as he clumsily tried to bring the horn to his mouth. His eyes grew wide with fear as he saw me rise and began to swing my sling. He simply froze in terror as the stone struck him in the forehead. He fell prostrate on his back and began to moan in distress.

I straddled him in an instant and placed my foot on the horn. My staff was at his throat. I thought how the iron points on my staff had turned this tool of shepherding into a formidable weapon. The young man soon regained his senses and began to weep softly as he felt sure his fate was sealed.

I realized it was time for the lookout to sound his "all clear" or the Khah-vah would be alerted. I reached for the horn and stepped back.

"Rise and give the signal that all is well" I ordered.

A spark of hope flashed in the young man's eyes and he eagerly reached for the horn. I pulled it away. I realized that only a familiar "all clear" blast would suffice. I could not take a chance with the Assyrian on the ram's horn.

I stood at the side of the young Assyrian as he lay on the ground and once again placed the point of my staff against his throat. His eyes grew wide with the anxiety of death.

It was a new sensation for me. I had never held the life of another human in my hands. The feeling of power and control was overwhelming. There was no need to be concerned about this enemy, all I had to do was push my staff into his throat and he would be no more.

The young Assyrian shut his eyes and with a set of his jaw turned his head as if to welcome the lance. I thought, how brave this young man was, to simply accept death as inevitable. I could see the tears begin to squeeze past his clinched eye lids.

I raised the horn to my lips and blew with all my might. There was no sound, only the escaping air as it exited the open horn. My blood ran cold.

I quickly looked at the approaching shepherds and Roman soldiers. They had no idea of the precarious situation the existed on this hill top. I played a flute and blowing on it produced a melodious tone that could be change with your fingers on a series of holes. This horn had only a small funnel shaped hole on one end and then curved and grew into a large opening from which the soulful sound projected.

Was the ram's horn broken or did I, simply, not know how to blow it? I had seen it done many times and grew a mental picture of the puffed cheeks of the men and tight lips of the men that blew it.

I pressed the tip of my staff into the taught flesh of the prostrate Assyrian. I leaned close and hissed. "Would you die for the lack of a proper sound from a ram's horn?

He clinched his eyes even tighter and as the tears began to puddle in the corner of his eye he pursed his lips in a tight line and with puffed cheeks made a distinct "PTTTP" sound. I had the key to sounding a ram's horn.

I raised the horn to my mouth again and with tightly clinched lips blew with all my might. The sound was very flat, but with little effort and relaxing of the lips, a blast ensued that would have made the bugler at King Herod's Palace proud. It sounded so good and felt so powerful that I almost sounded it too long. The khah-vah had their "all clear" signal. The young Assyrian's body went limp. He had resigned himself to a martyr's death.

The Roman soldiers thinking they had been discovered lost all thought of sneaking and charged the hills in a vee formation that bore the full impression of years of training. I began to cry in a loud but still subdued voice that it was I, Jaacov and not the enemy that sounded the horn.

The soldiers numbered seven in this first detachment that arrived. There was scarcely time to explain the situation when the others began to arrive.

Cornelius, Appias and the Romans listened to my account of taking the hill and my nemesis, Brutus, commented on my cowardice in not killing the young Assyrian straight away.

It was late sunset and the decision was made for me to simply join the shepherds in taking the sheep to the khah-vah. I was to simply note how many Assyrians were on guard and where they were located. The Romans would remain in the darkness near the khah-vah and await my report.

I knew none of the shepherds, but when they heard my name, they became quite excited. It seems I had become a legend in

110

the shepherding world. One of the youngest thought I had been in the "olden days" and voiced that I was surely not the real "Jaacov." He asked me what caracal milk tasted like, as it was now legend that I was raised by an "'ol momma lion." I laughed, but the laughter died as Cornelius led the Young Assyrian away.

"The youth was bound with his hands behind his back and his feet hobbled to prevent running. Cornelius prodded him with his sword as he called back over his shoulder. "Go with Elohim – Jaacov" we will await your call!"

It is not an easy task to move sheep when it gets dark. The half hour trip took nearly an hour and as we progressed in the darkness I heard the "all Clear signal blast from the ram's horn. The Roman soldier did a fine job of duplicating the Assyrians signal.

The torch lights of the Khah-vah loomed into view. It was very dark. The moon had not yet appeared.

I was afraid the Assyrians would find it odd that we moved the sheep after dark and would become suspicious. The shepherds had heard nothing of the hostile takeover by the Assyrians and had simply brought the sheep in, as instructed by the Master's overseer. The overseer was also Malisch's and Rachel's father. We still had no idea of their fate.

The shepherds agreed for me to do the talking and I proceeded to open the gates of the sheep enclosure when a call of challenge went up from the nearby thatched roof shed. In the darkness were a half dozen men with raised lances spread out in a pattern that would kill us all in short order. My heart began to thump wildly in my chest. "Oh great Elohim! – We need you now !" I prayed.

The silence was deafening as my mind played on a response that would not get us immediately slaughtered. In the distance wafted a long blast of the ram's horn, then two short blast.

The laughter of the Assyrians sounded as the lances were lowered and they began to curse that young lookout for deliberately waiting to signal a flock coming in, just to frighten them. They departed toward the khah-vah vowing revenge in many different ways.

My mind raced. "Who had known the proper signal?" This God, Elohim, was indeed a most wonderful and wise God.

We placed the sheep in the enclosure and a smelly Assyrian began to count them. He raised his staff and dealt a swift blow to a young Hebrew that was helping to move the sheep for counting. "Keep them moving - you Hebrew khazeer!"

The young man had been standing and staring at me. I froze again with terror. I really wished I was still out in the fields with only sheep, wolves, caracals and lions. I never felt terror there. The youth recognized me from when I lived at the khah-vah.

He move swiftly and as he rubbed his bruised arm he looked back at me and motioned to the thatched roof shed with his head.

I had fortunately removed my finely woven tunic and put on my old fleece tunic from my shepherding days. I carried all my worldly possessions in my pack slung across my back. They were few and did not hinder me in any way.

The smelly Assyrian was an example of a man that did not care for anything, not even himself. Shepherds stink from their close association with smelly sheep. This Assyrian stank from his close association with everything he had touched for his entire life. He smelled of stink that a sheep would avoid. He gruffly told us to go to the shed for some food.

The food was leftover from the Assyrian's evening meal. It was simply dumped on a rough hewn table in the thatched roof shed and we had to pick through it for morsels to eat. It was fare, I suppose for a starving man, but I had no desire to partake of it at all.

I sat on a bale and the young shepherd that received the blow from the Assyrian came and sat beside me. He spoke. "I know you – you are Jaacov – the brave shepherd – we thought you dead!" He flashed a smile. "You have come to rescue us – We knew Elohim would hear our prayers!"

I looked around slowly as not to raise suspicion. "Tell me of Rachel and Malisch?" I steeled myself for his answer. " Malisch and his father are dead – they died fighting the Assyrians - Rachel is one of the women that delight the Assyrians when they dine at night." My heart stopped beating and I could not take a breath.

The young shepherd looked at me intently. "Jacoov – will you defeat the Assyrians alone?" I came to my senses and whispered. "No – We have Roman friends!"

The boy's eyes widened with astonishment. I realized his only association with Romans was to occasionally see them pass in military formation and hear the wild stories of how cruel and powerful they were. I had lost all fear and awe of them. I still had a great deal of admiration for their courage and dedication. But they were really very human to me now.

How many Assyrians are here now and is there any sign of an army. I needed this information for Cornelius.

He briefly informed me of what had transpired. Some Assyrian businessmen had approached the overseer with a proposition to buy the khah-vah. Upon finding the Master was in Gaul and left someone they perceived to be a servant in charge, they formulated a plan to take over the khah-vah. They asked the overseer for the proper papers authorizing him to manage the place and the papers that proved ownership of the khah-vah. The overseer refused and ordered them from the property.

In the early hours of the morning there was the sound of fighting and the household was suddenly in control of the Assyrians. The overseer and Malisch were nowhere to be found and everyone was told they were called to Gaul to serve the Master and the khah-vah was sold to the Assyrians. Rachel was told she was now the property of the Assyrians at the order of her father and would become a member of Prince Aricho's harem in the near future.

"Did you not say Malisch and his father were dead?" I asked the servant.

"Yes – we did not see the bodies – but servants and slaves were ordered to clean the blood from the floors of their rooms and I know where two fresh graves are hidden." His eyes bore witness to his sorrow. "Jaacov we are in great distress – please tell us what to do!"

"Answer my questions as accurately as you can!" I lowered my voice making sure the slovenly Assyrian could not hear. " How many Assyrians are here in the Khah-vah?"

"Maybe ten or twelve – but there are lookouts along the road to Jerusalem and the road to the coast - I am sure all the Assyrians in this part of Judea are aware of what has happened!" The young servant was indeed a keen observer.

I thought of what Cornelius would need to know. I asked the servant. 'Where are the guards stationed here at the khah-vah"

"One at each corner of the outer wall at the rear of the khah-vah and one at the main gate in the front - there is no guard at the front door to the house – but a guard is at each of the side doors of the main house - they are very secure as they feel that any danger will come from Jerusalem or the coast – they also have a lookout in the desert to the east in case they come from Bethlehem." The servant was almost breathless in his narration.

I again grew quiet in contemplation. I thought the smelly Assyrian was nowhere around and suddenly he loomed into the light of the torch and his staff fell on my shoulder with a blow that stunned my arm.

"You Hebrew khazeers are all alike! – as soon as a back is turned you lay about as if you own the world!" He was not prepared for what happened next. I was not prepared either, by this I mean, I did not plan this nor was I calculating in my actions. I grabbed his staff from his hand and smacked him full in the face with a short jab. The staff was not sharpened and the blunt end simply broke his nose. He was now that familiar wolf as he fell flat on his back from the shock. His nose had no time to tell him it was broken and his brain had no time to tell him to cry out. My blows that fell about his head rendered him unconscious in short order.

The servant stood dumbfounded as he watched. I too, was somewhat dumbfounded. I had sparred with the Romans in Jerusalem and staff fighting was almost a game to them. But my reflexes had suddenly proven the staff to be a formidable weapon again.

I looked at the unconscious Assyrian and thought how ironic it was that in a single day I had the lives of two men in my hands. I did not kill the lookout in the desert; his fate was left to Cornelius. I was not going to kill this man, his fate is in someone else's hand.

"Tell me my friend?" I looked into the stunned face of the young servant. "What are the signals of the ram's horn?"

I had to shake the boy by the arm as he was still stunned by the fall of the Assyrian.

He spoke hesitantly. "A long blast means all is well – a long blast followed by two short blast means someone comes but there is no threat – a series of repeated short blasts means danger!"

"The lookouts along the roads – how would they be called in?" I had to know this.

"I think it is a series of long blasts – at least three – Yes I am sure! - It is at least three long blasts!"

"You have done well my friend! – Elohim - I am sure - is proud of you – I will tell the Romans of how well you have done – now I must depart – tell all the servants and slaves - they will be liberated tonight – tell them to stay clear and they will be safe!" I patted the shoulder of my new friend and gave him a reassuring smile.

As I arose to leave a thought struck me. I turned to the young servant and whispered. "Tell all the slaves and servants, you can trust - to wear white robes or gowns - The Assyrians do not care for anything that is not brightly colored and it may help to keep them safe!" He nodded as I departed.

Cornelius and Appias were well pleased with my report. I assured them the smelly Assyrian would be no threat. He had no idea I was nothing more than an upstart Hebrew. He probably would say nothing for fear of being shamed that a young Hebrew shepherd got the best of him.

"Sire Cornelius? I asked. "Who blew the ram's horn with the signal that a flock was arriving?"

Cornelius voice gave evidence to his compassion. The young Assyrian was ready to die but when offered freedom he gladly gave us the signal."

"But Sire! ---------------- He placed his hand to my mouth.

"Later – Jaacov – We will talk later - We must plan now!"

The decision was made to take the khah-vah as silently as possible. We would have no problem as we had close to forty soldiers to overpower only ten or twelve Assyrians. If all went well we would only loose a few of our troops.

The plan was for me to try and take the guard at the front gate of the khah-vah with my sling. Five soldiers were waiting at the rear wall, should the guards decide to jump down and run.

We would then take each guard at the three doors of the villa before they could enter and shut the doors.

The night was still dark. The moon would not rise until well after midnight. We had over an hour of complete darkness.

The guard at the main gate was a clear shot as the torch provided ample light. The Assyrian wore no turban upon his head. The stone struck his temple and he fell in a heap. The Roman that ran along the base of the wall drove his sword between the Assyrians shoulder blades and then twisted the weapon to cause massive bleeding in his chest. He held his poise only long enough to assure no one saw or heard the deed.

The Romans moved with great stealth and speed. It was unusual for them to fight unencumbered by armor. They moved silently and swiftly. Over twenty swept through the gate with no more noise than a slight breeze on a warm summer night.

I headed straight for the great hall of the Master. The sound of the surprised guards was only brief and if a guard heard the noise of his fellow guard in his battle with death, it only perked his interest and accelerated his own demise.

I was only a few steps ahead of the Romans as they entered by all four doors. We were inside and there was no resistance. Surely the Assyrians in the villa had to have heard something. We heard the surprised cries of the guards on the wall as they realized an attack was in progress. They too were now silent.

I heard a distinctive "Ugh! From the door on my left and I turned to see an Assyrian guard with his lance through the shoulder of a Roman. The Roman was on his back and had both hands on the lance to prevent the Assyrian from pulling it out and stabbing again.

In a flash my staff fell on the side of the Assyrians face and he stumbled to the side. Dazed and confused he turned his head toward me and pulled his sword from its sheath. He took one step my way and froze with a look of amazement on his face. His body convulsed with shock as his own lance suddenly protruded from his chest. He slowly looked at the bloody point and collapsed on the floor.

I looked into the face of Brutus as he released the lance. It was Brutus that had been impaled on the floor. The blow I delivered to the Assyrian had given him time to pull the lance from his shoulder and drive it through the back and chest of his attacker. Gone was the look of hatred as he gazed at me. He gave a weak hand salute across his chest as he slumped to the floor in pain from the shoulder wound. He would live.

Slowly the torches were lighted in the great house and cautiously we approached the rooms where the Assyrians would have been asleep. Had they been alerted and fled before we arrived? Had the smelly Assyrians been much sharper than we thought and alerted them to danger.

The door to the Masters bedroom was slowly opened and there upon the cushions of the massive bed laid the body of the Assyrian that ruled the house. His throat was cleanly cut from ear to ear and his hands folded neatly across his massive chest. There was no one else in the room.

Three more Assyrians bodies were found in the same manner. They had not perished at the hands of the Romans.

We entered the great dining hall and there sat the entire staff of slaves and servants around the long low table. They were all dressed in white and calmly arose, offering their seats to the Roman soldiers. It was a solemn moment as these oppressed people gave the only thing they had to give to their liberators. They freely gave their servitude.

We suddenly realized not all Hebrews were meek and humble people. There were many white gowns speckled with deep red blood stains.

I thought of the young servant that had spoke with me in the thatched roof shed. He was not among the others. I thought of Rachel. She was not there either.

My desire to find Rachel was overwhelming, but the immediate fate of the young servant was pressing. Rachel's fate was already decided as she was not there. The servant's fate may still be in balance.

I dashed from the house. As I passed the door leading out to the sheep enclosure I stooped to picked up the sword of the slain guard that lay on the stone steps. The sword was somewhat longer than the Roman's weapon, but I could wield it just the same.

I could see the torch light flickering in the shed as I cautiously approached. My heart pounded in my chest and I thought perhaps the smelly Assyrian had regained consciousness and vented his rage on the servant.

As I looked hesitantly into the shed, my fears fell away as I observed the young servant sitting calmly on the bale with the Assyrian's staff in his hands. Every time the smelly man made a move or groaned the youth would deliver a smack to his head. The smelly Assyrian still lay exactly as I left him hours ago.

I told Cornelius of my fears for Rachel. He smiled as he looked at me and softly said. "Ahh! – perhaps my young friend has found a sweetheart!"   I felt my ears burn as the blood of embarrassment rushed to my head.

Cornelius called the women in to the great room and assured them that all were safe and told them of my concern for Rachel.

One of the young girls stepped forward and with lowered head softly whispered. "She has fled – she left early this morning in the dim light of dawn – she said she had rather die than become the wife of an Assyrian!"

I rushed to the young girl and knelt before her. "Where did she flee – tell me – where did she flee?" My voiced cracked in despair.

She pointed east toward the desert. "She went to seek you – Jaacov! – you are all she ever talked about – she would not believe you were dead – she said she would find you living with your mother, the great caracal that raised you in the rocky plains!"

I quickly gathered my possessions and filled my pack with dried fruits and water. Cornelius watched me intently. As I rose to leave the room, two Romans stepped to block the door. Cornelius raised his hand and motioned them to step aside.

Our eyes met and Cornelius nodded his head in understanding.

As I briskly departed I heard the voice of my one time nemesis, Brutus, call. "Return to us mighty "fortis" for we are not whole without you!" I felt my first rush of that special love that bonds men together.

CHAPTER V

RACHEL

I reached the hill only a horn's blast from the khah-vah. A brief search revealed no Rachel. I was not surprised as she had no way of knowing I had been there or the Romans were coming to her rescue.

I found some rope that had been burned in two by pig's fat. I did not know the significance of the rope. I did know that pig's fat burned very slowly and if soaked into a rope would act as a slow fuse. I put the discovery out of my mind and struck out for the oasis on the road from Jerusalem to Bethlehem.

My mind was filled with all the woes that could befall a young woman alone in the wilderness. It was less than twenty miles from the khah-vah to the spring that formed the oasis. If Rachel had continued at a moderate pace, she would have made it to the oasis around nightfall, about six hours ago.

Our conquest of the khah-vah had taken only minutes after my report on its vulnerability. Little time was lost in my search for Rachel. I could make considerable better time in my travel across the rocky desert than Rachel.

The moon began to rise and the country side was taking on an aura of early dawn. I was making good time. I threw all caution to the wind and would occasionally stop to catch my breath. I would call Rachels's name and listen for any signs of an answer. I felt sure every wolf, caracal and lion within hearing range was on my trail. I began to feel the heaviness of exhaustion. Still I pressed on, my heart growing heavier with every labored breath.

The sun rose and still I raced on. The stops to call Rachel's name did little to refresh me. It seemed that each time it was more difficult to resume my race to the oasis. As I reached the low ridge of hills west of the spring, I ceased my calls for Rachel.

Soon the silhouettes of the tall date palms surrounding the spring loomed into view. I could see the smoke of a campfire rising and drifting in the morning breeze. If Rachel had made the oasis, at least she would not be alone.

I was still dressed in my shepherd's tunic. It was a good disguise the night before, but I became aware that it was really too small for me now. It had been close to three years since I had worn it.

As I raced toward the spring I became aware that the Assyrian's sword I had pick up at the khah-vah had been striking my left leg at the thigh as I ran through the desert. I had simply tucked it into my belt.

My eagerness and concern for Rachel had blocked the pain as the sword had repeatedly struck my left leg. The leg was not seriously injured but had bled quite a bit. The leg looked as if it was seriously wounded, with the blood drying as it flowed down and the fresh blood causing the dried blood to crust and crack. My perspiration had collected dust from my long run and my hair was wild and matted.

My eyes scanned the near side of the oasis for any signs of Rachel. I glanced only briefly at the two tents on the far side with the dying campfire between them.

Two men in robes and Assyrian turbans were busy about the camp. It was evident they were breaking camp and preparing to leave. I thought how odd it was to be leaving so late in the morning. The men had not seen me, but they were Assyrian and I was suddenly very wary.

I slowed long enough to take the sword from my belt and place it on my back. I simply placed it under my tunic with the handle behind my neck. The blade was under my tunic and my belt held it close to my body. The presence of the sword restricted my movements somewhat, but I did not want to convey any threat to the Assyrians.

I turned my attention back to scanning the near side of the spring. I approached a group of small boulders, where I had slept many a peaceful night and my eyes saw, indeed, someone had slept there recently.

I squatted and looked closely at the ground. My scrutiny indicated a struggle had ensued. There were deep gouges in the sand and then two deep impressions led toward the opposite side of the spring. My eyes caught a bit of color in the sand and I reached down to retrieve a small bit of colored twine. It was the twine that Hebrew women weave into their hair.

My blood ran cold. Rachel had been here and now she was gone. My mind raced as I envisioned her being dragged away by - --------------------! My heart stopped. The two Assyrians were standing across the pool of water gazing at me.

I slowly rose from my squatted position. I said nothing but my gaze was intense. I only saw two men, but there were two tents. How many were hidden from view.

"Shepherd!" One of the men called. Where are your sheep?"

I said nothing.

"Have you battled a lion? - Have you lost your sheep to a pack of wolves"? Both men now laughed at this comment.

My mind raced as I had no idea as to what to do.

The two men removed their flowing robes and began to move around the lake toward me.

One of the Assyrians called back to the tents. "Mudir! - We must take care of this shepherd; he seems to be injured and will not speak.

A man's voiced answered. "Make haste- we have wasted much time!"

I knew nothing of fighting in the reality of the world. I had sparred with all the Roman soldiers at the compound and had become quite a combatant in the sparring sense. I had never fought in anger or had malice in my heart toward any man until yesterday.

"Elohim! – Why will you not simply give me back my sheep?" My prayer was in earnest. I did not want to be part of this plan, God's Plan or any plan.

I realized this was for real. There was no time for wishes or second guesses. If this was God's plan, it was unfolding right now.

The Assyrians were approaching. Whatever was going to transpire was going to happen now. I suddenly knew I had to be closer to those tents. There was a least one more man and if Rachel was also there, I had to be close enough to reach her before he could do her harm.

I began to move toward the men as they skirted the pond. I stumbled a bit. It may have been from exhaustion on perhaps I stubbed my foot.

The Assyrians noticed and began to laugh. "He's looks almost dead – if he seeks the girl – he definitely cannot do her any good!" Both men laughed maliciously.

I chilled at the thought. "They had Rachel!" Instinctively I stumbled a bit more and turned my head as if confused. I continued my advance toward the men.

We would meet at the midpoint of the far end of the spring fed oasis. As they drew nearer the Assyrians drew their swords and I knew there would be no questions. They were just going to kill me and be done with it.

I used my staff as if I needed it to steady my walk. The Assyrians had no idea that it was fitted with iron points on both ends. I had affixed an adornment at the center of the shaft of some fine threads. The threads acted like the feathers on an arrow and kept the shaft straight if it was used as a throwing lance.

The Assyrian that led the way had only enough time to widen his eyes in disbelief as the staff's iron tip pierced his heart and protrude through his back.

The second Assyrian raised his sword. I do not know if he was trying to defend himself or if he was going to attack me. I did not look at him. As I released my staff, I drew my sword from my back and brought it down in the top of his turban with all the strength I could muster. I looked at his turban only. The sword sunk through the thick fabric with a soft sound that had no indication that it was instant death. My body was already in motion toward the tents. I pulled the sword from the top of the toppling Assyrian's head and flew with the speed of the caracal toward the tents.

The flap of the farthest tent opened and a very heavy man dressed only in the flowing trousers of an Arab stepped out. It took him only a glance to see what had transpired. He moved with a swiftness that surprised me as he dove into the nearest tent.

The screams of women brought sheer terror to my heart. I would have expected a scream from Rachel, but the screams were from many women and it was the pitiful screams of futility. I wanted to dive into the tent and protect them, but I had no idea of what lay behind the flap.

I stopped and waited. I had spoken no words since my arrival at the oasis. I stood about fifteen feet from the tent flap and waited. The screams subsided and the sounds of scuffling could be heard. I was dying inside thinking that perhaps he was stabbing the women. Something made me remain still.

Slowly the tent flap began to move. The sharp edge of a huge curved Arabian sword emerged as it was used to push the tent flap aside. The heavy man emerged with the raven haired beauty, Rachel, held as a shield before him.

He looked around warily and then addressed me. "You seek this Hebrew woman don't you? - Your master sent you and if you return without her - you will lose your life - won't you?" His eyes darted around. He had not yet realized I had killed both his associates. He still thought they may be others.

I still had not spoken. The eyes of Rachel were on me and there was no sign of recognition. She was in pain as the Arab held her by the back of her hair. If she squirmmed even the slightest he would twist his grip and her eyes would shut with the pain.

"Am I right young shepherd - is this the prize you seek? - What if she has no head young shepherd? – What then - young shepherd? - I can remove her head in an instant!" He was beginning to feel sure I was alone.

I could see the hair on his chest as it now began to glisten with the perspiration of anxiety. I could see that he had body hair all over. Hair was visible on his shoulders and as he turned to stress his grip on Rachel's hair, I could see that his back was also covered with hair.

"You have caused me great strife this morning" – you – you – Hebrew rag man!" He was beginning to become angry at the loss of his two men. "I don't know how you managed to kill my friends but I assure you – that will not be my case as I will kill this woman and all the women if you are not careful!"

He questions were demanding. "You do not speak – what do you want – is it this woman?"

I did not answer. I did not answer because I did not know what to say. I had no experience in arbitrating or mediating. My total experience had been answering questions about sheep. I had no years of experience in conversation. I simply stood, sword in hand.

He looked at me and his eyes spoke of his confusion. I had seen that look in the eyes of the wolf and caracal when I did not run. It was not what they were accustomed to dealing with. It suddenly occurred to me that the man was no different from the wild creatures that prey upon the weak.

I managed a slight smile while gazing intently to his eyes. Yes, this man was afraid. The smile had a profound effect and the man's voice grew shrill.

"Now – my friend – let us not be hasty here! – You see we found this woman asleep this morning and we naturally assumed she was a runaway slave! - We have bought these other women and are taking them to the west for a great profit.

His brow lifted as a thought came to him. "You see – we have done your master a great service and have captured his slave! – Uh! – You see – Uh! - For a small profit we- Uh! - I will gladly return this woman or any of the women we have!" He raised his eyebrows in an appeal for a settlement.

I stood mute and silently gazed at him. He rolled his eyes and grunted in exasperation.

"Can you not speak – you! – you!" He was clearly searching for some profanity, but caught himself and returned to his mealy mouthed persona. "Shepherd"

I slowly placed my sword on the ground and with the other hand, held my palm to him with a sign to wait. I carefully removed my rolled pack from my back and reached into the folds and retrieved my pouch.

The words of the robed man from the unclean mountains rang in my ears. It had been close to five years. "Your people place great value on these stones." I opened the pouch and poured the stones and denariuses into my hand.

The eyes of the Arab grew wide as he looked at the stones and coins. I closed my hand and drew it back in a clear sign that there were conditions. The fat Arab looked at me.

"I must see the stones more closely!" He spoke as his eyes turned to coals of covetness.

I spoke for the first time. "All – the women – all!"

He stepped aside the tent flat and ordered all the women out. "Out! – Out – Now ! – Out – All of you! – Now - or you will feel my whip!"

The tent flap opened and there proceeded out four of the most pitiful women I had ever seen. They were dressed in tattered rags and covered in the filth of neglect. It was evident they had not been starved. I suppose that if they were to be sold as slaves, their physical condition should not be wanting. The women showed severe signs of physical mistreatment.

The women squinted their eyes in the bright sunshine. Their hands were free, but they were shackled at the feet. There was no way they could have run away.

A gasp of amazement ensued as one of them caught sight of the bodies of the two Assyrians. As looks passed between the women, and it became evident the two men were dead, a definite air of relief passed through them. One of the women raised her eyes to heaven and began to chant in a tongue I knew to be from the east.

The fat Arab drew his scimitar back in a threatening fashion and the woman cowered. I could see the intense hatred in the face of the chanting women as she drew back.

I lay the bag on the ground and stepped aside while motioning him to examine the stones. He released his grip on Rachel's hair and she slumped to the ground. Her hands went immediately to the back of her head. This Hebrew beauty had probably never felt any pain at the hand of a man. My heart went out to her.

I heard the gasp of astonishment as the Arab knelt to examine the stones. He gazed at them while giggling sounds came from his bearded face. He looked at me with the fire of coveted wealth gleaming in his eyes. He placed the stones and coins back in the bag and clutched them to his chest.

His gaze was straight at me as he moved his foot and kicked my sword toward the tent door. He placed the bag in his trousers and casually lifted his giant scimitar. He slowly began to swing the sword in a playful manner and a gurgling laugh passed his lips.

I had moved to the side and watched him carefully. I had no experience with deceit. I had never seen blatant betrayal. I still never thought to lie. The truth always seemed best. What was this man doing?

"You are a fool – shepherd!" He hissed as his eyes grew intense. He was no longer in doubt about the situation. He slowly stepped my way.

I saw my sword on the ground by the tent flap. My staff still protruded from the chest of one of the Assyrians. My pack lay on the ground. I had no weapon. The Arab was by far too huge for me to physically fight. I began to feel weak and my vision became blurry. I fought to keep my concentration.

The huge Arab once again issued a gurgling laugh as he raised the giant curved sword and advanced toward me. Everything began to swirl as the exhaustion and anxiety of pending death overcame my consciousness. My last view, as I fell forward, was of this Arab. His eyes were wide with surprise and the point of my sword was protruding from his chest. The sand in my mouth was tasteless as blackness shut everything out.

The sand under my face felt smooth. It had a cool soothing sensation to it. The blackness began to turn to a hazy grey and I felt the gentle touch of a woman's hand as a cool damp cloth caressed my cheek. Slowly reality began to return and I feared opening my eyes would reveal a horrendous scene.

I clinched my eyes and prayed. "Oh Great Elohim! – Let me awake amidst my sheep and return to my simple life!" I wanted no more treachery, deceit and conflict. "Why? – Oh Great Elohim – must you make me part of your Great Plan?"

The sound could have been from an angel as Rachel's sweet voice whispered. "Jaacov – you brave man – Please wake up! – Wake up!"

My mind slowly focused as I lay on the sand with my head cradled in Rachel's lap. She had bathed my leg and washed away the dust of nearly three days of no sleep, no food and constant anxiety. My mind raced with the thought of the present situation.

Three days ago the only violence I had ever known was being nearly kicked by an Assyrian, and an altercation with a young Roman soldier who now relished my friendship. I had never considered my encounters with wolves, caracals and lions as violence.

My thoughts went to the last two days. I had witnessed the death of a dozen or so Assyrians and had killed two, myself.

I was now fully awake and sat up with a start, expecting to see the giant Arab standing over me with his scimitar poised in a death blow.

"All is well! – My Jaacov! – All is well!" Rachel's voice was calm as she pulled me close. I was not used to being cuddled and instinctively pushed away to assess my situation.

"Please! – Jaacov! – Have no fear! - The slave-trader is dead! - The woman killed him with your sword - He is gone – Jaacov – they are all gone! – God sent you to deliver us! – Oh! – Jaacov – you are so wild and so wonderful and I love you so!" Rachel pulled me close and began to weep. I felt a new sensation.

I gently pulled from her embrace and arose to find we were still near the oasis, but on the western side behind the low ridge of rocks I had used so often for shelter.

The oasis scene was normal. Gone were the tents, camels and donkey cart. The bodies of the Arab and his Assyrian allies were nowhere to be seen. I saw no carrion to betray the location of bodies. It was simply a deserted oasis, with a cool, welcome, spring fed pond for refreshment.

Rachel's weeping brought me back to reality. I knelt and winched as the now dried chaffed skin on my left thigh gave me some pain. I took her in my arms. She went limp with emotion.

I instantly thought how the hand of God had brought me here and protected me. I reflected on my attack on the lookout at the hill east of the khah-vah. I then thought of the battle at the khah-vah and my encounter here at the oasis with the two Assyrians and the giant Arab. The only injury I had was from my own sword as it swung against my leg as I ran.

Rachel was safe! Elohim is, truly, great!

I had been asleep for nearly six hours after I had collapsed. Rachel told me how the haggard woman who had chanted a prayer picked up my sword and drove it through the Arabs back as he advanced on me.

The woman stood over the Arab as his life slowly ebbed away and recounted all the atrocities he had forced upon her. She truly took great delight in his painful death.

The women then conferred and quickly carried all the bodies far into the desert and buried them deep in the sand to hide them forever. They deftly went through the tents and possessions, removing any items that would identify the men.

Rachel then related how the woman offered her the opportunity to join them as they were going back to the eastern lands where they had been sold into slavery. The women seemed very happy as apparently they found great wealth among the stores of the Arab.

Rachel continued her tale as we began to pack for the trek back to the khah-vah.

The four women had bathed leisurely at the oasis. They seemed to have no fear, now that their captors were dead and disposed off.

After their bath they dressed and prepared themselves as the beauties they were. Rachel told me as innocently as she could that the Arab would present the woman as pawns of pleasure for men as they traveled west. I assumed the women were now in business for themselves.

As innocent as I was in the atrocities of man, I was no stranger as to man's desires. For three years, I had been a free servant in the employ of a Roman officer and at the beck and call of forty Roman soldiers. I witnessed the passionate nature of the Roman soldier and found the women that came and went did so of their own free will. I was quite young and obviously of Hebrew descent and some of the woman considered it their duty to see that I was trained in the fine arts of pleasuring a woman. They seemed to take much delight in my innocence.

I never felt the fire that some of the men felt in their pursuit of pleasure, however, their fire seemed never to bring to a women the depth of satisfaction that soft, gentle considerate love can bring. I had felt that fire as I had embraced Rachel.   I put it out of my mind as I gathered my few belongings.

The women had retrieved my staff and cleaned it. The sword I had taken from the Assyrian at the khah-vah was there as well. As I rolled my pack, I heard a soft clink and my pouch with the stones and coins fell to the ground. These women were truly thankful for their rescue.

The Roman's were true to their word.   Upon returning to the khah-vah, we were told of what transpired.   I had heard three long blasts on the great horn as I struck out to find Rachel.   I knew the returning lookouts would be discreetly killed. All the bodies were disposed of in the desert, buried deep in the sand to prevent the scavengers from getting to them.

Romans had some of the male servants and slaves dressed as Assyrians, because of their beards.   These imposters manned the guard positions and any Assyrians that came to the Khah-vah were quietly killed and disposed off.   When officials would come with questions concerning missing residents they were simply told the Assyrians had sold the khah-vah and had left the country with their new wealth. The Roman's presence was obscured.

Cornelius was careful and instructed the servants and slaves to tell no one that Romans had delivered them from the oppressors.

The answer was simple. The Assyrians had sold the khah-vah and departed with their wealth.   The mystic of the khah-vah at Al-walabe had begun.

The word was sent out that any Assyrians who had an interest in the khah-vah, simply needed to identify themselves and they too, would receive their reward. There were no takers.

Within three days the khah-vah was back to normal. Cornelius and all but six of the Romans returned to Jerusalem. I stayed at Cornelius's request to get the sheep herding back to a normal routine.

Brutus pleaded with Cornelius to stay as his shoulder healed. I felt somewhat apprehensive about Brutus, but he now, obviously felt he owed me his life.

It was no problem at all for the Hebrew servants to understand the importance of silence concerning the Roman involvement in returning the khah-vah to Hebrew ownership.

Cornelius made it quite clear that any slaves were now free. The men and women in attendance looked confused and it was evident no one knew the difference between slave and servant. The young, in attendance, were born at the khah-vah and knew nowhere else. The older had been hired many years before or had also been born there when the parents of the Master owned the giant complex. Everyone had a job or task to fulfill every day and none seemed to want for anything. No one left.

As Cornelius was preparing to leave I asked him to step aside for a question. "Sire – I know you to be an honorable man – but – the Assyrian lookout on the hill to the east ---------?

Cornelius raised his eyebrows in amazement. "You worry that I offered freedom for the signal on the ram's horn - then killed him anyway?"

I lowered my head and nodded.

"Jaacov – I keep my word – even to my enemies! – The boy lives – I tied him with rope and soaked a piece with pig's fat. It burns very slowly and would release him hours later – long after we had taken the Khah-vah. I told him if I ever heard a single word about this event – the entire Roman army would seek him out! - I think we need not worry!"

As the days went by, Brutus was my shadow. I was not much at conversation, so Brutus did most of the talking. I had no experiences to relate. All I had known was sheep and there is not much to say about them, except they stank and must be kept on the move.

Rachel had an uncle that lived to the west of Al-walabe. The uncle and his family came to assume the master's role at the Khah-vah. According to the instructions of the Master, Rachel's father would inherit the Kah-vah if anything happened to him, therefore since his son Malisch was dead the next nearest male relative was to assume the rule of the khah-vah. Few women in Judea had any power.

All was going well. I had the shepherds cull the spotted and black sheep and sent two shepherds to take the tainted sheep east to the pass that leads to the Great Salt Sea. I told them to not pass the giant boulder that blocks the trail. They were to simply leave the sheep and call out, "THE SHEEP ARE FROM JAACOV!"

I directed the shepherds and sheep herders to never kill or discard any spotted or black sheep anymore. We would keep them with the flocks and tend them as we did all the white sheep. When the shepherds made the eastern swing at the height of the winter grazing they were to leave the tainted sheep at the great rock at the pass to the Great Salt Sea.

Rachel soon returned to her daily routine and assumed control of the Khah-vah's household. It was quite evident she was infatuated with me.

I became aware of many new sensations when I was near Rachel, it frightened me. I did not like new sensations.

We received some beautiful horses Cornelius bought from a caravan that passed through Jerusalem. We had ample pasture around the khah-vah and the fields of wheat and barley supplied ample grain.   The khah-vah was prospering under its new management.

CHAPTER VI

STRIFE IN JUDEA

The Roman messenger was clearly stressed as he handed me the parchment from Cornelius. He welcomed my offering of cool wine and a couch to rest upon. The khah-vah at Al-walabe was only about twelve miles from Jerusalem, but it was a tough trip if you had to make great haste.

There was great turbulence in Judea. King Herod was deposed and exiled to a city called Vienne in Gaul. The political situation was vexed as Herod's brother, Antipas, was planning to assume temporary control from his domain in Galilee.

Cornelius and the Centurion, Flavius, in Jerusalem had long requested the presence of a Prefect to assert Roman authority. This was an example of how important it was for Rome's interest to be represented.

Cornelius felt the khah-vah was safe for now, but he needed me in Jerusalem to tend to the Roman complex while he and the soldiers were off attending to the squabbles that abounded throughout Judea.

It seems the Herodian family, although, born in the southern part of Judea had no ties with any Hebrew heritage and was only in power because they had aligned themselves with Rome during Rome's early conquest of Judea.

Herod the Great's past was stained with intrigue and treachery. He had assumed the throne of Judea after killing his nephew. Herod adopted Judaism as his religion and deposed his own wife and son in hopes of gaining support from the Hebrew clergy. He was never held in high regard by the Hebrews and now there was great pressure on Rome to satisfy the Hebrew Sanhedrin.

Herod Archelaus, his son, had only ruled for about ten years. The atrocity of killing all the Hebrew males under two years of age around Bethlehem, also placed him in deep disrespect among the Hebrews.

Cornelius received word that Rome was going to honor Flavius's request and send a Roman prefect to govern Judea. The Hebrew Sanhedrin feared they would lose their power and voiced many complaints.

Cornelius and Appias were promoted to Centurions and additional troops arrived in Caesarea. Flavius went to the coastal port and selected the men he wanted and established a Centurion complex there, in order to be closer to the pirate problem that existed around the busy port.

The fresh troops arrived in Jerusalem and great fanfare was made to welcome the Roman Prefect, Coponius. Cornelius and Appias ordered a week of games and Roman festivities. It was quite an affair and many Judean dignitaries attended.

One of the major reasons for the great affair was for the new Centurions, Cornelius and Appias, to get acquainted with the Prefect, Coponius, and the dignitaries from Judea.

The Roman soldiers put on quite a show of their prowess in combat. It seems many of the soldiers had been gladiators and volunteered for military service to try and add some longevity to their lives. Their art at hand to hand combat with various weapons was very valuable in the training of the younger soldiers.

The guest Judeans did not care for the military display at all, but despite their obvious piety, the dancing girls were the center of their attention.

My friend, Brutus, was the son of a gladiator. His father was now dead but had sired Brutus by a slave girl that attended the men. The women were not allowed to raise their children so

Brutus had been raised at a children's complex that groomed young men for the gladiator coliseum or the military. He was a good warrior but never achieved the size to allow him to match the men that fought in the Coliseum.

A Hebrew, named Judas from Gamala was causing great strife in the relationship between the Romans and Hebrews. He was from a section of Judea that was not heavily occupied by Romans and resented the taxes.

The Hebrews did the tax collecting and paid Rome for the privilege of being a part of the Roman Empire. A great amount of the taxes went for the lavish lifestyle of the Hebrew Kings and the Clergy.

The tax collectors blamed the high taxes on Rome's demands. Judas of Gamala, located in Galilee, claimed that taxes to any nation that did not follow God was the same as slavery and was calling for a revolt. This situation kept the Romans on edge.

The new Prefect, Coponius was an accomplished horseman and brought his own private stock of horses to Judea. The animals were beautiful and full of spirit. It proved difficult to properly care for them in the confines of Jerusalem so when I suggested we care for them at the khah-vah, he was elated.

Coponius accompanied Cornelius and me, along with Brutus and two more soldiers on the trip to Al-walabe and the khah-vah. We had twenty of the most beautiful white horses in all of Judea.

Cornelius would answer the many questions the new Prefect had about the Hebrews and their way of life. The two men were fast becoming close friends.

The khah-vah looked magnificent as spring had brought new blooms on everything that grew. The stock was fat and sleek and the sheep had provided a banner year of wool.

Rachel threw all protocol to the wind as she ran from the house to climb upon my horse and shower me with kisses and embraces. I nearly fell to the ground as she cared for nothing else, but to embrace me. My ears grew hot with the rush of blood from embarrassment.

I could hear Cornelius explain to Coponius that he need not expect a Hebrew to show him any honor above common courtesy. "They bow only to their God and no man has their allegiance unless he fears their God."

Coponius seemed to be interested in this one God idea and asked Cornelius how he knew so much about him. Cornelius spoke softly as he leaned on his mount to be close to the Prefects ear. "If you are really interested - My Lord – I have a most remarkable story for you! – but it must be told in private and at a later time."

Coponius cocked his head in anticipation and with a wink he dismounted and looking around the khah-vah answered. "Cornelius – my noble Centurion – I feel we will have more than enough time while we are here!"

The situation did, indeed worsen over the next few years. The zealot Judas of Gamala aligned himself with a Pharisee. The Pharasee, Zadok, took the zealots cause probably due to Coponius's close scrutiny of tax collections.

Coponius refused to deduct claims the Sanhedrin demanded for expenses they felt were the responsibility of Rome. Coponius simply replied that any expenses due to political or religious reasons were to be borne by the country and not Rome.

The zealot further took offence when Rome demanded payment for expenses incurred when the soldiers had to quell disputes resulting from the disagreement.

The King, Herod Antipas, brother of Archelaus, was allowed to assume rule of Jerusalem. He had ruled over Galilee and Rome thought it would be wiser to deal with a King that had already proven his loyalty.

King Herod Antipas moved his palace to Jerusalem. Galilee was somewhat relaxed from Roman influence and in a few short years Judas had risen in revolt.

Everything the Hebrews did had religious overtones. This seemed to fascinate Coponius and he sought to learn more of this one God persuasion.

Coponius and Cornelius had become close friends and Cornelius was very protective of the Prefect. Coponius had no military training, but was an astute politician. He left the military control in the hands of the three Centurions that were in Judea.

Coponius had gained complete favor with King Herod Antipas and the Clergy in Jerusalem. When the revolt finally came to a battle the Romans defeated Judas and his followers and put the insurgents to death.

I was sent to the Khah-vah along with Brutus. Brutus was now a Decanus and took half of his unit to guard Rome's interest. The khah-vah had become the haven and retreat for Coponius and the Romans.

The number of fine horses had greatly increased and the rich lords and sheiks from the south placed great value in them. I was far from being an accomplished horseman, but Coponius took an interest in teaching me the finer points of good horsemanship.

Cornelius had told Coponius the entire story of all that had transpired with the birth of Jesus. He told how the hand of God had guided us in our appointed tasks. He related the story with full disclosure of his belief in God.

Coponius was not concerned with Cornelius's religious beliefs. Cornelius had proven his loyalty and valor to the Prefect when he led the Romans to victory against the rebel Judas.

The Prefect showed great interest in me. He could not understand how a common shepherd could play any part in anything except caring for sheep. I told him I did not understand it either.

Coponius was astounded with my ability to do financial affairs. I had learned my ciphering from the everyday demand of keeping up with sheep. It was easy to learn what the names of coins were and the values men placed on them. It was all part of the same system and was constant. Ciphering was an exact science and just came naturally to me.

Having been around the Romans for over ten years now had given me the ability to read. Cornelius had provided tutors for the troops to learn to read Arabic. He felt it very important for his men to be aware of all that transpired around them. I would be present at some of the sessions and was now pretty functional in reading the local writings and some Greek as well.

Coponius became infatuated with Judaism. The stories Cornelius related and his firm belief in miracles had captured Coponius's imagination.

Coponius held me in awe. He knew I was nothing more than a simple shepherd, yet I was chosen to witness the night the Christ Child was born. I had been the one to escort the Magi from the grasp of Herod and deliver the Christ Child from the King's swordsman. Rachel and the servants at the khah-vah took great joy in telling Coponius of the mystique that surrounded my childhood.

Coponius believed that every man decided his own destiny and the miracles that forced me to act as I did meant that God had me pick out for a reason. He developed a close relationship with some of the Rabbis at the Temple in Jerusalem. The Rabbis had a special section constructed for Coponius in the court of the Gentiles and he would spend many hours listening to the reading of the Scriptures.

The Prefect was obsessed with the Prophesy and would spend hours with the Rabbis searching through the scriptures and asking questions about the happenings that surrounded the time of Jesus birth.

Judea was not considered the best of assignments for any Roman. The officers of the Roman army assigned to Judea seldom advanced in rank. Cornelius told me he was satisfied to live out his life here, where men understood the power of a great God.

CHAPTER VII

THE TEMPLE

Coponius was the first Roman Prefect to be assigned to Judea. I don't know if his assignment was some type of punitive measure or if he volunteered, but the order came for him to return to Rome. He had been in Judea for only four years and it seemed as if we had known him forever.

Coponius ordered only two of his great horses to accompany him back to Rome. The khah-vah had become his second home and even the Roman soldiers sought the comforts of the sprawling haven on their leaves. The Romans never brought any debauchery and simply sought rest and solitude.

I must admit that some romances were spawned during the soldier's visits. The soldiers wounded in the rebellion of Judas sought their recuperation at the Khah-vah.

Two of the soldiers including Brutus fell deeply in love with the girls that attended their wounds and asked permission to marry them. The ceremony was a simple affair. The couples signed some agreements and exchanged rings. They then drank a toast and threw the fine wine goblets on the ground.

I must admit the marriages made us all very happy, but that happiness went no further than the khah-vah and the compound in Jerusalem. The women were virtually shunned by the Hebrew women they came in contact with.

Rachel and I were pledged to each other. We had not talked of marriage, in fact I had not even thought of it. Rachel, on the other hand, was forever talking about how we could make changes at the khah-vah and how a family could really make a difference in the atmosphere.

I found nothing lacking with the atmosphere as it was. We had ample food. The complex provided more than enough room for us, the servants and the Romans as they came and went. The crops were plenteous and the horses and cattle were fat and healthy. The many shepherds that herded our flocks around Bethlehem were all well trained and loyal. The fields of date palms, olive trees, wheat and barley yielded ample supplies and sent many profitable shipments to Rome. I saw no reason to complicate things with marriage.

Rachel would pout and shed some tears from time to time. I really did not know what to do or say. I was a shepherd and had been drawn into serving a Roman centurion. I now had to frequently come to the khah-vah to manage the horses and arrange for sale of beef and mutton. The appetites of Rome were insatiable, but paid very well.

I did love Rachel and thought of her often when we were apart. She knew my feelings as my passion was no secret when we were alone, yet she longed for our marriage.

I was relieved when word arrived that I was needed back in Jerusalem immediately. I was gathering my things as Rachel came in with her bags. She promptly announced she was going to Jerusalem with me. I would not have it and told her so. She was adamant and I was at a distinct disadvantage. I had no experience at arguing. I simply stood mute and looked at her. She spoke confidently as she explained how she could run my household and it would leave me free to conduct my business with the Romans. She could cook my meals and take care of my needs. She finally stood looking at me with her hands on her hips as if to say, "There it is settled!"

I stood silently, collecting my thoughts. What could I say, to this beautiful woman who loved me so? I had nothing to offer her.

My eyes caught our images in the great mirror as Rachel stood beside me. I seldom ever looked in a mirror and each time my reflection caught me by surprise. I was, by far, a different image from four years ago when I first saw myself.

I no longer wore the tattered woolen tunic that was stored in my pack along with the pouch of stones and coins. The pack consisted of everything rolled in my fleeced robe and tied around my shoulders by rawhide straps. My other belongings were usually carried on my belt, and consisted of a larger pouch containing my flints. I always carried my staff and a small dagger in my belt.

I stood tall and my body was long, lean and muscular. I, now, had much hair upon my face and hair was beginning to show upon my chest.

I would ride a Roman horse from time to time, but usually walked everywhere I went. I preferred walking as the care and attention a mount required was sometimes a hindrance. The Romans would simply have a servant, like me, or someone nearby take care of their horse and give them a small gratuity for the service. I had no servants and placed no value on money.

Rachel came close and looked at our reflections, she was a radiant beauty. He body was now fully matured as she was a picture of an alluring young woman.

I spoke hesitantly, for fear of hurting her. "Rachel – I have no household - I sleep in a room at the rear of Cornelius's villa - I have no belongings, only the clothes I wear and my thoughts of you!"

The tears welled in her eyes as she stood silently. She slowly approached me and with a warm embrace and tears flooding down her cheeks, she spoke. "No – You are wrong – my wild Jaacov - you are a wealthy man – you have great wealth hidden away in your pouch and you have me and this khah-vah. We will always be here for you!"

She raised her face and standing on her tiptoes, gently pressed her warm sweet lips on mine and lingered only a moment. She quickly pushed away, bid me goodbye and fled the room.

That feeling when I first fled the khah-vah many years ago was pressing in my chest again. I knew it would not kill me, but the pain was intense. I left for Jerusalem.

If I had purpose in my travel I would generally run. I could maintain a moderate run that in ten miles could well outstrip a horse. A horse could run much faster than me, but would tire and had to rest. I could set my pace and the twelve mile trip to Jerusalem took me scarcely two hours.

The pain in my chest did not subside until I neared Jerusalem and became aware of great fanfare in the city.

The new Roman Prefect was arriving soon and a splendid welcome was being prepared. I arrived at the Roman complex and Cornelius was in a foul mood.

"The new Prefect is arriving soon and he will like nothing the way it is! Cornelius was curt in his speech. "He sends word that he must have his own house and will not be satisfied with a dwelling in the complex

The present situation of the people in Judea was a mixture of all the countries past influences. Over the centuries the mass of people were a mixture of Greek, Assyrian, Italian, Egyptian and Hebrew.

The Hebrews had made great effort to keep their blood line pure but over the centuries a great deal of Hebrew blood was in almost all the people. I suppose that is why Rome saw fit to favor the Hebrew interest in Judea.

Most of the people were ordinary with no drive other than to live comfortably and survive. This simplicity was deeply rooted in me as I longed to be back with my sheep, sleeping under the stars and keeping my eyes open for the wolf, caracal and lion. It had been years, now, since those simple days and I still wondered why Elohim would not leave me be.

The Hebrews were very possessive about their Temple and felt that Elohim was for Hebrews only. There was a part of the Temple called the court of the Gentiles, but even if one converted to Judaism, he was still set apart from the pure Hebrew.

The majority of the citizens of Jerusalem were simple people that feared God, but had no knowledge of Prophesy or ritual and simply followed what the Priests and Rabbis told them. Most could not trace their origin to any particular tribe of the ancient Hebrews.

Still Rome sought to be fair to everyone and dealt with its provinces in like manner. I respected this, but still I thought it odd, because any dealing, with the people of Judea, was done with the tax money that was collected from them in the first place.

I deposited my pack in my small room and sat for a lengthy discussion with Cornelius and Appias. The new Prefect was Marcus Ambivilus. He was a politician with a Cavalry background in the Roman army.

Cornelius was concerned that the new prefect would not approve of me and other servants being treated as free men to come and go as we see fit.

Marcus Ambivilus was a strange man. Cornelius expected him to be very military minded due to his past cavalry career, but it was quite the opposite. The new Prefect was quite and stayed to himself most all the time. He was very reluctant to act in Rome's behalf and most decisions were left to the Centurions. Judea was coming under more control of the Judean Sanhedrin. This was not a bad thing as Judaism was a religion that stressed goodness toward mankind; however the downside was the aloofness of the Hebrews and their reluctance to accept gentiles.

Cornelius always felt alone due to his belief in God. Coponius was infatuated with the history and miraculous past of Judaism, but never openly accepted the concept. Cornelius was now very alone since his friend had returned to Rome. He would spend hours telling me of how it was so evident the Hebrews were God's chosen people.

Caesarea had ceased to be a pirate problem. The presence of Flavius and his centurion detachment brought Roman security to the bustling port. Judea was in a peaceful stage and it was close to twelve years since that magnificent night the great star appeared and the Christ child was born.

I was in my twenty fourth year and as I looked at myself in the mirror in the great room of the khah-vah I saw a fully grown young Hebrew. My hair was much neater now than as a youth. The Romans wore their hair very short and very few Roman had beards. The Romans had a Hebrew gallab that cut their hair. Gallab was the Hebrew name for sah-Pahr, the Arabic name for one who cuts hair. The gallab saw to it that I maintained a tradition Hebrew hair style.

Rachel came into the room and stood by my side. We looked in the mirror and I remarked. "You are the most beautiful woman in all of Judea, Rachel!" She placed her hand on my arm and gently caressed the muscle as her other hand reached around my waist. She pulled me close.

She lowered her head as she softly whispered. "You need not try to woo me, wild Jaacov – I have never been anyone's but yours." I did not understand what she meant by woo. I only spoke the truth. I asked. "What is woo – Rachel?"

She looked at me in astonishment. Her eyes grew moist and began to glisten. She softly said. " Jaacov – how can a man be so wild and yet as innocent as a newborn lamb?" I stood mute. I still did not understand anything about this woman I loved. She fled the room.

I was at the khah-vah at the request of Rachel's uncle now acting as the Master. Two of the shepherds were very late in bringing in their sheep. I was going to search for them. Cornelius had a great interest in the khah-vah as it was his refuge from the strains of policing Jerusalem.

The khah-vah also was now the center of horse trading in Judea. The great white horses of Coponius were very popular with the Arabs and Sheiks throughout the land. The Hebrews collected great taxes from the khah-vah, but the taxes were no problem as Elohim blessed the khah-vah with great wealth and success.

The Nubian boys from years ago had grown into fine stockmen. They were particularly given to caring for the cattle at the khah-vah. The great bulls that were in the herds of cattle could sometimes be quite a challenge, but the Nubians could control them when others would retreat in terror.

It was early and the sky was faintly aglow with a pale light as we set out for the plains between Bethlehem and the hills before the Great Salt Sea. The Nubians and I traveled light as the search should not take over a week even if the flock was spread to the farthest point of the territory.

The Nubians carried their packs across their backs and their staffs were always in their hands. The staffs were now equipped with sharp iron points and made a most formidable weapon. The Romans did not consider the staff to be a weapon to be taken seriously and the shepherds of the khah-vah had adapted the iron points to all their staffs.

Our plan of search was taking us east to the oasis before Bethlehem and then south to the old trail that led to the valley of the unclean. The report was the flock had last been seen south of Bethlehem and would have been heading east to fatten the flock on the fields near the great rock that blocked the path through the land of the unclean.

By late evening we were east of Bethlehem and saw no evidence of the flock nor had they passed this way. We made camp for the night and built a small fire, simply to comfort us against the chill that night in this desert always brought.

I lay on my blanket and gazed at the stars. It had been many years since I had shepherded my sheep and the ground seemed noticeably harder. I laughed at my thought when I realized it was not the ground that was harder, but my body was softer and I simply noticed it more. It was still comforting to let my mind go back to those simple times.

I covered myself with my cloak as the night chill set in. I could feel the heat radiating from the Nubians as they lay close. They had no cloaks and seemed to be resting as comfortably as me.

It was amazing to see how the years had changed my lifestyle. I had trouble going to sleep as my mind began to explore the many ways the missing flock could have met peril. Rachel entered my mind and sleep enveloped me with bliss.

We crossed the trail of the flock the next morning as we reached the eastern trail to the Great Salt Sea. It was not hard to follow the trail of grazing sheep. In a very short time we found the reason for the flock to be late. The decaying sheep were nearly a week old and only partially eaten. The signs indicated the shepherds had hastily moved the flock further east in hope of discouraging the lion that was wreaking such havoc. We increased our paced as we knew the shepherds were in trouble.

I felt my heart drop as I reflected on my past encounter with a young lion on a killing rampage. A young lion will sometimes leave a pride out of necessity. The dominate male will sense a threat and drive the young male away before he reaches a size to be dangerous. The young lion will sometimes stray into a sparsely gamed area and will suffer extreme hunger. When he reaches a flock of docile sheep his hunger will drive him to kill indiscriminately. The fear of future hunger will force him to continue to kill in this fashion.

As we pressed on I began to fear for the lives of the shepherds. My fears were not in vain. We approached a low rise and could see the carrion in the distance as they circled and then swooped down out of site over the rise.

We cautiously topped the small ridge and surveyed the grisly site below. We could see at least ten sheep's carcasses and the mangled body of a shepherd. The carrion was as thick as a flock themselves. The dead sheep were now numbering sixteen with the six from the first kill site. The poor shepherd had been dead for about three days.

The information given us at the khah-vah was that two shepherds were to combine their flocks south of Bethlehem and graze them up the eastern side of the plain and then head west between Bethlehem and Jerusalem to the khah-vah. I was very familiar with this plan.

I was sure the shepherds had combined the flocks and perhaps the other shepherd still was out there somewhere in the plains with the rest of the flock.

We made our way through the carnage as the carrion all but ignored us. The giant birds would amble away only to begin to feast on a different carcass. The dead shepherd had fallen under the giant jaws of a lion, but showed no signs of being ravaged. This was a relief, as a lion that had developed a taste for human flesh was a great danger.

We gathered the belongings of the shepherd and my blood suddenly ran cold. The belonging indicated that the missing shepherd had left his wine skin, water and belongings behind. He had fled or was carried away. This was not good. The shepherd had little chance if the lion pursued him.

We hastily dug a shallow grave for the slain shepherd and immediately set out on the trail of the remaining flock. A few miles of tracking told us that the flock was not being shepherded. The ground was fallow as the sheep simply ate everything down to the ground and even pulled the roots from the earth.

"JAACOV – AYEEE!" The frantic cry was from one of the Nubians as he raced across the top of a rocky dune to my right. He was about two hundred feet from me. The other Nubian was to my left about the same distance as we searched the rocky plain for the flock and other shepherd.

The young black man was screaming for his life. I readied my staff. The Nubian looked over his shoulder as he fled my way. Suddenly the lion topped the rocky dune as it prepared to leap at the fleeing man. My training with the Romans was now second nature to me. My staff, now a formidable weapon, sped with deadly accuracy. The lions lunge and the staffs flight met in mid air as the iron tip on the missile pierced the young lion's chest with such force that his leap was stopped in mid flight. The fierce beast fell to the ground clawing at the rigged shaft that protruded through its flailing body.

I pulled my sword from its sheath on my back and raced to the great cat to end its frenzied misery. The howls and screeches were deafening as the giant feline struggled to rise to its feet. It did not see me in its agony and my sword found the heart of the hapless animal. It relaxed and the body began its final few convulsions as death overshadowed its last breath of life. How strange, the ground still seemed to tremble with the stride of the great cat as he made his charge.

"JAACOV – THE LION – THERE IS ANOTHER! -- I heard the scream as a shadow passed over me. I felt no pain but a giant claw sank deep in my left shoulder and I felt myself being thrown through the air by a power that made me feel weightless. I rolled on the ground and immediately faced the jaws of another lion.

There were two, brother lions, exiled by a great beast that could not bear their competition. The lion sprang and I knew not to extend my arms. The jaws of a lion would simply bit an arm off. I thrust my wounded shoulder at him. I still felt no pain as the long fangs of the beast ground in to my left shoulder. I could actually hear the crunch as the bone gave way under the massive jaws.

"Oh- Great Elohim – is this how Jaacov will die" My mind was reaching for some hope in this hopeless situation. The massive cat stood, holding me as if I were a sheep and looked at his brother lying motionless on the ground. I did not move. The lion did not realize its brother was dead, and proceeded to drag me toward the beast sprawled upon the ground.

I was heavy enough that as I dragged across the ground the lion did not sense my sword movement as a threat. The Romans were very wise in their choice of the short sword. My weapon was the Assyrian version and only a few inches longer than a Roman sword. Had my weapon been any longer, I could not have maneuvered it to a thrust position as I hung from the jaws of this lion. I drove the blade into the chest of the cat and had to use my left shoulder as leverage for strength to force the blade deep into the heart of the cat. The shock of the sword caused the great beast to jump straight in the air. The massive fangs tore my flesh as they pulled from my body. I felt, for the first time the pain. My left shoulder had been grasped in the lion's giant claw and torn open. The lions jaw had crushed the shoulder bone and the massive teeth pulled away even more flesh.

The spastic leap of the lion had pulled my sword from its chest and it fell to the ground in confusion. I staggered to the flailing cat and with a mighty stab of my sword drove the blade as deep into its chest as I could. The blackness closed in on me and I rested.

In my rest I had night mares of flesh eating lions and swords with blades of leaves that would not penetrate a lion's flesh. I could smell the hot musky breath of the great cats as they would lick me and play with me as if I were a mouse. I slept on. I tried to wake up, but the blissful comfort of sleep would pull me back down into the depths of peaceful slumber.

The water was cool and sweet. "Drink –Jaacov – Drink deeply – my friend!" The voice of one of the Nubians came into my dream world. Again I tried to waken, but that blissful power of rest pulled me under its cloud of blackness again.

"Rachel? – Is that you –Rachel - I hear you? - Why are you screaming - Rachel?" The nightmares continued.

The voice of Cornelius was comforting. "I'm sure his father was a Roman – he had to have been a Roman soldier that stayed here in Judea and married a shepherd woman and started shepherding himself - Only a Roman could be that brave!" I smiled in my dream and suddenly a great clamor arouse. I could feel soft arms around me and I tried to wake up.

This time the arms of slumber did not reach out for me and I opened my eyes to a great brightness. I saw only the swirl of bright colors and could hear the tinkling of cascading water. It was cool as I felt the tears of Rachel fall upon my cheeks. "He lives! - Oh Great Elohim! – My Jaacov lives! – Thank You – Thank You - Elohim – You have answered my prayers!"   Rachel embraced me as I lay upon a pallet by the great pool at the khah-vah.

I flinched with the pain in my left shoulder, it was an involuntary action, but Rachel became quite upset and fled the room in tears. I did not react to the pain on purpose but she felt she had hurt me and fled. I thought how often I made this woman I loved, cry.

Cornelius came close and sat by my side. He spoke softly. "Jaacov – can you hear and understand me?"

I nodded with a winch, I simply could not help it, every move made my shoulder hurt. I turned my head to see the wound, but the pain was too great to see more than the wounds where the lion's teeth had sunk into the front of my upper chest. I squinted my eyes in the pain. I suddenly felt very tired again. I wanted Rachel.

"Jaacov – don't try to talk – just listen – you had a close call my friend – The Nubians sing your praises and even now the people here at the khah-vah have made songs of your prowess!"

A clamor arose as all the people began to talk and ask questions at the same time. Cornelius called for quiet and proceeded. "They tell how you tracked the lost flock and found the signs of the lion's attack – they then tell how you tracked the lions and saved the life of one Nubian and then attacked and killed two lions!" – Jaacov - how could you do this?"

I painfully shrugged my uninjured shoulder. I wanted Rachel.

Cornelius continued. "The Nubians found the rest of the flock and the body of the other shepherd – Jaccov – the lions had tasted of his flesh! – They had to die! - The Nubians brought you back but left the sheep in care of a strange man in a crimson robe - He said he knew you and you would understand. – Do we send for the sheep?"

I slowly shook my head.

"You mean – just leave them?" Cornelius asked.

I nodded.

My reluctance to speak often offended Cornelius and he threw up his hands in exasperation. He turned to me and his face softened.

"Jaacov - my friend – do you need anything?"

I nodded.

Cornelius stood transfixed for a moment and then sputtered. "Well!" There was a brief pause. "Well – What in the name of Zeus do you need?"

I twisted my body in a painful effort to gain some comfort and spoke. "Peace and quiet – and Rachel!"

The room erupted in howls of laughter and glee.

Cornelius rose and with a flourish, ordered everyone out. Quiet fell on the great room, Cornelius called in a loud voice. "Rachel – come girl – your wild man awaits you!"

Cornelius left the room. I could hear her quiet sniffles as Rachel approached and stood at the side of my pallet. I painfully moved my body to make room for her and patted the mat. She eagerly sat and gently fell into my arms with a great sigh of relief. Her hair smelled of lilac and her skins was as soft as fleece. The deep blackness of her eyes reflected a flash of fire that spawned from love. Her lips met mine with a softness that only angels possess. The healing was on the way.

Rachel and I wed two weeks after my ordeal with the lions. I simply had no will to resist the woman any longer. Rachel's uncle was a most honorable man and even though the overseer' job was his, he insisted that all rights and privileges of a daughter was due Rachel and as her husband, I had a share in the khah-vah.

Rachel was a devout Hebrew and began to insist that we go to the Temple in Jerusalem for the Celebration of the Passover. I really had no desire to go and knew very little about what a faithful Hebrew should or should not do. Rachel told me just to do as she said and everything would be alright.

I never went near the Temple if I could help it. The Temple guards always seemed to be watchful of all that went on. If a person was not dressed well or seemed to be ailing, they were refused admittance. I always felt pity for these people and felt they were the ones that should be most acceptable in the Temple.

The area around the Temple was charged with excitement. Inside the Temple there was quite a stir and the people were milling about trying to get a better look at what was transpiring. I had no interest in the situation, but Rachel was all the more insistent that we get closer.

The activity that was drawing attention was inside the Temple where women were not allowed and Rachel grew quite angry. She never could understand why a woman could not do anything a man could do. It quite often got her into arguments with Hebrew men and I would have to physically drag her away, kicking and taunting the men with challenges as if she were a man.

Rachel was now a true professional at beguiling me. My shoulder had healed but the damaged of the crushing lion bite had severely restricted its movement. I was not the warrior I had been.

Rachel started on me to find out what was the cause of the excitement inside the Temple. I agreed only if she would order me a dish of the delicious melon slices that were being sold in the courtyard of the Temple. She agreed and I set my course to the inner Temple.

I pressed my way through the crowd and drew some contemptuous looks. I reached a point where I saw a circle of Pharisees and Priests. Inside the circle was a youth about age twelve. The lad was talking and the men were nodding their heads in wonder and amazement. I thought it odd that these great men would give so much attention to a youth. The youth had a familiar flair and I reasoned he was one of the many boys I had seen around Jerusalem. Young men had to prove themselves in Hebrew culture as in almost all cultures. This was a mere boy holding the attention of all these learned and great men.

I returned to find Rachel seated under a shady covering with a bowl of cool melon slices. She was most skeptical with my telling of only a boy talking to a group of men. She asked question after question in an effort to make something more exciting than a boy talking to a group of men, but in my mind, that was all it was.

The melon was wonderful and I toyed with Rachel by placing a slice sideways in my mouth and smiling as if I had green teeth. She rolled her eyes and whispered. "So much for kissing you!" I quickly sucked the melon slice in and swallowed it, smiling as if nothing had happened. She dipped her head and I could see her laughing in forgiveness.

My gaze wandered through the crowd and I played a little game of "Where is this person from?" It was amusing to scrutinize the people and from their clothing, hair style and demeanor, try to picture where they were from or where they were going.

My left arm hung limply at my side as I sat in the shade. I had some movement in it, but I could not lift it higher than my chest and reaching behind me was impossible. I tried not to carry it in a noticeable invalid fashion. I had no desire for sympathy.

Rachel knew my plight and with never a word spoken, would walk on my left side holding my arm as if nothing was wrong. No man had a better wife and I was only a simple shepherd.

I turned to view the crowded street as it approached from the north. It was not as business orientated on the north and not as crowded. It was getting near mid-day and the people were finding their way home or to the many food booths for the noon meal.

My eyes caught site of a man walking and leading a cart pulled by a donkey. This was the way of travel of the moderate family. The walk of the man was most familiar. The man would stop and briefly speak to passersby. My body began to buzz with a feeling I had not had for many years. I slowly rose from my seat. Rachel started to speak, but seeing my gaze she took my left arm and pulled it close to her bosom.

I stepped into the street and Rachel turned her gaze to the man leading the cart. I knew this man. My eye caught sight of the woman seated in the cart; she was casting pensive glances about as they approached. A young boy of about four sat beside her and three more boys, between six and ten walked behind the man. My heart jumped in my chest and the tears swelled in my eyes. I knew this woman.

As the cart drew nearer, it was no mistake. The man was slumped from when I saw him last, but the twelve years that passed could not hide the radiant beauty of the woman seated in the cart.

It was Mary and Joseph. Rachel clung to my arm as I clumsily stumbled toward the cart. She did not speak, for she knew something traumatic was transpiring in me. She wanted to share it.

Mary's face still glowed with that inner love, compassion and strength that had brought her to the attention of God. Her eyes glanced my way and her face exploded with recognition. The look of concern that had been there was gone and she cried. "Joseph! – Look – it is Jaacov - Oh Joseph! He will help us!" My tears could be contained no longer.

I know the people on the street thought I had lost my mind as I sobbed my joy at seeing these two old friends.

Mary introduced me to her children. "This is James, Jude, Simon, and Joses and would you believe we have lost Jesus?" Mary's look of concern returned. I immediately knew the answer.

Joseph had walked to my side and placed his hand on my shoulder. I was now a little taller than Joseph, but still felt like that little boys of twelve years ago.

I turned to Joseph and he embraced me with a great hug that only men can understand.

"Mary – Joseph – This beautiful woman here is my wife – Rachel!" I pulled her close to my side. "Rachel this is Joseph and Mary! – Remember I told you of the great star and the Christ Child!"

Rachel gasped in astonishment then stood mute as if stunned by the encounter.

"Mary – you need not worry – for I have seen Jesus – he is in the Temple! – He is talking with the Priests."

Joseph and Mary both drew a breath of relief and Mary immediately began to grow angry. "I knew this would happen – Jesus gets so engrossed that he forgets all about his obligations – OHHH! - Just wait until I talk to him!" Joseph looked at me and with a wink shrugged his shoulders.

We escorted the small group back to the Temple and waited until Joseph emerged with the young lad. Jesus looked like any other boy of twelve. His walk spoke of confidence and his stride was one of deliberation.   His eye caught mine as Mary spoke harshly but with love.   "Jesus – How could you do this to us? – We thought you were with friends and spent a whole day on the road home and had to turn back to come find you!" Mary paused to catch her breath.

Jesus spoke. "Mother – why do you search for me – you know I must be in my Father's house!" Mary and Joseph stood silent as if struck dumb.

Jesus turned and looked again at me. As usual, I did not speak. Jesus took a pensive step my way and Mary spoke. "Jesus this is - -----------------."

"Jaacov! – Yes I know!" Jesus replied softly and continued to walk to me. He looked at Rachel and smiled, then reached up to pull my tunic from my left shoulder. He lightly traced around the scars of the lions fangs and then pulled my left shoulder forward to expose the massive scars from the torn flesh on my back. His touch was as if a searing poker from the smithy's furnace was on my skin, yet was as cooling as a comforting balm. My body began to buzz with that now familiar feeling when I was near him.

"You still have much to do Jaacov!" Jesus spoke as he turned back to his parents. "Come! – Let us leave and I will be obedient now!

We walked along with the family as they left Jerusalem, I told Mary and Joseph of how well Cornelius was doing and how he was studying the scriptures and was a true believer. They asked me to give him their best wishes and for him to stay safe and well.

Rachel had been by my side the entire time and had not spoken. I stood and waved as the family disappeared across the rise to the north of Jerusalem.

I turned my attention to Rachel. She was silently weeping with her hands held pensively to her mouth. She always placed her hands over her mouth when she was astonished.

"Rachel! – It's alright – they will be safe – I am sorry if I upset you – but it was such a shock to see my old friends and the Christ again! – You must understand how special he is! – Remember all the stories I told you?"

She nodded and through her silent sobs she said. "You waved at them – Jaacov - you waved at them!"

"Yes Rachel - I waved." I answered.

"Jaacov!– You waved with your left arm!" She sobbed.

I stood transfixed. The scars remained but my left had full movement with no pain. I also wept!

CHAPTER VIII

LOST LOVE

Rachel gave me a son in the second spring of our marriage. He was a beautiful child and I told Rachel he would turn out to be a fine shepherd. Rachel scolded me for not having higher hopes for our son. I did not understand this thinking.

My daily routines were boring. I was constantly dealing with the sale and transport of sheep, the shearing and shipping of wool, the harvesting of the fields, gathering the dates, olives and figs.

The horses left by Coponius had started a great enterprise and the khah-vah now had great status and was much renowned.

The Romans still took great pleasure in spending their furloughs there and many villas had been added. The khah-vah had become a sprawling complex. Cornelius saw to it that the Romans brought none of their paganism with them. The khah-vah was for relaxation and rest. It became quite famous for its peaceful and pleasant atmosphere. Everyone treated each other with respect.

My nemesis, Brutus, from years ago had become a fast friend. Brutus had married one of the Hebrew girls at the khah-vah. She had nursed him back to health from wounds he suffered in the, Judas led, Hebrew revolution. Brutus had finished his ten year enlistment in the Roman army and remained in Judea with his wife. He now took care of the horses and was quite a horseman. We often took lengthy rides and reflected on our earlier lives. Brutus could never understand why I longed to be back in the plains with my sheep. I felt it was a very honest and rewarding profession.

Rachel and I would ride sometimes to visit the shepherds in the fields and would spend a night or two under the stars. It brought back many memories and I often longed to remain. Our son, Adam, was a natural with the sheep. He would wander amidst the docile animals and pick out a young lamb. After a short period to become familiar they would then romp and play as if they were the same creations.

It was always Rachel that prompted us to return to the business of the khah-vah. It seemed as if there were not nearly as many wild creatures as years ago. The legend abounded that the wild Jaacov had vanquished the last of the lions when he slew the exiled brothers years ago.

Cornelius summoned me to Jerusalem to assist in welcoming a new prefect to Judea. Marcus Ambivius had returned to Rome and Annius Rufus was arriving.

The preparations were always left to me to arrange. I was much more adept at dealing with the shrewd Hebrew merchants. The Hebrews knew I was in the employ of the Romans and I was not held in high regard. I had never cared for what people said or thought of me. It did not matter. I knew how I felt and thought and what I wanted and needed in life. What anyone else thought had no effect on me. I simply ignored the snide remarks and innuendos and never let them bother me.

Dishonesty, on the other hand was a different matter. I had drawn some large baskets of grain from the warehouse in Jerusalem. The khah-vah allowed the warehouse to store and market its grain. I noticed the large mat containers had a peculiar sound when they were unloaded on the stone pavilion at the Roman complex.

The containers were large wicker baskets lined with linen to keep the grain from sifting through the wicker. As the grain was being unloaded and lightly dropped to the stone floor, the sound was different.

I moved a wicker container and it felt normal. I bent and picked the container up and again it felt normal. I dropped the container in frustration and a bit angry at myself for focusing on such a trivial thing. The sound of the wicker container as it fell on the stone was not normal. I noticed something else, when the wicker struck the stone, a bit of sand puffed away. I bent and found a small stream of sand flowing from a corner of the wicker container.

I could feel my fury rising. I seldom ever grew angry. Most situations that provoke anger are a result of a person's sensitivity. Most situations do not matter. This mattered.

The wicker containers had an inner layer of wicker on the bottom. The containers, each, had a false bottom that held nearly two inches of sand. The merchants at the warehouse were skimming grain from all its customers.

The warehouse was paid a fee for handling the grain, and the additional grain that was being skimmed was going into the merchant's pocket.

My fury quickly subsided, but I knew this had to stop and the merchants must be punished. If I told Cornelius, he would be furious and possibly order the merchants put to death. I had no way of knowing if the merchants were cheating everyone or just the Romans.

I reasoned that the skimming was being done only to customers that returned the wickers to the warehouse. The chance of discovery was too great if the wicker containers were put onto circulation for reuse elsewhere.

I examined the containers carefully and found them all to have the sand filled bottoms. I also noticed each container had the Hebrew symbol for Roman on the side.

I strapped my sword to my back and picked up my staff. As I departed, Cornelius called. "Jaacov! — Come I need you!" I simply raised my hand in a "Later wave" and left the compound. Cornelius watched in mute curiosity.

I made my way to the warehouse and entered with a determined stride. The attendant broke into a huge facetious smile and boldly stated. "Ahh! – The Roman lackey has come for some more grain for his Roman lords. He stepped into my path as I rounded the long counter and headed for the rear of the giant warehouse.

I placed my open hand over his entire face and with all my strength pushed him to the side. I seldom ever used all my strength knowingly, I simply responded to the situation, but the man fairly flew against the far wall and collapsed in a heap on the floor. The commotion aroused four other men from various parts of the warehouse and the man I had pushed began to shout insults and profanity. I began to search through the stacks of wicker containers in a staging area waiting for delivery. I found none with the Roman symbol.

The din of comments and vulgarity was now at a crescendo. "What is the meaning of this outrage? - Who do think you are? - Wait until Herod hears of this! – What do you seek?"

I did not speak, my fury was rising again. I had not thought this through. What if I found no proof? The merchants could say we had added the sand in an attempt to harass them.

There were hundreds of containers in various stacks throughout the warehouse, but none with the Roman symbol.

A huge stack of containers sat against a far wall with the Star of David on the side. These were set aside as the tithe of grain for the Temple. The warehouse stored the grain for the Temple and the handling fees were paid by the donator.

My fury was unbearable and in my frustration I plunged my staff into the bottom of a wicker container bearing the Star. I had struck out at my people and the symbol of my people, whom I felt should be the most trustworthy of all men.

I pulled my staff from the wicker and turned to leave in frustration. I looked up to see the eyes of the attendants open wide with fear. They were not in fear of me, but of something behind me. I turned to see a steady trickle of sand flowing from the hole in the bottom of the wicker container destined for the Temple. The warehouse was skimming the Temple as well. All went silent. The attendants stood motionless.

I slowly walked to the wicker as the sand ceased flowing. I pulled my sword from its scabbard on my back and gently prodded the container. The sand flowed again. I drove my sword into a half dozen containers and now the sand flowed freely. These men were even cheating the Temple.

I slowly turned and from the corner off my eye I saw an attendant reaching for a sickle hanging on the wall. My staff was in instant flight and struck the wall where the sickle hung. The attendant dropped to the floor and cowered. Silence again.

I did not speak. I stood motionless and gathered my thoughts. Two of the attendants turned and dove from the platform that opened into the loading yard. I could hear the rapid patter of their feet as they sped away.

The silence was uncomfortable. The remaining men began to squirm. One of the men that had emerged from a room nearby cautiously stepped forward. He spoke. His voice squeaked from fear and he had to clear his throat. He began to stammer in a pleading manner. "Look now – you are Hebrew and we are Hebrew! – Why is a little extra profit so great a grievance? – The Temple loses nothing and your Roman friends could care less – all this grain is a result of taxes anyway!" The man was wheedling.

I had heard enough. I slowly walked to my staff and the man on the floor covered his head and began to call on Elohim for help. I pulled the staff from the wall and turned to face the remaining men.

I spoke distinctly with measured words. "If the Romans hear of this - you may very well die! – If King Herod hears of this – you will surely die! – If justice is not done here I will personally take each of you to the eastern pass to the Great Salt Sea and deliver you to the land of the unclean!" One of the men's eyes rolled into his head and he fainted to the floor. The man that spoke clutched his chest and began to stumble backwards.

"Justice must be done before the moon fills again!" I turned on my heel and as I drove my sword into its scabbard I departed. Silence reigned.

The Feast of the Passover was near and the word was spread that due to abundance of grain, all would receive a free supply of grain from the warehouse for the holiday. Justice prevailed. My association with the Hebrews in Jerusalem was on a much higher level after the incident. I would think that such a deed would be best kept secret, but nevertheless, I was no longer considered a Roman lackey.

The new Roman Prefect arrived at a perfect time. The Festival of the Passover was in full swing and with the bonus of extra grain the people's mood was jovial.

Annius Rufus commented he had never seen people so happy to be conquered. Cornelius leaned close and told him how important it was to keep the people happy.

Annuis questioned why and Cornelius answered. "When they are happy – we do not have to fight them and when we do not have to fight them – we are happy!" Annius found this very humorous and roared with laughter.

The Festival of the Passover impressed Annuis . Cornelius told him of the miraculous freeing of the Hebrews from the clutches of Pharaoh. Annius was again impressed by Cornelius's knowledge of local lore. He was indifferent when Cornelius confided he was a believer in the one true God of Judea. It was amazing how tolerant the Romans were of religious beliefs.

Annuis Rufus spent only two years in Judea before he was replaced by Valerius Gratus, and again a great celebration was held to welcome the New Prefect. The Hebrew King Herod Antipas still ruled Judea and Galilee. King Herod Philip ruled the far northeastern country. Rome was satisfied with the royal role the Herodians played in their Empire. The Hebrew royalty fully realized their power depended entirely on Rome's approval. The reception for the new Prefect was a gala affair, but Cornelius was very subdued during the entire event.

Cornelius had finished his ten year enlistment in the Roman army and decided to extend his enlistment for the privilege of staying in Judea and being advanced to Senior Centurion. He was already five years into his second enlistment. Rome placed a great deal of trust in Cornelius and his knowledge of the Hebrews kept open a trusted path of communication with the Hebrew Sanhedrin

The Romans had sent a bevy of Germanic slave girls for the Roman soldiers in Judea. It was very difficult for the Romans to find romance in Judea due to the aloofness of the Hebrews.

Cornelius had grown fond of one particularly young girl with hair as yellow as the bloom of the narcissus. Her eyes were as blue as the sky. She was so young that she had been spared the ravages of Roman soldiers. Cornelius took her as his personal attendant and it was evident she had fallen deeply in love with the brave, wise, gallant and tender hearted Roman.

Rachel did a fine job raising our son, Adam, and we would spend many nights under the stars listening to the infrequent howl of the wolves. Only rarely did we hear the haunting cry of a caracal, but we were together and Rachel seemed to need nothing more than to be near me with Adam.

I prayed quite often to Elohim and asked him to reveal what it was he wanted of me. I was happy in my life, but felt as if it was a life set apart for someone else and I was living it. All I ever wanted was my sheep and the rocky plains.

Perhaps I asked Elohim too many questions, for in my twenty eighth year of life, Elohim sent a great fever throughout the land.

My Rachel had insisted on going to Jerusalem and aiding those dying from the fever. My protests were to no avail. She returned to the khah-vah hardly able to stand.

I sat by my Rachel and watched her life slowly burn away. Adam fully understood what was happening to his mother , but resented not being able to come near her. He blamed me, because I never left her side. I held her close as she would shiver in the chill of fever and I would tend the small wounds as the physicians removed the leeches.

Rachel would gaze at wonders that I could not see, as the fever burned in her body. The great room by the pool always had a cool breeze and I felt she would be comfortable there. She asked to be placed back in our bed and draw the curtains shut.

She pulled me close and I lay my head upon her burning breast. She began to soothingly wind her fingers in the long locks that hung from my temples. This was one of her many little things she did that brought me great pleasure.

She spoke weakly. "Jaacov – my wild love – I have loved you since I first saw you eating melon at the Masters table - you threatened me with your staff the first time I spoke to you - You may as well have cast the staff for you penetrated my heart all the same - Uhhh!"

She startled me with a low moan. "Rachel – please don't tire yourself!" I was trembling with emotion. That indescribable pain in my chest was back. This time it was more intense than ever.

"Jaacov – I hear the voices calling! - They tell me all is well and it is alright to go with them - Jaacov I hear the voice of Malisch – he is near and Father – they are calling – Jaacov I must go! – Uhhh!" Another low moan and she relaxed.

"Rachel – Please be strong – I need you!" My heart hurt so badly I could hardly speak. The pain in my chest was unbearable.

She gently pulled me to her face and whispered. "You are the one to be strong – Jaacov - care for Adam and ----------!"

She paused as if listening. "Jaacov! – The voices say Elohim still has great need of you!" Her lips met mine and I felt her spirit leave her body. My heart went with her and the pain was gone.

The sadness of losing my Rachel drained all emotion from me and I withdrew into a state of emotional isolation. The days that followed were a blur. I don't know if I ate or slept or even dressed. I found myself in the shed by the sheep pens where I first spoke to Rachel. I was sitting on a bale of straw exactly where we had our first conversation.

I could feel eyes upon me. I felt no threat, but the intensity of the feeling brought me back to the real world. I realized I had no weapon. I slowly looked around and caught the flash of dark eyes peering from the blackness of a storage room. It was my son, Adam.

The pain in my chest suddenly returned as guilt overpowered me. One of the last things my Rachel had asked was for me to care for Adam. I had not even sought him out in the days after Rachel's death. I was absorbed in my sorrow and suddenly realized my son had lost his mother.

Rachel was the one that held him on cold nights. Rachel soothed his bruises and calmed his fears. It was his mother's tears that washed away his doubts. It was Rachel's words that kept his young inquisitive mind focused on the right way to grow up. I was his father and I was failing him.

Rachel's soft voice whispered through my pain. "Care for Adam!" I opened my arms and the lad burst forth from the darkness of the storage room and threw himself into my waiting embrace.

Gone was his resentment of the last days. Gone was my pain of guilt. His strong young body convulsed with the sobs of sorrow and he clung to me with a grip that reflected his need for security.

We wept together, two men weeping over the loss of their most precious love.

The days that followed were consumed in a new relationship with my son. I sometimes wondered if he missed the softness of his mother. Words cannot describe how much I missed her, but I began to realize that she lived on in my son. His gaze reflected the blazing intensity of her dark eyes. His stubbornness reminded me of how useless it was to try and persuade his mother to change her mind.

Rachel would invade my dreams and she was always near when Adam and I would retreat to the fields to spend time with the sheep. Adam loved the simple life as much as I did.

My son was now my shadow. I saw to it he was tutored in the languages that prevailed in Judea. He was gifted in ciphering and accompanied me on my frequent trips to Jerusalem to tend the administrative business of the Roman complex.

There were many families at the complex now as Roman soldiers sought a more docile life and took wives from among the women sent to serve them. Some even took Hebrew wives. Adam found ample companionship among the boys and girls that now dwelled in the complex.

The khah-vah also had numerous children and at both locations the Roman military influence was prevalent. Brutus had a son that was near the age of Adam and they became fast friends. Brutus would spend many hours playing and training the boys in the art of combat. Brutus had been a gifted soldier and was also the son of a gladiator. His association with the gladiators greatly enhanced his art of individual combat. I had profited by his training as well.

Cornelius had a great interest in the young Germanic girl that attended him. The girl had suffered the same fever that ravaged the land and took my Rachel. Cornelius stayed by the girl's bed as Elohim's will was done and she recovered. Cornelius took the maiden as his wife. There was a considerable age difference between the two, but the girl, Bridget, was thrilled and made Cornelius a wonderful mate.

Bridget had been taken into slavery at a very young age and had witnessed the treatment that went along with serving unsatisfactorily. She recognized Cornelius's kind nature and instinctively was drawn to him. She took great pride in his position as Senior Centurion and now being free as the wife of a Centurion, she began to press her influence. Her authority was never challenged, and her wise conduct really improved the moral state of the complex.

The young woman did all she could to please Cornelius and began a study of Judaism. She and Cornelius would spend hours discussing the many commandments and rules that meant so much to a Hebrew. They both agreed that many of the requirements were simply not relevant to worship and service and would apply only to a Hebrew. They sometimes felt very alone, because even though they were believers they were simply not welcomed in the Hebrew society. The words spoken that night the Christ Child was born was their only assurance. "DO NOT BE AFRAID FOR I BRING YOU GOOD NEWS THAT SHALL BE FOR ALL PEOPLE!"

Cornelius would lament. "All people! – where are all the people! – Are we the only ones that believe in this new king and where is he! Elohim was listening and I warned Cornelius that asking Elohim too many questions would often bring unwelcomed answers.

A great celebration was planned for Cornelius's fiftieth birthday. I had no idea of when I was born and for the years I had served as Cornelius aid, he had included me in the celebration as an equal. I was now over forty years of age. Rachel had been gone for twelve years now and Adam was quite the man at eighteen.

We had received a message from the Master in Gaul. He was getting quite old now and needed an aid. He also wanted ten of the great horses from our stable. He felt the great abundance of grass and grain in his new land would be a great advantage in raising these fine animals. He was quite insistent that I come to Gaul and help with the great enterprise there and to assist in the formation of a Roman – Hebrew sheepherding endeavor on the island of Britannia.

Cornelius was consulted and again informed me I was free to do as I see fit. I did not care to leave Judea. I just wanted to tend my sheep. I sat and considered my life. Tending sheep was all I ever wanted. Everything else had been thrust upon me. I was a Roman aid, a widower, a father and one of the managers of the khah-vah. I had not asked for any of this. My son, Adam, was of a different mind altogether.

"Father! – I will go!" His face was aglow with the thought of a great adventure. "You have taught me well – Father – about the sheep and the ways of the wild - I have learned to cipher and read the Greek words and you know how I love the horses!" He was correct in all he said. He too was a free man and eighteen years of age.

Adam did a magnificent job of picking the horses to make the trip. The horses he chose were not what I would have picked, but his reasoning was well founded. I would have picked the finest of the animals. Adam instead picked the ones that were more docile and favored the food trough. His reasoning was that the fat and lack of exercise would allow them to suffer less on the long sea voyage. After their arrival they would be in better shape than an animal that was lean and required daily exercise. He was a wise young man.

Adam handled the entire procedure for the horse delivery. Cornelius and I escorted the caravan on the four day trek to the seaport of Caesarea. It was the farthest I had ever been from the country side where I had dwelt.

The arrangements were no problem due to the blessings of Rome over the entire affair. The Caesar, Tiberius, was in his sixteenth year of rule and spent considerable time in the northern part of Gaul. His interest in this new fertile land was as intense as was Augustus'. There was a great deal of conflict with the Germanic tribes and Roman colonization was greatly encouraged.

I had never seen the sea and stood in awe as my son sailed away on a great ship. It appeared the water ended only a short distance away and I became quite alarmed when I noticed the silhouette of the ship seemed to be sinking. Cornelius laughed and assured me that it was normal for things in the distance to seem to sink in the water as they grew more distant. He offered no reason for this strange occurrence and I spent many hours trying to reason how it could be.

My mind was filled with the sight of so much water. It was very salty to the taste and very deep. I had never been in water over my head and realized that it was very difficult to stay on the top of the water. Cornelius and the other Romans had a great laugh at my inexperience with water. I vowed to stay as far away from deep water as I could.

The next few weeks were very lonely and I spent many nights in the solitude of the fields. I was not needed to tend the sheep but I would often stay a night and share the watch with the shepherds. The wolves and caracals were not nearly as prevalent as years past. I never saw or heard a lion again nor did I even hear of one in our land.

Cornelius sent word for me to come at once to Jerusalem. I now chose to ride one of the fine horses whenever I journeyed. Most of the great animals were white, but we had some fine black horses as a result of the animals brought to us by the Arab Sheiks. I chose a sleek gelding that had seen his day as stud. He was a magnificent animal and very dependable in strange territory.

The trip from the khah-vah to Jerusalem was now very short due to having traveled it so many times.

I arrived and found Cornelius had not returned from a summoned visit to the new Prefect, Pontius Pilate.

I immediately set about rectifying some obvious deviations in the complex that I knew would cause problems. The guard post on the walls had become play areas for the many children that now lived in the complex. This had to be remedied. I brought this to the attention of the provost marshal and he took issue with me, a Hebrew, telling him his job. I quietly pointed out that regardless of who pointed out the defects, whoever corrected the problem would certainly get credit for it. He immediately set about having the children's toys and playthings removed and placing the areas off limits to all but the guards attending their posts.

Cornelius returned and noticed the activity. He flashed a knowing smile upon seeing me. Cornelius was no longer the young Roman warrior I had met so many years before at the oasis. The years had been good to him as he grew in his knowledge of God.

Pontius Pilate had been in Judea for about four years and a new prophet was causing turmoil in Galilee. This area of Judea was not in Pilate's district but he was very curious of this new prophet preaching of the coming of a savior.

This prophet was named John and went through the countryside preaching the importance of redemption and was baptizing the multitudes in a Hebrew tradition of cleansing with water. This new prophet seldom preached in a synagogue, and had brought some complaints from the Priests because the Temples suffered in attendance whenever he was in the vicinity.

Cornelius seldom took an active military role anymore. He was now a Senior Centurion and was mostly used for inspections and as an advisor. His knowledge of Judaism was a great help in keeping a peaceful attitude between Rome and Judea.

Pilate had asked Cornelius to investigate this new prophet and assess his impact on Rome's position in Judea.

Cornelius was intrigued with the thought of the Prophesy and was truly convinced he had a part to play in Elohim's plan.

Cornelius eyes grew bright with the flame of a spirit that seemed to ignite him whenever he spoke of God and the Prophesy.

Cornelius spoke. "Listen to me Jaacov – this man – John- may be the one! – he lives in the wilderness and the ancient prophesy in the scrolls of Isaiah say the voice will come from the wilderness – and the scrolls of Malachi speaks of the coming of one called Elijah! - Oh! – Jaacov come with me and let us see for ourselves and – Uh! - Rome of course!" His face glowed with excitement.

CHAPTER IX

JOHN

I still traveled light, all I had to do was pick up my pack and sling it over my shoulders. My old tunic was only a memory now as I was a picture of an average Hebrew man in his forties. My pack was still the woolen cape that was used to ward off the night chill, along with items of personal use. One of my prize items was a comb made from the bone of a large fish. My Rachel had made it for me and she would spend hours pulling it through my tangled locks, when I would return from some wild adventure.

Thoughts of Rachel would cause me great pain from time to time. She had loved me in spite of my reclusive ways and had given me Adam, a fine son, who had departed on his own adventure to Gaul and Britannia.

I still preferred the wilderness of sheepherding. It was a simple life and required nothing more than caring for sheep and myself. It seemed as if everyday a new task was laid before me. I felt a deep drive to do anything that was asked of me. Cornelius was my friend and benefactor and I felt the urge to do his bidding.

I slung my pack over my shoulder and instinctively felt for the small bulge from the pouch containing the stones and coins of many years ago. I seldom ever looked at them and carried them only because of the memory they would bring to my mind. My sword was in its scabbard between my shoulders and my small knife was in my belt. I was ready for travel.

Cornelius chose two soldiers to accompany us; one was the young son of my old friend Brutus. The lad was only seventeen but quite the fine specimen of a young Roman. The Hebrew blood that flowed in his veins gave him a tenacity to achieve any quest he took on. Brutus had named him Joseph, a Hebrew name, but the young man's demeanor prevented any remarks about the name from his peers.

Joseph indicated a strong desire to know more about Judaism and the Prophesy; I suppose it was a result of being at Cornelius feet, as a child, when the mighty Roman would tell the story of that wonderful night the Savior was born.

Cornelius was now a magnificent story teller and you would have thought he was a Hebrew as his eyes would fairly glisten with a fire from within. He was still suffering from the pain of exclusion from the inner circles of the Hebrews. I simply reasoned it was natural for a people to resent those that were their conquerors even though their lives were probably better for it.

I made a quick trip to the khah-vah, accompanied by Joseph and chose some mounts for our journey. We were privileged at Cornelius's complex because of our involvement with the khah-vah. The Roman detachments in Judea were Infantry and the use of horses was a blessing for those of us that could ride.

The four of us departed at early dawn and found the four day trip to the Jordan valley uneventful. We found a great deal of traffic on the roads and paths as we progressed. It was not difficult to make our way as the people were all fixed on the same location.

The word had traveled fast of this wild man that was preaching in the wilderness. His simplicity seemed to hold some mystic with the people. It seems only natural for a person to want comfort and convenience in their everyday life, but here was a man that shunned anything that resembled comfort. He dressed in un-tanned skins and ate wild honey. His roof was God's sky and his wine was the waters of the springs. His hair was matted, but his eyes blazed with the fire of Elohim.

The valley of the Jordan ran from the base of the Sea of Galilee for about fifty miles to the Great Salt Sea. We had heard that this man John was baptizing in the river Jordan, so our strategy was to simply ride up the river until we found him. It did not take long. The crowds of people seemed to know exactly where to go.

We were scarcely five mile from the Great Salt Sea when we came across a large encampment of people. There was an air of celebration that was contagious and Cornelius immediately began to mingle with the people asking questions about this man John.

It was obvious most of our group was Roman, but Cornelius had advised us not to wear helmets, carry lances or shields, for this was a peaceful mission and not a military venture. The fire that burned in Cornelius eyes and his command of the Hebrew tongue quickly put the people at ease.

The people numbered almost five hundred as the night set in. We built a small fire and prepared some of the Roman stew that was popular with the soldiers. The Romans would dry some meat in the hot sun on the tile roofs of the complex. The meat could be mutton, beef or sometimes the flesh of the swine. The Hebrews would not eat swine, but the Romans found it quite tasty and I also had eaten it as long as I could remember, shepherds are not picky eaters. The dried meat is placed in water and slowly boiled until the meat texture softened once again. If vegetables or grain was available, they were simply added to the mixture and the result would be a savory stew that quite often varied in flavor according to the ingredients.

This night the people around us began to react to the fragrance of the stew and began to offer a variety of ingredients, if allowed to partake of the stew. Soon the pot would not hold the offered ingredients. A merchant had stopped in an effort to do a little business and brought over a huge copper pot and the ingredients were transferred. Soon this pot was almost filled to capacity. As the darkness began to settle an atmosphere of gaiety began to prevail. Some people from the fareast put some spices in the stew and some salt from the mines near the Salt Sea was added.

A woman with very dark skin brought a pouch filled with a large white grain called cavala. The grain began to swell in the liquid and soon the huge pot was a thick mixture that was most pleasing to the eye. The woman stirred the pot and upon tasting it, raised her eyes to heaven and called loudly. "TAIYAAR!" We had no idea what she meant but what started as our meager evening meal was now a giant feast and it was time to eat.

The power of God is unexplainable and the tears came to Cornelius eyes as he sat among this multitude of people sharing a common meal and he was totally accepted. He slowly raised his eyes to the heavens and I could see his lips move as he gave thanks to God, Elohim, the God of the Hebrews. This great Roman embraced Elohim as his own.

It was a most festive night as the people rejoiced. The singing and dancing was of a joyous nature and soon all were quite content and silence fell over the group.

A voice called out. "Where is this John the Baptist – surely he must be hungry?"

Another voice answered. "He is resting in a cave nearby and it is of no use to call him – he will not come forth for he is fasting – he says the days ahead will bring a great moment and he must prepare himself!"

The people were spread over the countryside in small groups representing families, friends or just a group that had somehow bonded in the past few days.

We took turns standing watch and my turn was early the next morning. As the first light of the sun began to soften the black of the eastern sky, I could see the many small groups as they lay huddled in the rocks and scrub brush of the wilderness. I felt a wave of nostalgia as my mind went back to my young days of shepherding.   Life was so simple and I longed for that sense of well being that self-confidence can bring.

The night the Great Star appeared and the voice from Heaven announced the birth of the Christ Child had changed everything. I did not regret what my life had brought, but I still longed for the freedom of shepherding. I was being driven by an unspoken force and seemed to have little control of the situations that God placed me in. I did not want the responsibility that was placed upon me, but somehow I always managed to perform whatever was asked of me.

The people began to stir with the dawn and an air of excitement prevailed as word spread that the Baptist was up and preparing to preach.

I made my way to the giant copper pot only to find it gone. Cornelius laughed as he saw the look of disappointment on my face. I had, indeed, relished the thought of another taste of that delicious stew from the night before.

"The merchant only loaned the pot – Jaacov - as soon as it was emptied he took it back!" Cornelius laughed again and it was evident he too felt the air of jubilation.

We ate some of our dried grain and dates that was a staple of travelers. The waters of the Jordan were clear and clean as it cascaded over a layer of rocks a little north of where we camped. A few miles south of where we were the waters took on that salty taste as the salt and minerals from the rock deposits began to dissolve in the river.

The man called the "Baptist" began to climb a small rise to gain a vantage point so the people could hear.

The crowd grew silent as he stood motionless and seemed to be contemplating. His hair was matted and his broad shoulders were slumped as if he carried the weight of the world. His tunic was of camel hair and his wide leather belt supported a small pouch. These were apparently his only possessions. I could identify with not owning many possessions; they only required more care and this man did not seem to care for worldly things.

He began to speak and his words did, indeed, call for repentance and forgiveness before the cleansing of the baptizing water.

There were, among the crowd, a number of Priests and Publicans from Jerusalem. They began to grow uneasy as John did not seem to exclude them from God's demands for repentance.

This Prophet, John, set the record straight. He informed the crowd that he was not Elijah nor was he the Messiah. "I AM THE VOICE OF ONE CRYING IN THE WILDERNESS - PREPARE YE THE WAY OF THE LORD – MAKE HIS PATHS STRAIGHT!"

The great man continued with his preaching and stated that all shall see the salvation of God. Cornelius became extremely excited and whispered to me. "Did you hear him – Jaacov? – He too said all – that includes me – I too am one of the ALL!" I nodded and realized that my friend Cornelius, the great Roman Centurion, was a true believer and suffered at his exclusion from the social family of the Hebrews.

The "Baptist" began to make his way down to the river and the crowd pressed in on him. As he drew closer I could see the fire of the Holy Spirit burning in his eyes.

One of the Publicans shouted. "Master! – What shall we do?"

John looked directly at the group and with deliberation in his voice, softly, but sternly stated. "EXACT NO MORE THAN THAT WHICH IS APPOINTED YOU!"

The murmur that passed through the group of Publicans was not one of approval. The tax collectors were public officials and made their living from a share of taxes. They were often guilty of taking more than their share and were not popular with the people. The Publicans dealt closely with the Romans, therefore the Hebrew Clergy held them in low esteem. A look of piety swept over the Priest's faces as they felt excluded from this remark.

The "Baptist" slowly turned his head and paused for the crowd to recognized his attention was now focused on the Priests as well as the Publicans.

His voice now rose so all could hear clearly. "O GENERATION OF VIPERS – WHO HATH WARNED YOU TO FLEE FROM THE WRATH TO COME? – BRING FORTH FRUITS WORTHY OF REPENTANCE!" He continued to scold the Priests about their attitude of superiority because of their heritage back to Abraham.

Questions began to be called from the crowd as he spoke of bringing forth fruits worthy of repentance. A voice called. "What shall we do then?"

John paused and stated. "HE THAT HATH TWO CLOAKS – LET HIM IMPART TO HIM THAT HATH NONE – HE THAT HATH MEAT – LET HIM DO LIKEWISE!"

Cornelius could contain himself no longer and my heart jumped into my throat as he called in a demanding voice. "And what shall we do?"

The "Baptist" looked knowingly at Cornelius and softly answered. "DO VIOLENCE TO NO MAN – NEITHER ACCUSE ANY FALSELY - AND BE CONTENT WITH YOUR WAGES!" Cornelius dropped to his knees as John moved away, continuing to speak to the crowd.

Again the Priests began to question John. "You say you are not the Messiah and you are not Elijah – why do you baptize?"

John admonished the Priests again for not following the ancient scriptures requirements to repent and cleanse their sins with water. He boldly stated. "I BAPTIZE WITH WATER - BUT THERE STANDITH ONE AMONG YOU - WHOM YE KNOW NOT; - HE IS IT – WHO COMING AFTER ME IS PREFERED BEFORE ME – WHOSE SHOE'S LATCHET IN AM NOT WORTHY TO UNLOOSE!"

A murmur of excitement rushed through the crowd and heads began to turn and people began to gaze at each other with curiosity. The day waned on with many being baptized. The Priests and Pharisees mingled with the people trying to discredit the "Baptist" but the charisma of the man was, by far, too great.

The night was as festive as before, with the people's spirits soaring with the words of the Prophet. Yes! There was no doubt. John said; the one that was "IT" stood with us this day. Many people, that normally would be cleansed with the water and begin their trek home, simple stayed, hoping to meet the Messiah.

The night grew cool and very quiet as an air of security seemed to blanket the countryside. Cornelius had grown quiet and called me to his side. "Jaacov – do you see any threat here, with this man, John the Baptist?"

I answered. "No – Master Cornelius – but he does upset the Priest and Publicans – You know they will complain to Herod and he will demand Pilate take action."

Cornelius agreed. "King Herod will use that old conspiracy to rebel ploy that seems to be so effective!" Cornelius spoke softly. "Jaacov – you heard the Prophet today – he said to accuse no man falsely – I will report absolutely no threat from this man and urge Pilate to not be influenced by the religious insecurities of the Priests and King Herod.

The Roman grew wistful and his voice took on the tone of a child. His eyes glistened with tears of compassion. "Jaacov – the Prophet said I was to be content with my wages – he means I am in my place as a soldier in the Roman army – OH! Jaacov! – my soul sings with the knowledge that I am still part of this great Plan of Elohim!" He drifted back into a deep stillness as he communed with God.

I left him to his thoughts. It was simple for me. Elohim simply sent me to do his will. He never asked me to do wrong. I was here because God willed it. I slept soundly until my watch.

The dawn came with the promise of another great sermon as the "Baptist" was seeking to quench his hunger. He was moving through the mass of people as if searching and eagerly eating any food offered by the people.

It was noticed the Priests and Publicans had departed. I suppose they were disappointed with their efforts to discredit the "Baptist" and simply returned to Jerusalem to seek an audience with Herod.

I urged Cornelius to make haste on our return so he could forewarn Pilate of the "no threat" condition.

Cornelius was most reluctant to leave. He argued that the Priests would have to arrange an audience with Herod and then plan their strategy, so one more day before returning would still allow ample time to forewarn Pilate.

A wave of activity move through the mass of people as John made his way to the river. This day he did not mount the rise to speak. He immediately began to preach and baptize people.

The river had a most serene look to it. The current that had been present the day before was gone and   stillness lay upon the valley.   We could head the soft ripples of the water as people moved to John and the splash of the water as they were submerged and the sins of life were washed away.

Cornelius, Joseph, the other soldier and me, were standing on the small rise where John had spoken the day before. A quiet fell over the multitude and John found he was alone in the water.

As he looked up to welcome the next person, he saw the crowd had parted on the river bank and a lone man stood waiting. There seemed to be a glow around the figure of the man as he stood dressed in a simple white robe that draped over one shoulder and tied at the waist. There was nothing special about the figure; however, every eye was on him.

The people stood transfixed and I felt a shiver sweep through my body that penetrated my very soul. I knew this figure. There was something about the way the man carried himself that I knew so well.

I placed my hand on Cornelius arm and he softly whispered. "Yes – I know – Jaacov – It is Jesus."

There was no mistaking the way he carried himself and the way he walked. I had seen it as a young child and again as a youth when he was in the Temple.

Jesus stood upon the river bank and John spoke to the crowd. "BEHOLD THE LAMB OF GOD - WHICH TAKETH AWAY THE SIN OF THE WORLD!" Not a sound could be heard.

Jesus moved toward John and he held up his hand to forbid Jesus. "I HAVE NEED TO BE BAPTIZED OF THEE – AND COMEST THOU TO ME?"

Jesus spoke as he continued toward John. "SUFFER IT TO BE SO NOW: - FOR THUS IT BECOMETH US TO FULFIL ALL RIGHTEOUSNESS!"

John baptized Jesus and without another word Jesus walked back to the river bank. The silence was overpowering as all stood transfixed, gazing at the figure of the man on the river bank.

Suddenly the sound of fluttering wings could be heard and a glowing light could be seen descending on Jesus. Within the light was a dove and the beautiful creature landed on Jesus shoulder.

The fluttering ceased and the silence was again shattered as the sound of a great wind came, but there was no wind blowing. The sky grew very bright and we had to lower our eyes so as not to be blinded.

Suddenly the wind ceased and once again I heard the voice from Heaven speak. "THIS IS MY BELOVED SON – IN WHOM I AM WELL PLEASED!"

The multitude of people closed around Jesus and John continued with his baptizing. Cornelius and I decided not to seek out Jesus as he was now for the people and seemed to be set on his chosen path.

We made preparations to depart for Jerusalem the next morning and as we were leaving we saw Jesus walking among the people. John was nearby preaching and commented to his disciples. "BEHOLD THE LAMB OF GOD!"

Two disciples of John immediately began to follow Jesus. Jesus turned and asked. "WHAT SEEK YE?"

They replied. "Rabbi – where dwellest thou?"

Jesus answered simply. "COME AND SEE."

They walked away and we departed for Jerusalem. The trip was very quick as we stopped only to rest the horses. An audience was arranged with Pilate before we even went to the complex. The whole city was a stir with the news of the Prophet and the coming of a new King.

The visit from Herod went as predicted. Pilate placed no credibility on any rebellion and left the course of action in Herod's hands.

Cornelius was furious at the decision of Pilate not to protect John and his movement, but Pilate was convinced that the Hebrew's should handle their own religious differences.

In a few weeks John was arrested. He had been arrested before and released. John had admonished Herod over his marital situation. King Herod had divorced his wife and took, his brother, Phillip's wife as his own. John had publicly held the new wife, Herodias, to be equally sinful.

Cornelius found that Jesus wanted to visit John in Herod's prison and used his influence to arrange the visit. Cornelius said that Joseph, his old friend, had died a few years after Jesus' visit to the

Temple many years ago. Mary still lived in Nazareth and was cared for by Jesus brothers and sister. Cornelius told Jesus I was well and said. "Jesus just smiled as if he knew."

I voiced my concern that Jesus may also be in danger. Cornelius calmed my concern by telling me that Jesus had departed back to his home and the land of Galilee.

Queen Herodias' daughter, Salome, was an accomplished dancer and Herod held her in high regard. Herodias vexed Herod into granting her a favor if Salome would dance a special dance for him. The King agreed and Herodias demanded John's head on a silver platter as the favor. Rumors from the palace indicated that Herod really was not in favor of killing John but had made the promise and was bound to his word.

Cornelius was livid at this act and called for Pilate to take punitive action against Herod. Pilate would not hear of it and it seemed the relationship between Cornelius and Pilate was somewhat strained after that. I really felt sorry for Cornelius as he was torn between his love for God's chosen people and his Roman vows.

The words of John were his only consolation and he lived every day being just in all he did. I felt privileged in serving him.

CHAPTER X

PIRATES

The khah-vah continued to prosper. I suppose the blessings of Rome had something to do with the success, but we treated everyone with respect. I do not remember anyone that was connected with the khah-vah ever leaving to do anything else. The only exceptions were the children of the Roman soldiers that grew up at the khah-vah. The people at the Khah-vah were mostly Hebrew. If there was any Assyrian blood, it was from long ago and there was no Assyrian kinship felt at all. We all believed in Elohim, but the strict Hebrew culture that prevailed in Jerusalem and in the structured Hebrew families did not exist.

We observed the Sabbath and relaxed, but since we had no slaves, the work that had to be done every day, simply was done with no regard as to who had to do it.

Our crops were very abundant as were all the endeavors at the khah-vah. We had no problem paying the taxes. The khah-vah had a network of people that knew the status of all who lived nearby and quite often we would furnish the grain and even the money for taxes for those that fell on hard times.

We still cared for the blemished sheep and annually delivered them to the unclean hills near the Great Salt Sea. I often thought of the robed man in the tattered maroon cloak trimmed with the magnificent gold braid and his words to me about God's Plan. I often wondered if they really did eat people.

A messenger arrived with the news of the Masters death. Adam, my son had arrived in time to keep the vast holdings of the Romans and the Master from falling into the greedy hands of the other business men that profited from Rome's ventures. It seems as Adam had chose the very life he wanted.

This new frontier offered adventure and wealth. It seems the Master upon his death kept his word and the khah-vah was now the property of Rachel's family. Rachel's father and brother were dead and the Uncle had passed away. The next blood relation in line was Adam and he was in Gaul. I was his father and even though I was not a blood relation of the family, the ownership of the khah-vah was indisputably mine. I went to Elohim in prayer, asking why he chose me.

My mind was still in touch with God as I realized I was in the vast wilderness beyond the khah-vah. I had retreated to the wilderness in my desperation to escape the responsibilities placed upon me. My mind screamed in prayer, I was tormented for answers. All I ever really wanted was to tend sheep. I sat upon the sand in the low hills east of the khah-vah and assessed my life.

I still felt as if I were a lad and wanted no burdens, but I did, indeed, have many burdens. I was no longer a lad, but in my forties. I still had much body strength and great endurance. My body was lean and my muscles supple. I was well trained in the use of the sword, lance and in the art of wrestling. I was an equal to any of the skilled Roman warriors. I took no pride in these attributes, but still I knew I possessed them and felt no fear of any man.

I often thought how the Hebrew men sat around and mulled over the plight they felt they were in. The land offered many jobs and the Romans kept peace among the many people around Judea. The khah-vah was a prime example of how people can benefit from working together and sharing equally in the bounty and privileges of the khah-vah. It seemed as Elohim blessed our every effort.

I slept under the stars that night and dreamed of my Rachel. I could feel the warmth of her bosom and embrace as my mind raced back over the years that had passed so quickly. I wondered if I would ever see my son, Adam, again. I placed my head upon my pack and became aware of the leather pouch that held the stones given me by the robed man and the coins from the Master. I reflected on his honesty and good will toward my parents and how he had passed that profit on to me. I hardly ever looked at these valuables as they held only sentimental value of past memories.

I had never shown them to anyone since the Arab man, who had kidnapped Rachel. The contents of that pouch had actually saved my life that day. The stones and denarius had distracted him enough for the terrorized slave woman to drive my sword through his heart.

The blast of the ram's horn startled me from my slumber and I instantly knew it was the call from the khah-vah. I was needed, called the three long blasts. It was not the continuous blasts of imminent danger, but nevertheless the sound brought me back from my nostalgic melancholy. I departed my wilderness haven and within the hour the giant complex loomed into view.

I remembered the site from my youth and reflected on how much it had grown. Outside the walls were numerous small cottages that workers and retired Roman soldiers called home and raised their families.

Cornelius wife had a small dwelling built atop a low hill and often stayed for weeks at a time. She never exercised her assumed authority here as she did at the complex in Jerusalem. Cornelius and Bridget never had children. The woman although considerably younger than Cornelius, was, nevertheless devoted to the great Roman.

Bridget probably had never known freedom. She was taken into servitude by the Romans at an early age. She was apparently of slave descent in her own country and never knew any different, except to serve. She had been too young to have been subjected to that ravages of man and Cornelius was the first man she had ever known. Bridget had grown into a rare beauty and was the center of attention when she shopped for the Roman complex. Everyone knew she was Cornelius's wife and Cornelius was held in high esteem by the Hebrews. Her fair skin, yellow hair and flashing blue eyes were a great curiosity in Jerusalem.

The Hebrews still stayed distant from Cornelius and he had to be satisfied with his small group of servants, soldiers, wife and friends as comrades in worship for Elohim. I too was a believer, but was never perplexed by delusions or the pressures of religious preference.

Pontius Pilate was a typical Roman. He publically showed no preference to any God, but I would notice the graven images of Roman deities around the great home of the Governor.

The constant rumors of the Messiah were growing more prevalent and we knew Jesus was about his Father's business in Galilee.

The people were continually talking about the latest miracle this new prophet performed. There was a story told by the wine merchants that this man could change water into wine and they all wanted him in their employ. It seems that the new Prophet had quite a following. One of the men who followed Jesus, when he was baptized by John, had brothers and they too became his disciples. The Pharisees were particularly concerned with Jesus and had him under constant scrutiny.

The ram's horn had summoned me to the khah-vah and I found a message from Cornelius. The pirates had raised their ugly flag of treachery again in Caesarea. Cornelius was requested to once again go and quell the threat. I was not asked to go, but as I lay on my pallet at the Roman complex, I knew my place was at the side of Cornelius, my mighty Roman benefactor.

Cornelius took a detachment of the younger Romans from both complexes in Jerusalem. He knew that the pirates would be formidable foes and he chose his men carefully. The men mostly were single and relished combat. This was evident by their attitudes in the practice arena. My council was welcome here as I had spared many times with the young Romans.

We departed Jerusalem with a detachment of fifty men for Caesarea. All the men could swim except for me. I elected to march with the troops while Cornelius rode his magnificent white mount. We were an impressive group as we marched in quick time and exited the city. The steps were short but very rapid. The impact of the soldier's feet would shake the ground and brought many people out to witness the march. Many questions were asked and an air of suspicion prevailed. I knew better than to tell of our mission against the pirates so I told a little lie and confided that Cornelius was going to spring a surprise inspection on the troops in Caesarea. He was going to show them what a real Roman soldier was like.

The Roman soldier is a perfect example of a warrior. They are skilled in forming what they call a wedge. The soldiers form an impenetrable line with shields interlocked and lances protruding forward to impale the enemy. Should an adversary get by the lances, the short sword of the Roman will render him harm quickly. The soldiers from Jerusalem were very formidable due to the additional training from Brutus, his son, Joseph and me. We were skilled in close combat of the individual nature.

Brutus was the son of a gladiator and had passed his skill on to his son. Joseph. My friendship with Brutus had provided many friendly matches and my skill rivaled that of Brutus.

The march was pressed and the trip to Caesarea was shortened to only two days. I marched at the rear of the company and became aware of pounding footsteps behind me. I had frequently looked back to assure we were in no danger and the footsteps placed me on alert. I carried my trusty staff that was as effective as any lance. I prepared myself to thrust the lance as I quickly turned and stared straight into the smiling face of Brutus.

He was matching my rapid step and had the face of complete satisfaction, having successfully sneaked up on his old friend. My face revealed my surprise and he burst out in laughter. "My friend would go to war without his best weapon?" He asked.

I have my staff and my sword – Brutus – what more do I need?" I answered.

"Cornelius's wife told me of the rumor of the battle with the pirates –my wife said to remind you that you have Elohim and now you have Brutus!" We marched on in silence. My heart soared with the passion of friendship.

We stopped a few miles from Caesarea and had a meeting. Cornelius thought the idea of a surprise inspection was a good cover, but we needed to make sure of the pirate situation. From experience we knew that the city was in no great danger from the pirates as they used the city as a haven and the local businesses often profited by the ill gotten gains. In the long range, the word would spread that the waters were hazardous and soon trade would simply move elsewhere and then Rome would suffer. It was in Rome's best interest to keep this part of the great sea safe for trade.

Cornelius suggested we send a spy into the city and plant the idea of the inspection and observe if it caused any activity. I volunteered and reasoned it was a perfect cover. I was dressed as the average Hebrew man. My staff did not portray its deadly characteristics compared to the lance of the Romans. My short sword was strapped to my back under my pack and the handle protruding between my shoulder blades did not attract much attention. I was not a picture of threat. Brutus insisted in accompanying me.

Cornelius was very respectful of Brutus intent but strictly forbade him to accompany me. "Anyone can look at you and see Rome dripping from your pores - my friend – that could cause you great problems and may compromise our mission!" Brutus was retired and was here of his own will, but no ex-soldier would ever disobey his onetime commander. Brutus hung his head in disappointment and moved away from the group.

I sought Brutus out and thanked him for his support. Brutus was not fully dressed as a soldier but the leather armor he wore was a dead giveaway. His Roman short hair was also not in keeping with the long hair of the Judean people. I told him of an inn facing the sea and I would meet him there later. He embraced me and did not say a word. I saw his son Joseph walking our way and the two were conversing as I struck out for Caesarea.

My rapid run made short work of the journey and in less than a hour the city came into view. It sprawled along the blue-green shoreline of the Great Sea. The city was not directly on the sea, but back some way with a long sandy beach. The water was full of rock formations and there was only one open section in the reefs to accommodate the ships that were anchored.

It was a great enterprise to unload and reload the ships as many small boats and barges were necessary to move the cargo. The city was a hub of enterprise and every man that wanted work could find it.

I reasoned why the pirates chose this city for its haven. Lookouts could see for miles up and down the coast. Any ships approaching could be identified and the pirates could put to sea and flee before they could be attacked.

Cornelius was going to delay his entrance into the city long enough for me to place myself to observe any activity.

I found the inn and sat at a bench to observe the ships anchored. I counted nine ships of different types at anchor. There were no sails in sight and no small boat activity at all. The port activity was at a standstill.

I purchased a cup of wine and as I sipped the cool beverage a man in a hooded robe sat at the far end of the expanse in front of the inn. The proprietor came out again and the hooded man waved him away without ordering. The Innkeeper stood by my table and wiping his hands repeatedly with his towel said. "Cheap rabble – using my inn and shade to rest their worthless bones!" He directed his attention to me. "So where do you journey from – my paying friend?" His insult was directed at the hooded man.

I had not thought of conversation and had no experience at lying. The little lie I told concerning Cornelius visit to Caesarea was still in my mind. I didn't feel any guilt but I was concerned that I had uttered something that was not true. I reasoned that if you ever lie, you most always remember it and at some time either set it right or lie again to support it. Here was an example of just that. I could not tell the Innkeeper the truth and had to lie again. I knew I was at a disadvantage in lying. I decided to tell as much truth as possible.

I journey from Jerusalem. I answered.

The Innkeeper stood mute. I knew he expected more. I was experienced at listening and knew that in conversation, people give much information in the speaking. I had seldom ever offered more than an answer to the question.

"And your business here?" The Innkeeper continued to wipe his hands.

I answered with the only answer I had experience with. "Sheep"

The silence was uncomfortable. A man some few years older than me shuffled by and the Innkeeper growled a curse. The man stopped and gave the Innkeeper his attention. "All I ever get are the dregs of the earth from Jerusalem!" He motioned toward the hooded man. "That one will not speak and will not buy!" He now points at me. "This one has to have the words pulled from him – and you!" He now looks directly at the man. "You will not pay your debt – you must wait until you can take another ship!" He snapped his towel over his shoulder and stormed into the inn.

The passerby was vaguely familiar. His eyes had the look of a sleaze and I had seen those eyes before. My mind went back in time, but before I could reflect further the man spoke. "You journey from Jerusalem?" He asked.

I nodded.

What is the situation there – I too am from Jerusalem?" I could see his face and knew he was also searching for memory of me.

I answered with a lie, Elohim does not lie, he has no reason to lie, but he told me the lie to tell. "Jerusalem is quiet - the Romans are getting soft and are on the road to Caesarea to inspect the troops here."

The words were like lightening from the sky as the man dashed off kicking up sand from the ground. The Innkeeper stepped from the door and sneered. "Pirate swine – he is lucky to have his life – if the Pharisees knew he was here they would put him in prison or maybe take his life!"

The Innkeeper once again cast a look of disapproval at the hooded man and motioned with his hand for me to have another drink. I nodded in agreement.

It was only a short time when I noticed a great activity along the beach. Some of the skiffs were rowing out to the ships. I began to notice more activity down the beach. Soon there were at least a dozen small craft making their way to three of the ships at anchor.

The Inn keeper came to the door and with a whistle noticed the activity. "Ahhh – things are looking up – they must have spotted a merchant ship – soon – they will return and my pouch will be full once more. I had seen the look riches bring to the face of a leach before. I had seen it on the face of the Arab slave trader just before he died. The Innkeeper's mood greatly improved as he re-entered the inn, whistling the lilting notes of an Assyrian tune.

The hooded man sat silently, I assumed he was asleep as he sat motionless.

I looked down the beach and caught a glimpse of the man that had fled at the news of the Romans coming. His step was deliberate. I thought he was a pirate because of the comments from the Innkeeper, but he did not flee to the ships with the others. He was returning and it was evident he was on a mission.

The man stopped in front of the hooded man and stared at me. He spoke almost under his breath. His voice was trembling with anger and the words hissed as if filled with venom. "You – You – treacherous traitor against your kind!

He took a breath as I sat motionless and only gazed at him. Suddenly I knew the man. My mind went back to the Hebrew warehouse where the merchants were caught cheating on the grain. He was the young man that reached for the sickle on the wall. I had cast my staff to stop him. His face was livid with hatred.

"You have ruined my life!" He hissed. "I had to leave to escape the wrath of the Temple and now have to depend on piracy to fill my belly – I did no more than the corrupt officials that still live in the lap of luxury today!" He pulled a dagger from his belt and took a deliberate step my way.

In a flash the hooded man stood and with a sweep of his robed arm, encased the man in the robe and disappeared around the corner of the inn. I stood in mute astonishment. I gathered my wits and ran to the corner. All that was visible was two trails in the sand as the hooded man dragged the pirate away. I had to reflect in all I had seen. Was it a dream, did it really happen. How could this happen so fast. I returned to my seat and sat once again in mute astonishment.

The Innkeeper once again came out and seeing the hooded man gone, uttered a sigh of relief. He looked at me and realizing I was his only paying customer, softened his customer appeal. "Well! – my weary traveler from Jerusalem – how would you like a bowl of my mutton – who knows – it may be one of your sheep!" He roared with laughter at his humor.

I needed a reason to remain longer so I accepted. I suppose the meal was good, but my concentration was on the ships activities. The ships did not set sail but seemed to make ready for a rapid departure. I counted the men that went aboard the three pirate ships in the harbor. It looked as if the crew were near thirty men per ship. I found no activity on any of the other ships at anchor.

As dark approached a visitor came and engaged the Innkeeper in a brief conversation. He left shortly and began to set oil lamps on stands on the beach. The entire harbor area had lights to allow ships to maneuver at night, but it was obvious these lights were to signal the pirate's ships. There seemed to be no one on the beach that needed to be on the ships, so my reasoning was, at the sign of trouble the Innkeeper would light the signals and the ships would simply get underway and be safely out of the harbor before any harm could befall them.

The Innkeeper returned and assuming I cared nothing for what was transpiring began to give me valuable information. He knew from my attire I was Hebrew. He now observed my sword and noticed my staff. He had no knowledge of the hooded man and my accuser. He pressed close and whispered. "You are a zealot – are you not?" He looked expectantly at me. I am not a very suspicious person and had never realized my attire reflected a rebellious attitude. He took my silence as a positive answer.

He leaned close and whispered. "The pirates are wary of the Roman soldiers that arrived today! - they are ready to depart at the signal - these pirates are an evil lot - but business is business and the Romans want their tax - they cannot find their look out you met today - so I was selected to sound the alarm if the cursed Romans try to make trouble!".

I could not believe how Elohim had blessed me at being at the right place at the right time. I truly believed that we the Hebrew people were his chosen ones and he was simply using the Romans as his tools to do his will.

"Do you need a place to sleep - Sheep man? — I cannot stay up all night and I certainly cannot go to my bed with you sitting in my inn alone!" He was impolitely telling me he was closing. I was not accustomed to being devious and was not making a good spy. I needed to speak with Cornelius so I paid the Innkeeper with the few coins I had left and gave him the balance as a gratuity. He raised his brow in appreciation and bid me good-bye; glancing around to give the impression my imagined secret was safe with him.

Upon arriving at the Roman complex it was later than usual, but the compound was active with preparations for an inspection from Cornelius. Cornelius was a shrewd soldier and knew that a ruse had to be as real as possible to be effective. I had no trouble sneaking into the complex and caused quite a stir when I simply appeared at the conference table where the Romans were making their plans.

It was a simple effort. I scaled the wall at the one blind spot from the guard's tower. I once again scaled to a window by using the vines of ivy that grew on the side of the building. I crept to the room where the officers were gathered. I shed my pack and sword and set my lance against the wall. I stepped back in the darkness of a corner and as a servant walked by with a tray of wine and wafers I simple stepped out and made a hand sign to dismiss him and took the tray. I then proceeded into the room and set the tray on the table and simply stood there. No one, not even Cornelius look up at me. I moved closer and leaned over looking at the map spread before them.

The Centurion that commanded the complex spoke. "We really have no idea how many pirates there may be!" He spoke hesitantly.

"A good count would be close to a hundred or a little less." My voice caused a great reaction. I had good control of the Roman's tongue but it could not hide the guttural accent of the Hebrew. Hands went for swords and daggers in a flash.

The booming voice of Cornelius called out. "HOLD MY ROMAN HEROS!" His voice softened as he saw I was not going to be killed on the spot. "This upstart Hebrew is my friend and aid and now a most remarkable spy!"

The other Romans did not seem to approve of me. They obviously had heard that Cornelius had a Hebrew aid and my free movement among the Romans in Jerusalem was not the norm here. There was a definite air of resentment in the room. My diplomacy was truly going to be tested.

Cornelius spoke. "Romans – set aside your doubts and trust in me - for I tell you – this Hebrew is the match of any Roman and as truthful as your own spirit – now let us hear him!" He returned his focus to a crude map lying on the table.

"Come Jaacov - tell us what you have seen!" Cornelius made it plain that he would tolerate no further internal strife. His mission was to rid Rome of the pirate problem and that was going to happen.

I pointed out the anchored location of the three suspected pirate ships. I told of the manner the crews used for quick escape, using small boats, and of the Innkeeper being used as a lookout. The estimated number of pirates was a surprise to the Romans. They really thought that the count would be higher.

A long discussion followed and everyone offered what they knew of piracy and the methods involved. It was evident a large number of merchant businesses had to be aware and a part of the pirate enterprise.

Seeking information from merchants involved was considered useless as long as the pirates were around. It was decided the pirates must be removed first and then an investigation launched to find the collaborators.

The discussion waned as the night progressed. I began to think of my friend, Brutus, and left to seek him out. He was nowhere in the complex and Joseph, his son, had not seen him since I left them on the road to Caesarea. I wondered if Brutus became discouraged when Cornelius forbade him to accompany me and simply returned home.

I returned to the conference to find a plan had been formed. There would be a great fanfare staged about the inspection by Cornelius. The Romans from Jerusalem would then parade in grand form as they left Caesarea. The soldiers in the complex would stage a great party with much drink and festivities since the inspection was over. They would pretend to be drunk and late in the day begin to relax and fall asleep. Hopefully this would fool the pirate spies and they would send an all clear signal and the pirates would return to town.

The departing Romans that had marched from town would stop as soon as they were obscured from view.

I would stay in Caesarea to observe the pirates. If the plan worked the Pirates should return to the city and begin to quench their thirst from the tension of the last few days.

If this occurred I was to hoist a lantern high above the Inn and a lookout would report to the waiting Romans. Cornelius men would then shed all their armor and with only their short swords and daggers sneak back to the beach. The best swimmers would swim to the three ships and seize control as quietly as possible. A signal would then be sent and the remaining troops would slay the guards on the beach and hid in the boats.

The troops in the complex numbered close to a hundred and would now have stealthily placed themselves in a position to storm the beach. The plan called for all the Pirates to be on the beach. The Romans hiding in the boats would prevent them from fleeing to the ships and any that did make it would be killed by the Romans already on the ships. The troops in hiding would storm from behind and hopefully most all the Pirates would be handled in one decisive battle. Stealth and cunning was of the utmost importance.

The biggest obstacle was getting all the pirates on the beach. The plan now called for someone to raise the alarm and announce the Romans were returning at fast pace to catch the Pirates in town. Hopefully a signal would be sent and the pirates would rush to the beach in order to escape. The plan had to be executed early enough for the Pirates to react and run to the beach.

Cornelius did not want to have to sort through drunks to find pirates. He was very concerned about falsely accusing anyone. John the Baptist words still rang in his ears. Elohim's plan was in action. I stealthily made my way back to the Inn, very much aware of the coins in my pouch placed there by Cornelius. He had smiled as he told me. "I know this is new to you - these coins are the wheels on which society turns – pay your way - my friend!"

I made my way onto the beach as the first boats from the pirate ships slid onto the sand. The departing men began to make their way boastfully toward the Inn. Profanities rained against the Romans for interrupting their routine and many voiced their regret having not done battle. I thought how they would feel in a few hours.

I entered the inn and found the boats I saw were not the first. The inn was full of pirates well on their way to drunkenness. Elohim's plan was working, so far.

A seat was not to be found. I was grateful as the tables were full and there was great pushing and shoving. The profanities were flowing and I was amazed at how many gods were called on to damn the Romans. I was still convinced that even though Rome conquered and occupied, most people were far better off because of them.

Here was an example. Left to do as they see fit, these pirates chose to steal, kill and defame themselves. The very men they cursed were going to bring them to Roman justice. It was the second time I was involved in such an action. Soon the darkness set in and the boats ceased to run. The men in or around the inn numbered well over eighty and I felt that all the pirates that were coming ashore had already done so.

The rear of the inn was very dark and a small hill blocked the view from the approaching coast road to the south. I made my way through the crowded inn and casually took a lamp from the wall. I moved toward the rear door and held the lamp as if to see my way. A gnarled man was slumped against the wall next to the door and looked at me with curiosity. My legs shook from anxiety. I had no fear of the man, I feared no man, but I did fear failure of our plan. These pirates were killers and not the respecters of mankind. If all did not go as planned, the lives of many just men would be forfeited. Cornelius had made it plain that the pirates would be engaged this night.

I made a hand gesture to indicate I wanted to relieve myself. The man smirked knowingly and stepped away from the door. I exited into the cool night air. There was no one around and I trudged up the incline to the top of a low hill. I looked back at the inn and realized I had to be much higher for the lamp light to be seen from far down the coast road.

I quickly took my dagger and cut a bit of the rawhide lacing from my sandal. I tied the lamp to the top of my staff and removed my pack from my back. I unfold my woolen blanket and hung it from the iron tip of the staff to block the lamp light from being seen by the ships. I could still see the faint trace of light from the sunset as I raised the staff as high as I could and waved it from side to side. There was no way to know if the Romans saw me or not, but the plan was set in motion.

I lowered the staff and was refolding my blanket when I was aware of someone standing behind me. I turned and looked up into the snarling face of the gnarled man from the door. His sword was pointed at my throat.

"I knew you were up to no good when you took that lamp – Hebrew – no man takes a light when he seeks to pee!- and now I find a spy and from what I learned -you have connections with the Romans - AHHH! – That is it! –the signal is to the Romans!" His face suddenly changed and his eyes widened with surprise. He gasped and arched his back. The tip of a sword burst from his chest and the man slumped to the ground. Standing behind the man was the hooded figure I had seen before. The hooded man pulled the sword from the gnarled man's body and wiped the bloody shaft on the sandy ground.

"Quickly! - Help me get this pile of dung out of sight - my Hebrew friend!" It was the voice of Brutus, my Roman friend. He had not forsaken me. He had shadowed my every move and had twice saved me.

We carried the dead man to a spot where he could be covered with the reeds washed up on the beach. Brutus and I quickly returned to the inn and I re-hung the lantern on the wall. I ordered two drinks and we exited to the front of the inn.

The time passed slowly and some of the pirates began to leave. We did not attempt to engage them in conversation, but gathered that some had homes and families and where returning to that comfort. It seemed odd that criminals could have a life that was considered normal by some.

I turned my attention to the vague silhouettes of the small boats along the beach. Elohim saw fit to bring clouds that night and only occasionally was the beach washed with any light. I could see the shapes of fleeting figures as the Romans went about their grisly task. Only once did we hear a cry. The scream caught the attention of group of pirates at the front of the inn and one called out. "IS ALL WELL?"

The silence was torturing as Brutus and I prepared to attack the men if they went toward the beach.

Faintly from the boats came a crescendo of raucous laughter. One of the pirates laughed and stated. "I guess sometimes happiness can bring pains of pleasure!" All the pirates within earshot laughed and soon the cry was forgotten.

The waiting was unnerving and some of the pirates grew wary of Brutus and me. Brutus stayed wrapped in his robe and hood, but my obvious Hebrew dress seemed to attract some attention. I felt the eyes upon me and even some suspicious glances went to Brutus.

The noise of merrymaking seemed to diminish as a wave of caution swept through the inn.

From the distance came the cries of someone running and shouting. "The ROMANS RETURN! – THEY MARCH NOW ON THE COAST ROAD – THEY COME IN FULL FORCE - THE ROMANS – THE ROMANS RETURN!

The reaction was instantaneous. The mass of pirates began to flee the inn, stumbling over each other in the process. The Innkeeper made a mad dash to light the lamps along the beach and a bell from down the beach began to toll the warning. In the darkness we could see the figures dashing to the small boats. The sounds of conflict were minimal as the pirates did not suspect any Romans waiting at the boats that were supposed to be guarded.

From the town came the sound of marching feet and from the torches we could see groups of Roman wedges converging on the mass of confused men at the water's edge. The wedges had individual soldiers placed at the rear. These were the men best trained at hand to hand combat. These men were the ones picked by Joseph and myself. They were to engage the pirates that escaped the Romans at the beach. Soon all was quiet. The battle was quite successful and Cornelius had to admonish his men for being jubilant.

The Innkeeper sought refuge in the Inn and acted as if he did not know anything had happened at all.

The morning came and the Romans enlisted the help of every able bodied man in town. Cornelius felt it would be a lesson to the inhabitants and perhaps they would not allow such a lifestyle to invade their town again.

The bodies of all the dead pirates, numbering well over a hundred were placed on the oldest and least valuable of the pirate's ships. The ship had its sails set to take the ship straight out to sea and it was set afire. The thick black smoke from the pitch fed fire could be seen long after the vessel of death disappeared over the horizon. Once again I made note of how the vessel seemed to be sinking. This caused me great concern and I reflected on how I had noticed the same phenomenon on land.

Cornelius held a town meeting in the square at the entrance to the small Temple in town. There were many citizens casting accusations at other citizens, but Cornelius told the multitude that all cases would be heard in the established fashion of the Hebrew court.

I had told Cornelius of the definite involvement of the Innkeeper, but he was reluctant to take action against the man, however, Cornelius's wisdom was at its best that day.

Cornelius told the people that the conflict that day was not aimed at the city of Caesarea but at the pirates that made it their home. He did not apologize for any harm or damage that the town suffered as it was their fault to ever allow the situation to occur. He stressed this was the second time he had to vanquish pirates from Caesarea and if it happened again the town of Caesarea would be destroyed.

He bluntly told the people evil was real and if you allowed evil, then you too were evil. He then brought forth the Innkeeper and gave him a reward for graciously allowing the Roman spies to use his inn to co-ordinate the operation.

I was stunned and did not fully realize what wisdom Cornelius had until we were on the road south and looked back to see the smoke from the burning inn. I then realized that the town of Caesarea was executing their own justice.

Judea and Galilee were ablaze with the preaching of this new Prophet called Jesus. We few in Jerusalem knew he was the Messiah named in the Prophesy. It was of no use trying to tell anyone what we knew.

If a new king was coming, surly he would have a great army and the first thing he would do was rid Judea and Galilee of the Romans.

We heard the stories of how he healed the blind, made the lame to walk, cast out demons and fed the multitudes not just once, but twice. We even heard he had walked on the waters of the Sea of Galilee and brought a boy in Capernaum back to life while being carried to his grave.

Cornelius took particular interest in stories of how Jesus associated with sinners and people that were not Hebrews. He stressed the story Jesus told of how good a Samaritan was in helping a traveler. The Samaritans were despised by most Hebrews.

I began to need more rest than I normally did and shrugged it off to getting old. I was near forty five years of age and in much better shape than most of the Hebrew men, but I was tiring very quickly these last few weeks.

I sat at the table near Cornelius for our evening meal and he was excited about hearing of Jesus coming to Jerusalem to preach in the Temple. He told us the people that now followed Jesus numbered in the hundreds and he drew crowds in the thousands. The Temples and Synagogues welcomed him as the crowds always brought great offerings.

The down side was Jesus often attacked the Priests for their pious attitudes and lack of servitude to the people. There were many complaints from the Priests to Herod and Pilate.

I had no appetite and as I rose to leave the table many dark spots began to circle before my eyes and then blackness set in.

I vaguely remember Cornelius setting by me and praying to Elohim for my healing. I have a recollection of Rachel comforting me in her arms, yet I knew she was gone. The fever raged through my body and I would shake violently with the chill of the sickness deep within me. I had undoubtedly caught some vile disease from the cup of the Innkeeper when in Caesarea.

I was growing weaker as the days went by and have no conscious memory at all. I dreamed of being free in the wilderness with my sheep and of Adam romping with me as a child. Rachel would bring me cool water, but the cup was always just out of reach. I often saw the Great Star in the sky and voices from the heavens would tell me I still had much to do.

While everything was going on it seemed I was under water and was slowly drifting down toward the Great Salt Sea. The robed man would call to me and throw beautiful stones to me. I could hear sheep in the blackness calling for me. A sheep's bladder, fat with air, floated in the water and as it turned I noticed the bladder tubes would slowly seem to disappear into the bladder. The protrusions really did not disappear but as the bladder rolled on the water they would go out of site on the other side. This was repeated over and over as the hallucinations continued.

Days went by and Cornelius and Brutus were sure I was going to die. Occasionally I can remember leaving my stupor and seeing the sky from my window of the khah-vah. I can remember pointing to the terrace and everyone reacted and moved my pallet into the sunshine of the balcony.

Once again I sank into that deep blackness of the nether land and my dreams were plagued with the repetition of hallucination from fever. The slowly rolling bladder continued to plague my dreams. The days passed in a feverish fog.

I became aware of a bright light and the figure of a man in a simple white robe was centered in the light. I could not see his face but I knew the man to be Jesus. I felt a buzz going through my body. It was the same feeling I had so many years ago when, as an infant, he touched my arm. I had felt the surge like lightning when he was child and looked at me. The tingling was the same as a youth when I saw him in the Temple and then later as the dove descended on him at the river Jordan. In my fevered state I saw him raise his hands to heaven and then lower his face to look at me. It seemed as beams of light radiated from his fingertips and caressed my body. The chill of the fever left me and a sense of wellbeing overpowered me and I slept a deep sleep of comfort.

"His fever is gone! – His fever is gone!" The voice of Bridget roused me from my deep sleep. "Summon Cornelius! – Tell him Jaacov lives – JAACOV LIVES!" I heard the words and for the first time in many days I was fully aware of what was around me.

My pallet lay just inside the door to the terrace on the upper rear bedroom of the khah-vah. "Take me into the warmth of the sun!" I weakly asked.

Immediately Bridget and two young maidens pulled my pallet with me still on it out onto the balcony. Bridget brought me a cool cup of water and asked. "Do you hunger Jaaacov?" I thought how odd it was that food seemed to be the balm that soothed all pain.

I nodded and she produced a bowl of cool melon slices that I favored so much. She sat by me and took my head in her lap. She gently began to feed me the succulent melon and the taste instantly spurred my appetite. I grabbed the bowl and began to devour the fruit

"Easy! – Jaacov – Eat slowly – you have not eaten in days! – You will be ill again!" She pulled the bowl from my grasp and dangled a slice of the delight in front of me. I clinched my eyes in exasperation. She laughed. "I feel we have our Jaacov back again!"

The sound of pounding feet could be heard on the stone stairs as Cornelius burst into the room. He stood at the door with his brow dripping sweat from running. His massive chest heaved with the labor of catching his breath.

"Is it not wonderful – Jaacov – Is it not wonderful to know Jesus?" He almost shouted.

I answered feebly. "I saw him in my dream – Sire- He was in my dream and --------! Cornelius cut me off.

"I know – Jaacov! –I went to Jerusalem for herbs and there I spoke with the Pharisee - Nicodemas!" Cornelius eyes were bright with the fire of Elohim as he spoke.

"This Priest Nicodemas is well studied in the Prophesy and sympathizes with the new believers in Jesus - He told me my old friend Flavius the Centurion has retired in Capernaum - He too - is a believer in Elohim and has aided the Hebrews there in building a new synagogue - Flavius's old servant was quite ill and a Priest in Capernaum urged Jesus to go minister to him - Flavius sent a messenger to meet Jesus and said he only needed to say the words and his servant would be healed!" Cornelius words were full of exuberance and his eyes flashed with fire.

"Jaacov! – Nicodemas told me Jesus said; he had never seen such faith and this faith would heal the servant – I prayed there with Nicodemas and I asked Elohim to heal you – Jaacov – in the name of Jesus – I asked in the name of Jesus! – I knew you also were healed!" Cornelius fell to his knees at my pallet and pulled both Bridget and me into his massive arms. He raised his face to heaven and his voice rang with praises to Jesus and God. There was much joy at the khah-vah and I felt warm all over.

As the days passed my strength returned and as I lay on my pallet the dream of the sheep's bladder began to fascinate me. The hallucinations that accompanied the fever were still fresh in my mind. I rose and sat in the great chair on the balcony of my bedroom. I began to study the horizon to the east and noticed I could see just the top of the hill I had visited so many times. It was about an hour's quick walk from the khah-vah. I reasoned, logically, the father away something was it would be smaller, but why was it seemingly sunken in the ground. The rolling sheep's bladder with the small entrance tubes protruding flashed in my mind. In my fevered state I recalled the protrusions apparently were sinking into the bladder, but actually were disappearing due to the bladder being curved. A vision of the hills in the land of the unclean sinking as I moved away flashed in my mind. I sat up with a start. The earth was not flat, it was curved, yes, the earth was curved. It was the only solution that answered this question. Now another question entered my mind. If the earth was curved, why then, did everything not just roll away? OH! – My head began to ache. Enough of these fevered questions. I did not want to be wise. I only wanted my sheep, Rachel, Adam and some cool melon.

Once again I was about the task thrust upon me. Cornelius called upon me for all new dealings with Hebrews. I spent much time around the Temple.

The mistrust of years ago concerning my association with the Romans had disappeared. The people knew I was a simple man to deal with. I knew the values of the different coins and of the products used in everyday commerce.

My only nemeses were the zealots. There were a number of Hebrew men who felt they were not free. I simply could not understand this attitude. They could do as they saw fit as long as they obeyed the laws of Judea and Rome. The laws were for the good and safety of the people. The Romans simply did not harass the people as long as the people behaved.

I will admit that only a few Romans were really good. The attitude of most of the soldiers considered the world to be at their feet. These men were probably one of the main reasons the Hebrew zealots stayed active.

The attitude of Rome was passive as long as the occupied land yielded the resources to satisfy the enormous appetite of the Empire. If that situation was altered, Rome's punitive action was brutal, bold and conclusive. Rome's Centurions and Prefects were generally better educated and more sophisticated than the average soldier. If a situation occurred and it was found the soldier was the cause or used poor judgment, the reprisal was severe. Many soldiers bore the scars of the scourge whip.

The soldiers assigned to the prison were an entirely different breed of men. They had absolutely no feeling for mankind. I suppose this was a trait that was required and sought so the guards would never bond or feel sympathy for the prisoners. The comfort of these men was provided for and Rome discouraged their association with the people. They were the source of Rome's reputation of brutality. Soldiers committing serious offences dreaded being sent for discipline, because they bore the scars for a lifetime.

The average Roman soldier did little socializing in Judea. The complex where Cornelius was stationed had, by far, a mild atmosphere due to Cornelius attitude toward Judaism. The khah-vah was a perfect example of how people could live together in harmony without being bound by daily restrictions or requirements to attain some status of piety. Cornelius's wife, Bridget, was the moral enforcer and had no favorites when her judgment fell on some illicit affair.

She had forcefully removed many prostitutes that overstepped their status. If a soldier presented a problem she had only to bring the attention to Cornelius and he handled it.

Cornelius was a wise man and knew he could not influence every soldier that came onto his complex, but he was keen on instructing every man to respect everyone else's life choices. Cornelius was the senior Centurion in Judea and actually had no command under him, but over the years had collected a group of about forty soldiers that had a similar nature as his. These men were affectionately known as "Cornelius' Cowards." It definitely sounds strange to hear the term coward used in an affectionate manner, but it was, indeed, so.

The men in Cornelius's special group were the quiet and meek. These men were content to be still, considerate, compassionate and listen. It took time for this to occur and I do not think it was ever planned. I think it just happened. These men were like his personal warriors and were often sought for delicate missions. It was the inclusion of these special men that had proved so successful in the pirate venture in Caesarea.

The training of these men included being tutored by Brutus and his son Joseph in the art of man to man combat of the gladiator. I also enjoyed this action as well. The Romans had great respect for me.

Should a new soldier insult one of the "Cowards" or indulge in ridicule, the "Coward" simply took the abuse and would silently retreat. In short order a refresher in hand to hand combat would be scheduled and as luck would have it the offender found himself facing the very "Coward" he had insulted. Rarely did the insulter leave the field without a sound, painful and embarrassing drubbing.

The wave of enthusiasm over a new King continued in Judea.

We received word "JESUS WAS COMING TO JERUSALEM!" The city was buzzing with excitement and Cornelius was ecstatic.

CHAPTER XI

THE PASSION

The Passover was near and the city was filling with people coming to the Temple. All of Judea was murmuring about this new King. Most people knew nothing of the Prophesy, but national pride and patriotism kept the hope of freedom alive in everyone.

Jesus' ministry was not one of conquest or rebellion against Rome. The people on the streets only knew that a new Prophet was in Judea. Our information came from the Rabbis and Priests that constantly had spies watching Jesus and the disciples that followed him.

The ministry of Jesus was one of love, repentance and service to mankind. The Priests of the Temples were fearful that this approach to the welfare of the common man would disrupt their pious authority and somehow reduce their status in the eyes of the people.

One of Jesus followers came to Jerusalem and made preparations for a great reception. His name was Judas Iscariot and he was, from all appearances, the one who handled all the dealings for Jesus ministry. No one in Jerusalem knew the man, but his reputation was one of a zealot. He was reputed to have had dealings with the groups that wanted Hebrews free of Rome. He was most diligent in arranging for the entrance of Jesus into Jerusalem. These things I know for it was my duty to Cornelius to report anything that could cause strife between the Romans and the Hebrews. This man stressed how important it was for the people to welcome the new King.

Pontius Pilate sensed the enthusiasm of Cornelius when he heard Jesus was coming to Jerusalem. Pilate ordered Cornelius to move to Caesarea to keep a close eye on the city and avoid the pirate situation from developing again. Cornelius was furious and felt betrayed by the Prefect, but Pilate felt if any conflict developed between the Hebrews and the Romans over Jesus that Cornelius's judgment and dedication could be compromised. Cornelius obeyed and as a good Roman did a most remarkable job of hiding his disdain of Pilate. He made me promise to keep him informed of all developments.

The atmosphere at the Roman complex changed almost immediately upon Cornelius departure. The Centurion left in charge had no feeling for the Hebrew people at all. The aloofness of the Hebrews did not help the situation. The people of Jerusalem simply went about their daily business and ignored the presence of the soldiers. This attitude had an effect on the Romans and they began to become aggressive in their daily routines. An example being; the detachment of guards that changed four times daily at the Prefects headquarters would march through the streets and ruthlessly force people from their path. I had seen this same action with the simple minded sheep. A sheep would be peacefully grazing and another sheep would simply charge and butt the unsuspecting animal. It was a message that simply stated. "I am here - notice me!"

Tension began to develop in the city as the people grew in their anxiety to welcome the new king. Palm leaves were gathered and placed at intervals along the road leading to the north gate of the city. There was an air of expectancy among the people convinced that Jesus was the Messiah.

The Priests, however were very cautious. Spies sent by the Temple and Herod reported Jesus was not kind in his remarks about the Priests. It was rumored He even had a Publican among his followers. The rumors reported a sermon on a nearby mountain had glorified the poor, humble and peacemakers. Not a kind word or single accolade was directed at the Priests. The whispers of the Priests suggested heresy. This man carried the credentials of a Priest and yet he did not represent his position of piety.

The people of Jerusalem were all astir of the news that Jesus had visited an old friend named Lazarus in nearby Bethany   He found the man had been dead and in his grave for four days. Jesus had ordered the grave stone removed and he brought Lazarus back to life.

The word came that Jesus was on the way to the city. I made my way to the Gate that led to the north and east of Jerusalem. A short walk led to the small town of Bethany and the Mount of Olives. This would be the gate that Jesus would enter. The streets were packed with people.

I was well known by the residents of Jerusalem, but I realized that many of these people were in Jerusalem for the Passover Holiday and had heard of Jesus from far away. The Sadducees and Pharisees were in grand array as they had positions established along the way to greet Jesus. The excitement of the people grew to a fever pitch. The streets were crowded. Resident along the way charged fees for people to climb on their roofs. Some men were even climbing trees.   The Romans discreetly placed themselves along the side streets and simply observed the evolving situation.

I found a spot on a podium at the rear of a group of Temple Priests.   Among the Priests was an acquaintance of Cornelius named Nicodemus. A muted discussion was being held on the possibility of Jesus being the Messiah of the Prophesy. The Priests voiced discontent on the way Jesus' ministry was being conducted and were all in agreement that a true King would not have conducted such a humble ministry.

The Priest, Nicodemus, was unusually quiet and when questioned, he reminded the other Priests that the Prophesy foretold of how the Messiah would come. The group grew silent, but an attitude of sullenness prevailed.

A cry was heard outside the gate. "HE COMES! - HE COMES!" The crowd pressed closer and cheers could be heard. "HOSANNAH! – HOSANNAH TO THE HIGHEST!" People began to place palm branches on the street and some even placed their cloaks and robes for the Messiah to pass on.

I could not believe my eye as the crowd parted and I saw Jesus astride a donkey enter the north gate of Jerusalem. It was not what I expected. I suppose I expected him to be escorted by a multitude of attendants attired in finery and riding on magnificent horses. The scene was most humbling. The Priests were stunned.

Nicodemus uttered a gasp of astonishment. "He rides as our ancient Kings!" He mumbled. "The donkey and a foal of peace – not the mighty horse of War!"

The other Priests were livid and began to lament on how this charade would definitely convince the Romans that the Hebrews were truly a conquered people. Nicodemus said nothing; he simply watched Jesus intently as he slowly passed the podium and never even looked their way.

One of the Priests spoke in a loud voice. "He is nothing more than a peasant – I hear he even dined in the house of the Publican – Zacchaeus - in Jericho!" - Is this what a true King would do? – I think not!" The Priests left hurriedly and made their way to the Temple.

The crowd pressed in on Jesus and much music could be heard as the viols, cymbals and harps began to play. The people burst into song and many hymns were sung.

Jesus never looked my way, but I could see how he had changed from the vibrant young man that was baptized by John only three years ago. His face bore the weary look of his brief ministry. His eyes still blazed with that inner fire of conviction. In my eyes his whole countenance was glowing.

The people continued to shout and raise Jesus' name in praise. "BLESSED IS HE THAT COMES IN THE NAME OF THE LORD! – THE KING OF ISRAEL! - HOSANNAH!"

The crowd slowly made its way through Jerusalem toward the Temple. I followed at a distance and noticed the look of hope in the faces of the people. I looked at Jesus as he touched the extended hands of the pressing crowd and how he would reach out and caress the little children. These people wanted a leader. Here was a man they had never seen, riding on a donkey and they were declaring him a King. I was amazed.

The entourage arrived at the Temple and Jesus slowly made his way inside. He was followed by a group of men that I assumed were some of his closest followers. The Temple guards stopped the mass of people from following Jesus. The Temple guards always monitored the crowd that attended the Temple. A great many of the people began to make their way home or back to their shops as Jesus went into the courtyard of the Temple.

I sat in the shade of the Temple's outer wall and ate a snack of dried fruit and grain I always carried in my pouch.

I bought a small gourd of sweet wine and relaxed in the coolness of the shade. I was very near one of the entrances to the Temple. A hush fell on the usual noisy courtyard inside the entrance. It was as If Elohim had called for quiet.

The voice of Jesus was as I had never heard before. He spoke loudly but with great authority. "IT IS WRITTEN." He paused then continued. "MY HOUSE SHALL BE CALLED A HOUSE OF PRAYER FOR ALL NATIONS." He paused again. His voiced suddenly rose, clearly tinged with anger. "BUT YOU HAVE MADE IT A DEN OF ROBBERS!" The crescendo of chaos that followed brought nearby Roman soldiers at a fast pace, but they stopped abruptly at the entrance.

The Temple guards who had rushed inside as soon as the chaos began, suddenly rushed out while uttering curses against the crazed Prophet inside that had gone berserk with a small animal whip.

Jesus was furious and I stepped into the entrance in time to see him upset a table stacked with coins. The coins cascaded across the stone floor of the outer court as the money changers gave chase in an effort to keep from losing their small fortunes. Jesus continued as he bashed open cages of chickens and other fowls. The curses and vulgarities were definitely out of keeping with what a good Hebrew would expect in a Temple.

Jesus used the small whip to usher the animals from the Temple. The whip actually produced little pain but was mostly an attention getter for the animals. The Temple courtyard was in bedlam and I feared for Jesus' safety. I worried needlessly. Jesus' authority was overpowering. The Temple guards fled. The merchants were cursing but totally involved in recovering their fortunes. The Priests stood in mute astonishment as Jesus continued to clear the courtyard of the merchants and moneychangers. He then left as meekly as he had entered. The melee that occurred was completely out of character for Jesus ministry, but was totally in character of righteous indignation. The Priests immediately retreated into conference to access the situation.

I soon heard that Jesus had been to the Temple before and had angered the Priests by casting out the merchants. This had happened while I was ill. The Priests were incited by Caiaphas, the Chief Priest, to seize and kill him, but Jesus retreated to the wilderness for safety. Since then, Jesus had grown in great favor with the people and now the Priests had to be more subtle.

I followed Jesus and his Disciples a short distance as they left Jerusalem to stay the night in Bethany. I returned to the Roman Complex and wrote a report to Cornelius while the events of the day were still fresh in my mind. It was a most perplexing situation and I hoped Jesus had not caused a rift with the Priests that would present a problem. I still felt Rome had no reason to interfere in any way.

The next day found me at the Temple early. It was not long before Jesus and his Disciples arrived and once again the crowds began to gather. Jesus immediately began to teach and preach inside the walls of the Temple. The Priests gathered quietly in the corners and listened closely as Jesus spoke. I could see some heads nodding in agreement and some would seek another's ear to voice some comment. At times, frowns would pass over the face of the Priests and a discussion would ensue, but there was no effort made to disrupt Jesus' sermons.

A group of Priests moved to the front of a crowd and one of them spoke. His voice was loud, but clearly quivered with caution. "Under what authority do you preach, teacher?" A hush fell over the group. I looked at the faces of the Priests and their faces shown with expectation. "They had him now!" they thought. No man would dare declare they came straight from God.

Jesus calmly turned his attention from the people and looked directly at the Priests. His voice took on a tone of deliberation. "BY WHOSE AUTHORITY DID JOHN PREACH AND BAPTIZE?" – WAS IT OF GOD OR WAS IT OF MEN?" The question was addressed directly to the Priests. A murmur went through the people. John was a martyr and a Prophet; he had been killed by Herod. He was much revered and the Priests knew that denying John was from God would cause a riot. If they did acknowledge that John was sent by God, then why did they not believe him and stop his death.

The looks of dismay on the faces of the Priests gave evidence that this method of entrapment was to no avail. The Priest answered. "We cannot tell you of whose authority John preached."

Jesus' look was one of knowing and with a tone of complacency he answered. "THEN I WILL NOT TELL YOU OF WHOSE AUTHORITY

I DO THESE THINGS!" He immediately turned his attention back to the people and began to tell of a man that had a great orchard that was rich in abundance.

The man left and went afar, leaving the orchard in the care of the people. After some time he sent some servants to collect some of the fruits of the harvest and the people killed the servants. The great man sent more servants and they too were killed. The Lord of the orchard finally sent his son and the son, also was killed.

Jesus looked sad as he continued the story. The master then came and killed all the people and gave the riches of the orchard to others. The people lamented saying: "Heaven Forbid!"

Jesus told of a great stone that builders rejected. This stone then became a great cornerstone. He continued to say all who fell upon this cornerstone would be broken, but whosoever the cornerstone fell upon would be ground to powder.

The Priests had decided to seize Jesus, but were frightened that the people might turn on them. I saw one of their spies speaking to the man called Judas and they retreated into the Temple. Jesus left the Temple and continued to heal and preach as he left the city for the day.

My report to Cornelius was hurriedly sent on its way. It was clear that Jesus was no threat to Rome. He had even given his opinion on Rome's right to collect taxes. Jesus had called attention to Caesar's image on a coin and stated "ONE MUST RENDER UNTO CAESAR THAT WHICH IS CAESAR'S AND UNTO GOD THAT WHICH IS GOD'S!"

The day of the Passover was upon us. There was great jubilation in the city and Jesus continued his teaching and healing. The people were joyful. The Priests had spies everywhere, but no threats were made toward Jesus out of fear of the throngs of people.

As I made my way through the streets I caught site of a servant of the Arimathean a close friend of Cornelius. He was carrying a great jar of water from the city well. We spoke and he asked of word from Cornelius. The servant stated that Joseph the Arimathean missed his frequent discussions with Cornelius about this new Prophet called the Messiah. Joseph was a very rich member of the Sanhedrin. I was acquainted with this man through his close relationship with Cornelius. Joseph was from Arimathea, the north country of Israel.

Cornelius and this man would talk late into the nights about Jesus. He would relate stories from friends that knew Jesus as a youth and told us he followed in his father's footsteps as a carpenter. He also told us after his father's death, the family had bought a farm and was doing quite well.

He had made many visits to the island of Britannia and made his fortune in mining the metals that were there. He had met the Master and brought me letters from my son, Adam.

As we spoke I observed two of Jesus followers. They seemed to be searching the crowd for someone. I pointed the men out to the servant and told them they were Peter and John, close associates of the Prophet.

Without a word the servant shouldered the water and departed for his master's home. As he left the two Disciples caught sight of him and followed, I too followed at a distance. The servant stopped at the door to the Arimathean's home and I could hear the Prophet's followers speak. "The Master saith unto thee - where is the guest chamber that he may eat the Passover with his Disciples?" The men disappeared into the house.

I went to the Roman complex early with anticipation of a long hot bath in the pool of the Centurion. I felt no need to inform Cornelius of any of the day's occurrences. Jesus had preached and healed and now was going to enjoy a nice quiet Passover meal in the home of a friend.

I enjoyed my bath and was deep in a peaceful sleep, dreaming of a starry night sky, surrounded by contented sheep. I was lying by the fire with my head in Rachel's lap telling stories to my son, Adam. Rachel was slowly twinning my temple hair ringlets when I was suddenly awaked by shouts of activity in the complex courtyard.

I could hear the soldiers cursing the pompousness of the Temple Guards. "They had no business taking police action into their own hands!" A soldier shouted. It seems the Temple guards stealthily made their way through town to the Garden of Gethsemane to arrest some usurper. A ruckus had insured and now quite a crowd was gathered at the house of the Priest, Annas.

One of the Roman soldiers began to laugh and spoke. "One of the Prophet's followers cut off an ear of a guard and they say that the Prophet healed it!"

My legs went limp, the usurper was Jesus. My mind went immediately to Elohim. I prayed. "OH! – Mighty Elohim – I heard your voice from the heavens say this was your son – you must not let harm come to your son!"

I hastily dressed and accompanied a small contingent of six Roman soldiers. We raced through the streets in a rapid instep march. I wanted to burst ahead and could have easily done so, but reasoned, if I wanted help from the Romans I needed to reflect my willingness to be part of them.

We could see the mass of people at the gate of the High Priest's house. The misty night was aglow with the blaze of many torches. The air was filled with the pungent smell of the pitch that fueled the flames.

The Temple guards tensed from their relaxed poses as we approached. The Romans stopped and formed a line in the street facing the entrance gate. A Roman soldier from the private guard of Pontius Pilate stepped forward and in a low voice said. "Steady boys! – Steady now! – Pilate says do nothing – this is a religious situation and we must let the Priests and King Herod handle it!"

I silently stepped from the group and made my way to the gate. The guard nearest me took a half step forward as if to block me. I looked directly into his eyes and could see his fear of uncertainty. The man was frightened, not of me, but of the situation. I simply nodded as if I understood and he relaxed and allowed me to pass.

Inside the courtyard were small groups of people discussing the arrest of Jesus. "What has this man done?" A man asked.

"The Priests say he is a blasphemer!" Another whispered

"All he has ever done is good!" A young maiden cried.

A large fire was crackling in the center of the yard and a group was standing for warmth against the chill of the crisp night air. A man's voice asked. "Who brings these charges against this Prophet? – Someone must accuse him – it is the law!"

Another voice answered. "It was one of his own – the one called Judas Iscariot – he was the one who led the Temple guards to Gethsemane and accused the Prophet! – Now - the Prophet is inside being questioned by Annas and the Priests!"

I noticed a tall man near the fire, his face shadowed by the hood of his robe. I knew this man. I moved closer and discovered it was the man called Peter. It was obvious he was trying not to be conspicuous.

The young maiden moved closer to Peter. She too had recognized him. "This man also was with him!"

Peter turned from the fire and uttered. "Woman I know him not!"

Another man took Peter by the sleeve and stated. "Yes – thou art one of them!"

Peter snatched his sleeve from the man's grasp and replied. "Man – I am not!"

A great curtain was pulled aside and inside the room stood Jesus. He was not bound, but simply stood at the center of a group of Priests and Scribes as they hurled insults and questions at him. Also in the room was another of his disciples, the one called John.

In the next hour the questions and blasphemies cast at Jesus were heartbreaking. He was struck repeatedly. I wanted to hurl myself at his accusers and drive my sword into their hearts. It was a new feeling for me. I had never wanted to hurt or kill anyone. I controlled myself; knowing if Jesus could stand so noble and quiet, then I also, could keep my peace.

I moved closer to the group questioning Jesus and overheard a man telling another. "My cousin, Malchus, is a servant of Caiaphas and his ear was cut off by a follower of this Jesus - that follower is here!" He pointed at Peter, standing in the group. "That is the man!"

"Ah! – Yes!" – The other man stepped toward Peter and spoke with confidence. "This man also was with him for he is a Galilean!"

The group turned their gazes to Peter. Jesus raised his downcast eyes as Peter replied. "I know not what thou sayest!" As Peter and Jesus eyes met, a cock crowed in the distance. Peter's face went white and his eyes clinched, as if with pain, he suddenly fled the courtyard.

The Priests began to speak of taking Jesus to the house of the high Priest Caiaphas or King Herod or even Pontius Pilate.

I knew Pilot needed to be aware of the situation. I felt a strong desire to flee to Cornelius, for I knew that he would come and take some action to protect Jesus.

I hastily made my way through the early morning mist to the Roman stronghold of Pilate. The guards knew me as an aid to

Cornelius. I was accustomed to the proper wording of a request for an audience with Pilate. I'm sure the guards thought Cornelius was shortly behind me and soon I was ushered into Pilate's presence.

Pontius Pilate was still in his sleeping attire and clearly agitated at being awakened. He looked at me and leaned to the side as if to search for Cornelius.

I answered. "Sire – My Master is not here- I felt it best to come to you first – the Prophet Jesus has been arrested and ------!"

Pilate raised his eyes to heaven and issued a sigh of exasperation. "I know! – I know! – You Hebrews praise him one day and curse him the next! - Why come to me? – Cannot your Priests or Herod solve this one man crisis themselves?"

"Sire – I fear they will ask for his life and they must come to you for that!" My persona was wavering. I felt the tears of frustration welling in my eyes. I seldom cried, but the scenes of Jesus standing so calmly amid the questions and bearing the pain as men smote him was almost more than I could bear.

Pilate stood and stepped closer to me. He looked at me with an intensity I had never seen before. He spoke calmly. "Hebrew – I have never seen such dedication as I have seen from you to the Centurion Cornelius - yet I understand you are not a slave?"

The Prefect cocked his head in expectation. I answered hesitantly. "I am told I am a free man – I am told I am a wealthy man and I don't really know what that means – I lack for nothing – but Cornelius is my friend and I would die for him!"

"Ahh! – that is what I feared - and Cornelius would die for you and this Hebrew Prophet!" Pilate drew a breath and continued. "I have a great responsibility in this situation – I must keep Rome's interest above all else – I see no threat in this man they call Jesus – but if his sacrifice will ensure peace in Judea – so be it!"

My face showed my disappointment in this decision and I hung my head in desperation. My heart was breaking and I felt helpless for Jesus sake.

The Prefect noted this and with sternness in his voice, spoke lowly. "Hear this Hebrew – if you or Cornelius interferes in this situation and compromises Rome's interest – you lives will be sacrificed as well!   He raised his voice as he ordered. "NOW LEAVE ME!"

My mind reeled as I exited the complex. Dawn was breaking and in the distance I could see a small crowd following a group Priests and Temple guards as they escorted Jesus towards the home of Caiaphas.   I could bear the scene no longer and struck out for the southern gate of the city. My heart was pounding as I ran through the streets. The city was still sleeping, but it would be up and about soon. I wanted no conversation. I didn't want anyone to see me, not me, not this coward that was fleeing not his own death but possibly the death of a good and just Holy Man.

My mind turned to Cornelius. I was betraying my best friend in fleeing, yet my mind told me that Pilate would indeed call for Cornelius' death if he interfered. I ran on.

The miles flew by as I fled south and then to the east of Bethlehem, I avoided all contact with any people. I would seek asylum with the unclean people in the valley that led to the Great Salt Sea. Perhaps if I caught one of the dread diseases then God would pity me and forgive my betrayal.

My mind sought Elohim and I felt a great sense of self pity. Again I was being plagued with these new feelings. I was no longer a youth or even a young man. I was somewhere in my forty fifth year of age. I prayed. "Oh – Great Elohim – Why did you choose me for all these task? – all I ever wanted was to tend my sheep – I was content in the wilderness with only berries and fruits for food – I fought the caracal and the wolf and killed the lion – I loved my sheep – These great things you sent to me should have been sent to great men who were better prepared to handle them – Oh - Great Elohim – you must know – I am only a shepherd!"

I fell to my knees in exhaustion. As a young man I could have run well into the night, but my age prevented me running any further. In the distance I could see the hills around the valley of the unclean rising on the horizon.

A cold wind suddenly blew in my face and as I looked to the heavens I could see a great black cloud in the northwest toward Jerusalem. The clouds were boiling as if angry. The sky suddenly became very dark and the wind started whipping the sand into a frenzy. Exhaustion began to take over and I felt myself slipping into the blackness of unconsciousness. My last vision was of a great flash of light as the hand of Elohim cast a gigantic bolt of lightning that split the sky over Jerusalem. I lay prostrate as the wind blew the sand over my body and a warm rain began to fall.

As the hours passed, Rachel came to me and cradled my heard close to her bosom. As she twinned my locks she softly sang her song of "Brave Jaacov" I protested and told her. "Brave Jaacov is a coward!" It was as if she didn't hear and continued. I could feel the reality of consciousness beginning to take over and resisted. It was pleasant to be near Rachel and feel her caresses.

I was instantly aware I was not alone. I felt no fear. If Elohim saw fit to have a wild beast ready to tear at my throat or the lance of a warrior at my heart, it was the will of Elohim and a coward would not resist.

I opened my eyes and the faint glow of dawn was visible in the east. I slowly raised my head from the sand that half covered my body and scanned the area around me. I suddenly became aware of a robed figure standing on a low rise near my feet. His outline blended well into the darkness, but the dawn light reflected his face and hands as ghostly white. I slowly sat up and raised my hand in a greeting and sign of submission.

The robed figure moved closer and I simply sat to accept whatever fate Elohim had for me. The robed man spoke and chills went through my body. I knew the voice. It had been thirty three years but the voice was the same. It was the robed man from the valley of the unclean.

He spoke softly. "Well young shepherd – you have aged some – but the years seem to have been good to you."

The crimson robe seemed much more frayed than I remembered and the gold brocade was tarnished, but it was the same robe and man. "How do you know I am Jaacov?" I asked.

"One as old as I, knows many things and Elohim speaks to me often." The man was definitely older and as the dawn continued to brighten I saw for the first time his face in detail. It was wrinkled and drawn but clean and without blemish. The old robed man extended his hands and arms for me to see and slowly turned them over. They too were wrinkled and drawn but clean and without blemish.

I looked with astonishment and before I could speak the old man explained. "A great storm came last night and as we - the unclean - spread our skins to catch the fresh water we found it to be as salty as the great sea – the people began to cry out – BEHOLD! - OUR PESTILENCE – IS WASHING AWAY! – The rain was as the tears of God falling. Something was causing Elohim to shed his tears on the earth. His tears that fell as rain washed our sores and pestilence away. The lame walked – the blind could see – the mute could speak and the lepers were cleansed! – We are born again – kind shepherd – the land of the unclean is no more!" The robed man slumped to the ground and I sprang to his side to ease his fall.

"You must rest - my old friend!" I pulled a large rock and placed it behind his back. The robed man sat back and took a labored breath. We sat in profound silence for quite a while as I sorted out the details of his brief recitation. He too was placing this situation is what order he felt Elohim intended it to be.

After resting a bit the old men explained how the blemished sheep had made their lives much more tolerable, over the years and why, after all this time, did he find me, once again, asleep in the wilderness?

I told him all that had transpired over the years and he was particularly interested in the ministry of Jesus. He fully understood the situation that Jesus was in, because the unclean also were outcast. The old man then began to tell me of the significance of the recent occurrences.

The old robed man was a Priest and a Pharisee and had been outcast when he first contacted leprosy. He related how he could not help but minister to the sick and crippled people and the Priests had sent him away at the first signs of sickness. The Temple had never sent any help or sustenance of any kind. The unclean people had been supporting themselves in the hills for centuries and had become outcast to all mankind.

The old Priest was very familiar with the Prophesy and felt that this man, Jesus, was indeed the Messiah that was prophesied. He then told me the tears that fell from heaven were the tears of Elohim as he wept over the death of his Son.

I startled at this and the Priest calmed me by saying this was in the Prophesy. It is prophesied by Isaiah that he would die upon the tree. It is also prophesied that he will rise again and live among his followers. I started again. I and the old man laughed and agreed that this was wonderful news.

The man stopped for a few moments and I asked if he was alright. "Yes – I am well – but you my friend still have much to do."

My shoulders slumped at this statement and the Priest put his feeble arm around me and whispered. 'You have no choice – shepherd – God has chosen you and you must see it through –

believe me – shepherd – if it is a bargain you want – the reward Elohim has for you is well worth the sacrifice!"

I did not doubt the words of the Priest, but the thought that Jesus would live again was urging me to return to Jerusalem.

The people of the valley of the unclean were all going home. Some were old and were going home to die with family. The younger were going home to start new families. It was a wonderful miracle and I felt humble to be witness to it.

I assisted the old Priest in his short journey to Hebron, south of Bethlehem. He was born there and his family could not believe he was cleansed. I took a meal before setting off for Jerusalem. I took a westerly route that would take me to the khah-vah. I wanted to spend some time there before confronting Cornelius.

Along the way passerbies were full of news of a blasphemer being crucified by the Romans. I knew that the Romans only carried out the wishes of the Pharisees and Priests. I went limp upon hearing a witness tell of the scourging of Jesus by the Roman prison guards. I knew how terrible the scourging was as some of the Roman soldiers had endured it as a punishment for crimes against Rome.

Another group of travelers told of the disciple, Judas, hanging himself. They then told that his body was cut down and cast into a field and he lay there still.

The khah-vah was doing well under the management of Brutus. Brutus was an example of how a man can change. As a young man he was compulsive and sometimes a bully as I had witness when we first met. Slowly through his association with Cornelius and his marriage to a Hebrew girl he changed into a kind and gentle man. He was by no means any less a soldier. Being retired to the khah-vah gave him time to hold private classes on hand to hand combat for the Romans that took leave at the khah-vah. His father's training as a Gladiator made him a notable person to have as a friend. I knew this also from our escapade with the pirates in Caesarea.

I rested for a few days at the Khah-vah and the rumors began to arrive that the Messiah had rose from the grave. I wanted to believe it was true, but it is hard to believe that someone who is dead and buried can once again walk and talk. I spoke of my joy and happiness, but deep inside a small voice of reality said I would have to see it to believe it.

CHAPTER XII

SALVATION

I returned to the complex in Jerusalem to find Cornelius there. He was furious at me for not sending word that Jesus was arrested and crucified. He had arrived and immediately went to the tomb of Jesus to find it being guarded by Temple guards. The guards told Cornelius that Pilate refused Roman guards, but gave permission to seal the tomb as best they could. Cornelius found a large stone covered the grave entrance that would require numerous men to move. The Temple guards were very anxious about the followers of Jesus stealing his body.

The next day the tomb was found open and Jesus was gone. The guards had fled to the Priests with the story of a great earthquake that rolled away the stone and apparitions so gleaming white they caused them to fall into a trance. When they awoke the body of Jesus was gone. The Priests then spread the story the body of Jesus was stolen by his followers and bribed the guards to say no different. The Priests even promised to protect the guards if Herod should find out.

One of the Roman soldiers from the complex had been assigned duty at the crucifixion site on Golgotha where Jesus was hung from the cross. He told Cornelius of the last hours and said that he believed Jesus was truly the son of God. Cornelius embraced the man and they both wept. Cornelius was very cold toward me and it caused me great heartache.

Cornelius had confronted Pilate after his visit to the tomb. The meeting was confrontational and Cornelius was ordered from the complex and told to go back to Caesarea and be grateful he was not being punished for his actions.

The city of Jerusalem was alive with rumors of Jesus being alive. The Romans at the site of the crucifixion stated that he was truly dead. They knew death when they saw it.

The guard that had been closest to Jesus gave him some wine vinegar to sooth his thirst and said as soon as he drank it, he raised his eyes to Heaven and said. "IT IS FINISHED – FATHER - INTO THY HANDS I COMMEND MY SPIRIT!" and with a loud shout gave up his life. The soldier stated they thrust a lance into Jesus' side and the clear fluid of death issued from the lung.

Cornelius was still weeping as he departed for Caesarea; he never once spoke to me again. My heart broke and I once again sought refuge in the wilderness.

Weeks went by and I was beginning to look like John, the one who baptized Jesus. It is not hard to survive on the land. I was born in the hilly plains around Bethlehem and food sources were everywhere. Berries and grain grew wild. It was easy to take grain from the shaft and rub it in briskly between your hands. The chafe will release from the grain and you simply blow the chafe away. It is quite nourishing and spring water was abundant for those who know where to look.

It had been some weeks now as I roamed the countryside and I found myself obsessed with finding a lion. I had not seen a lion since I killed the maverick twins that had wreaked havoc with our sheep. I suppose the intensity of tracking such an adversary kept my mind off of Jesus and Cornelius. It was rumored a lion had been seen in the plains north of Bethany.

The road was unusually crowded so I took to the plains and made my way by the Mount of Olives and started west of Bethany. Off to my right was an expanse of olive trees atop a sprawling hill. I could hear singing and the sound of voices, many voices, from within the trees.

As I approached the woods, I began to see many people gathered and talking among themselves.   Nearby, a man spoke. "Remember what he said at the meal – GO YE UNTO ALL THE WORLD AND PREACH THE GOSPEL TO THE WHOLE CREATION!" I turned and to my amazement looked into the face of the man called Peter. He had spoken these words to John, another of Jesus' Apostles.

John spoke and said. "He was stern to us who did not believe until we saw – Jesus said we must remain in Jerusalem until the one the Father promised arrived!"

I looked around and saw many of his followers. I reached for the sleeve of Peter and asked. "Sire – does the Messiah live?" He uttered not a word, he simply pointed toward the hill.

There stood Jesus dressed in a simple white robe standing with his arms outstretched as if to embrace the multitude. My body began to buzz as I stood transfixed. The Savior lives. His face seemed to glow with light from within. I fell to my knees and placed my hands together and gave thanks to the Great Elohim. His son lives.

Jesus looked at me and with a smile he raised his hands and eyes to Heaven.   He raised his voice in prayer and asked the Father to bless us all.

I could not believe my eyes as the clouds above Jesus seemed to boil in the heavens.   A great wind blew and the sound was deafening. As I looked, the entire group fell to their knees and we watched, transfixed as Jesus slowly ascended upwards into the clouds.

Suddenly all was quiet and the soft murmurs of praise and worship could be heard from the people.

A voice called out. "YE MEN OF GALILEE!" We looked down to see two men dressed in gleaming white raiment standing where Jesus had ascended to Heaven. The men continued to speak.

"WHY DO YOU STILL GAZE AT THE HEAVENS?" – THIS SAME JESUS – TAKEN UP FROM YOU TODAY – SHALL COME AGAIN IN LIKE MANNER AS YOU SAW HIM GO UNTO HEAVEN!"

My mind was reeling from what I had seen and heard. Once again, I heard those words "whole creation." God and his son, Jesus was for all people, not just the Hebrews. Cornelius must hear of this. Many stayed and continued to worship as I quietly made my way from the woods and started west through the rugged hills for Caesarea and Cornelius.

Cornelius no longer lived at the Roman complex in Caesarea. His semi retirement had afforded him a home. His belief of the one true God of the Hebrews had put him in great favor with the Hebrew people. However the distance the Hebrews kept on a social level still plagued him. He longed to feel a part of the family of God. I had to seek his home.

Cornelius stood mute and looked at me as if I were a stranger. He had been terribly hurt while I did not inform him of Jesus' arrest. I never told him I fled to the wilderness and knew nothing of his crucifixion. Perhaps my appearance from my weeks in the wilderness rendered me unrecognizable. My heart was breaking as I felt he did not know me.

"He lives – Sire! – He lives!" I spoke with a trembling voice choking back my emotion.

The listless face of Cornelius slowly took on a tone of understanding. "Jaacov? – Is it you – my friend?"

I replied as the tears began. "It is I – Sire – I have seen him – Jesus lives!"

Cornelius and I met in a few steps and our embrace released the tears of two old friends as we shared the wonderful rejoicing of our Savior living.

I held Cornelius and realized he was not the massive man I had once known. He was not frail by any means, but his torso lacked the solid hardness of his youth. Cornelius was in his mid fifties by now and his age was telling. I suppose I had also passed my prime, for I could not maintain my runs for hours as I once did.

The sobs subsided and Cornelius spoke. "Jaacov – my Hebrew brother – I did not realize it at the time – but you probably saved my life by keeping Jesus arrest from me – I did you a terrible wrong – I am truly sorry – can you forgive me?"

I choke back the tears of joy in my heart and responded. "Forgiveness is not necessary when there is no transgression – Sire!".

Cornelius threw up his hands in exasperation. "Sire! – Sire! – I am not your master or your Sire – Jaacov – when will you call me Cornelius?"

My mind reeled with Cornelius' sudden outburst of indignation. I once again simply told how I felt. "I have but one ambition in life – tend my sheep – I had but one wife – Rachel – I have but one son – Adam – I have but one God – Elohim – I have but one Savior – Jesus and I have but one Sire- you! – Please – Sire – I beg of you - don't ask more of me than this!"

Cornelius' face changed into a broad smile as he spoke. "Jaacov – many people take your quiet demeanor for a slow wit – but you are – indeed - a very wise shepherd! – Come you must dine – We have some cool melon and then – for you – a long hot bath and a good grooming!" I noticed that Cornelius did not eat.

I told my old friend all the details of the courtyard happenings and the shameful way I fled when I couldn't cope. I relayed the encounter with the robed man of the unclean and of the magnificent ascension of Jesus. Cornelius was delighted and his face shown with expectation when he heard of Jesus instruction to preach to all creation. He was perplexed with the news that Jesus would return in the same manner as he left. He joked about what would people say when he spent all his time looking at the heavens. I laughed at this humor as well. It was a magnificent night and I slept well.

The next morning, Cornelius was unusually quiet. "Sire – are you well?" I asked.

He paused a moment as if deciding whether to answer or not. "I have been fasting as is the custom of the Hebrews and I had a vision last night – Jaacov – I was preparing for bed –and it was so real." He grew silent once again.

I continued to eat my breakfast. Cornelius spoke again. "Do you ever dream – Jaacov?"

"Yes." I answered simply.

Cornelius looked pensive as I continued eating. In a moment he rolled his eyes and said. "Oh! – I forgot – Jaacov – to get anything from you – it must be pulled from your mind with the rope of a winch.

I did not like to reason with my answers, so I simply tell the truth. "Yes! – Sire - I dream – it is usually only when I am ill and I do not like it - for it keeps me from hearing danger as it approaches!"

Cornelius slowly shook his head and uttered. "Oh! – Jaacov – if only life were that simple for me! – Do you ever dream while still awake?"

"No Sire! – I sometimes see that which I desire – but I always know it is only in my mind." I again answered honestly.

Cornelius went on. "My friend – this was real and I was not asleep! – A man dressed in gleaming white raiment came to me and called me by name – he said – CORNELIUS – YOUR PRAYERS AND GIFTS HAVE BEEN SEEN BY THE LORD AND HE IS REWARDING YOU – Jaacov - I trembled with fear!"

Cornelius continued. "The man told me to send men to Joppa and seek Simon – also called Peter – at the home of Simon the tanner – He will tell us what to do!"

I looked into the eyes of my Roman friend and saw his pleading soul as it reached out for the answer to this riddle. I spoke. "I will go – I will seek Peter for I know him – He is the one I spoke of that denied Jesus in the courtyard and is now his foremost Apostle. I have heard that he too has performed great miracles in the name of Jesus!"

Cornelius stretched forth his arm and placed it on my shoulder. "Jaacov – you are as faithful as the most devout soldier and you have served me continually – take two of my servants and seek this Simon Peter!"

Joppa was only a long day's journey to the south of Caesarea. The town was a resort on the sea shore and had many beautiful gleaming white houses that reflected sunlight far out in the Great Sea. We approached late in the day as the sun was setting in the west.

We made inquiries as to where Peter was lodging and presently stood before the gate of a large house on a cliff by the sea. We inquired for Peter and were told to wait.

The gate opened and there stood the familiar man who stood so tall. Simon Peter, the fisherman that Jesus called from the shore of the Sea of Galilee. He no longer had the look of one with no mission. Gone was the doubt that had perplexed him as he followed the Master. He now had that glow of commitment and true dedication to his new ministry.

"Enter my friends - for a vision has foretold of your coming!" He spoke as we were ushered in to the great hall of the house. We were shown to the seating area and reclined on soft cushions as Peter told of his vision from God.

Peter informed us we were the reason for the vision. He looked at me and said. "You are the strange soldier that is always with the Roman - are you not?"

I responded. "I am not a soldier but a simple shepherd that has served the Roman Centurion – Cornelius – he has been told by a messenger of God to seek you and beseech you come and speak your words to him and his household."

Peter bade us dine with him that night and stay until the morning.

When dawn arrived Peter and some of his followers packed their belongings and we proceeded to Caesarea. The journey took all day and well into the night.

When we arrived at Cornelius' home we found the entire household and many friends had gathered.

Cornelius ran and fell at Peter's feet as if to worship him. Peter commanded. "Standup – for I am also only a man!"

Cornelius rose and led Peter and his followers into his great hall. Upon seeing the large gathering and noticing there were many gentiles he began to preach.

Peter told of the many miracles Jesus performed and his walking on water. He spoke of Jesus' forgiveness of betrayal. Cornelius' eyes met mine and we knew we were also forgiven of our betrayals. Peter told of his vision when God sent a great sheet containing all the common, forbidden foods of the Hebrews. God told him to eat thereof for it was not unclean if God cleansed it.

Cornelius was entranced by Peter's words. Peter looked intensely into the eyes of Cornelius and seemed to choose his words carefully. "You know it is unlawful for a Hebrew to keep company with one that is a Gentile – but God showed me that no man should be called unclean or common."

He paused as if reflecting and then addressed the entire group. Again his words seemed measured. "Therefore I come unto you without seeking compensation as soon as I was sent for – I ask now – why have you sent for me?"

Cornelius spoke. Oh! – Simon Peter – Apostle of our Savior Jesus Christ - I too had a vision!" Cornelius unfolded his vision as Peter listened intently.

Peter opened his mouth and said. "A truth I have perceived from God that he is no respecter of persons: but in every nation the people that fear him and do works of righteousness shall be accepted by him – the word sent unto the children of Israel is to preach the peaceful message of his Son – Jesus Christ - for he is Lord of all!"

A murmur of joy swept through the great hall and Cornelius raised his face to Heaven as the tears streamed from his eyes.

Peter continued. "That word – I say – you now know – as it was taught all through Judea – the word began in Galilee and continued after Jesus was baptized by John – God anointed Jesus of Nazareth with the Holy Spirit and with power – He then went about doing good and healing all that were oppressed of the devil – for God was with him! – We are now witnesses to all these things which he did both in the Galilee and Judea where in Jerusalem they slew and hanged him on a tree!"

There were many there who had never heard of the works of Jesus to this extent and stood amazed.

Peter went on. "On the third day Jesus arose from his grave and did show himself often to us – his followers - and then to the others he chose to be his witnesses!" Peter's eyes met mine and suddenly I knew my purpose in life. My soul rejoiced: this new meaning gave a reason to take every breath, a desire to arise each day I wanted to tell what I knew of Jesus.

My body began to buzz with that feeling I felt each time I had encountered Jesus. I had the impulsion to look around to see if Jesus was there. That is when I noticed some of the people did not fully understand what Peter had said.

In my movements around Judea I had become familiar with many languages and dialects, so I began to explain Peter's words and soon others that could speak different tongues were interpreting as well.

Peter's voice rose above the murmuring of the people. "Jesus commanded us to preach unto all the people and to testify he is the one God ordained to be the judge of the quick and dead! – We the prophets are to give witness that whosoever believeth in him shall receive remission of sins!"

As Peter spoke these words a great rush of wind and thunder rushed through the great hall. Peter raised his hands to Heaven and told of the night they were gathered in Jerusalem for the Feast of Weeks called Shavuot. This feast in called Pentecost in Greek. It was the night God sent the promised comforter. He spoke of the tongues of fire that danced over the heads of the people.

As the people listened their faces began to glow with that inner light that comes from the Holy Spirit. The Spirit filled the souls of all in the hall, Gentile and Hebrew alike. The speaking of tongues continued until all present fully understood.

Soon the magnification of God by the people subsided and Peter once again spoke. "Can any man forbid the cleansing water of forgiveness and deny baptism to all who are here?" A cheer of acceptance resounded and Peter commanded all to be baptized in the name of the Lord.

Cornelius swooned as the water was poured over him and I too felt a rush as no other force could compare. Bridget sat with

Cornelius and lovingly wiped his brow with a cool cloth and then softly scolded him for appearing helpless in front of so many people. Cornelius reminded her he was far from being helpless while in the arms of the Lord. She embraced him and said she had never been so happy.

Peter tarried with us for some days and continued to preach and teach. It was a most wonderful time and we rejoiced continually. I found rejoicing a new feeling and this feeling I liked.

I stayed far too long in Caesarea and longed to be back at the khah-vah. I had ample time to reflect on my life as I took my time in traveling home. I realized I had never sought to deliberately do anything except tend my sheep. It seems as I was always called to do something. I was now called to testify about Jesus. When I met anyone along the way I would ask if they had heard of the Savior. I would tell the whole story if there was time and sometimes would only answer questions from those who had heard. I began to realize that most Hebrews refused to believe. They commented he was only a Prophet and had died. The Savior could not die and would lead the Hebrews back as a great Nation when he really came. I realized that witnessing to the Hebrews may not be effective. I continued, however, for I could not bear the thought that one could be lost for lack of hearing the word.

The years passed and the khah-vah continued to prosper. Brutus' son, Joseph, finished his ten year enlistment and returned to assist Brutus with the horses. The business of the khah-vah was growing as time went by, but Rome's tolerant attitude toward Judaism and the new religion, Christianity, was changing.

The new followers of Jesus were allowed to teach in the Temples for a while, but the Priests were not tolerant of the Christian's belief they could commune directly with God through his Son,

Jesus. The Temples definitely did not care for the reduction in sacrifices.

Rome's attitude had always been tolerant as long as Rome benefitted. As Christianity began to grow it caused great stress in the Roman Empire for there is no room in Christianity for the sins of man. The many temples to gods and goddesses of Rome were losing supporters to Christianity. The pagan cults of the Empire were constantly complaining and Christians were being persecuted in many places.

A new disciple of Jesus came directly from the order of the Pharisees. He was known as Saul and converted to Christianity after being a leader in the persecution movement. He was a great embarrassment to the Priests and they actively harassed him as well as all the other disciples. The Christian movement was forced to meet in seclusion. The man Saul changed his name to Paul and left to preach to the gentiles in the lands of Europe.

The wealthy Arimathean, Joseph, of the Sanhedrin, along with the Priest, Nicodemus, had suffered greatly at the hands of the Hebrew Priests. Joseph decided to conclude all his business in Judea and moved his family to Britannia and manage his mines of precious metals himself. The Priest Nicodemus accompanied him. Peter was crucified in Rome and Paul languished into oblivion in a Roman prison.

The Christians were suffering all over the Roman Empire now. The Emperor Nero had gone mad and set fire to Rome with intent to blame the Christians.

A number of Emperors were murdered at the hands of their own people and the present Emperor had been in power since his success in putting down another rebellion of Hebrew zealots. Jerusalem had suffered great loss when Emperor Vespasian's son, Titus, destroyed the Temple.

The khah-vah was spared due to the Emperor's family being great equestrians and had knowledge of the khah-vah's fine horses.

The Prefect in Judea had change so many times I could not name them all. The present Prefect was Salvienus. He also assumed the title of governor when King Herod Agrippa II died. Rome had much success with the Herodian line of Kings, therefore they would not allow any other family to claim kingship. Rome had a new Emperor, Domitian, brother of Titus that had destroyed the Temple in Jerusalem.

One morning I awoke and found Bridget at the khah-vah gate. She had all her possessions with her. She fell into my arms and sobbed that Cornelius was dead. My heart dropped as I held her in shock.

I carried her to a couch as she sobbed the drama of waking to find Cornelius sitting on the balcony of the terrace clutching to his chest a crude wooden cross he cherished as a symbol of Christ death. "He looked so happy and peaceful!" She cried. "He was my wonderful love and companion – Jaacov - and now - he is gone."

I comforted her by saying. "No! - He is simply not here – Bridget. – Think of him as having gone on a mission – for you will see him once again! – He has gone to be with Jesus and awaits you when you come! – Is it not wonderful to know this most magnificent thing?

"OH! –Yes – Jaacov – He is in Heaven with Jesus!" My heart was heavy, but I felt a sense of great joy knowing that this was, indeed, a true thing. Jesus had died, but I saw him alive and I saw him ascend to heaven and he said all who believed in him would share in that great glory.

Bridget slowly regained her composure and I remarked to myself how such a wild beauty had become such a cultural lady. She bore herself with a definite air of nobility.

I questioned her. "Bridget – why did you not send me word and I would have come to Caesarea?"

She hung her head. "The Romans have no respect for the desires of their dead. – The Romans sent Cornelius back to Rome for a royal burial at his family's Estate. - They have no concern for his wife – they would only think of me as a slave. I was not of Roman birth and could sense I would never be accepted. - I have sold our house and what I have here is yours. - She placed a pouch fat with coins at my side.

I said not a word, but pushed the bag of coins back to her and looked into her eyes as they glistened with tears. The blue of the sky held no match for the gleam they possessed.

"Please! – Jaacov! – Let me live out my remaining years here where Cornelius and I spent so many happy days! – I will be your most obedient servant!" She was almost pleading.

"Of course Bridget!" I answered. You are welcome to live here – but no one here is a servant – you know we all share and share equally."

The woman jumped to her feet and with a swoosh of her blond hair she darted from the room calling to her servants to bring the belongings for they were home and they were all now free. She added. "You are all free – as soon as you get everything packed away!"

I found myself laughing at her enthusiasm and was happy that some of her sadness was lessoned. I felt the deep loss of Cornelius. I was also very tired.

The next morning at breakfast I called all of the khah-vah into the great hall. There were so many people that the doors on the two sides had to be opened so the people could hear. One door opened and I could see the shed were I had first talked with Rachel. The other door opened to the east and the distant hill leading to the far oasis could be seen.

I never imagined so many people were living at the Khah-vah. I never heard harsh words or fits of temper. No one ever seemed angry although we took caution with strangers because we were all Christians.

I spoke of the death of Cornelius and recounted how his covert action saved us all from the tyranny of the Assyrians so many years ago.

Many of the people remembered Bridget and she was most welcome. She never requested the villa she shared with Cornelius many years ago.

Brutus son, Joseph and his family lived in the villa now. Bridget simply moved into the house with the single women and was accepted. She made herself my personal attendant and we had many long talks about life and our experiences. Her life in Gaul was exceptionally harsh and she confessed that even slavery was more comfortable. She was very grateful to Elohim for being spared the ravages of the Roman soldiers.

We spoke of Cornelius and she laughed at his crude actions the first time we met at the oasis. She confided that at first she favored Cornelius only out of gratitude, but as time went by she fell deeply in love with the mighty Roman warrior. We became great friends, this woman of Gaul and I. She attended me well.

I spent a great deal of time on the terrace of my room. The years passed pleasantly and the height gave a good view of the lookout hill and the broad expanse of wilderness that led to the old oasis before Bethlehem. I could not see as clearly as I used to, but spent many a relaxing hour reminiscing over my sheep.

I was transfixed one afternoon and was taking great pleasure in watching a vast flock of sheep coming from the eastern wilderness as the time for shearing was nigh.

Bridget entered the terrace and with her usual cherry voice proclaimed. "You have a caller – wild Jaacov!" Her remark brought instant memories of my Rachel.

I uttered a low growl and whispered gutturally. "Send them up - for I hunger!" She chirped with laughter and skipped away. Her attitude of life was much younger than her years that now numbered in the sixties. I thought for a moment and realized that I was somewhere in my mid eighties and sometimes I really felt the years. I found it uncomfortable sleeping in the wilderness and had long since stopped spending nights under the stars. If I sat for long lengths of time I had great difficulty getting up, and even a harder time walking for a few steps. I tired easily and running was completely out of the question. Still I had great pleasure in life, but spent many hours wondering what God had left for me to do.

A man of mid age stepped onto the terrace and I painfully pulled myself erect from my chair. He was very distinguished and carried a tablet of papyrus hanging in his pouch. There were numerous scrolls as well.

He spoke in very proper Greek. Thankfully I had learned Greek many years ago. It was the language of the merchant and traveler, as well as the scholar. It was also the universal language of the Roman officials. Greek was almost the only language that people wrote anymore.

He introduced himself as Luke from Antioch in the land of the Assyrians. He immediately informed me he was a Christian and had met Jesus' mother, Mary, many years ago. "Tell me – my new Christian friend – are you the one they call "Jaacov the Lion Slayer."

I felt a little embarrassed, but nodded without speaking.

He continued. "Mary the mother of Jesus told me a young shepherd called Jaacov was there the night the Christ Child was born – are you that Jaacov?"

I nodded again without speaking.

He pulled his stool closer and with great intensity looked into my eyes. "Oh! – Jaacov! – Please tell me you can remember that night?"

I spoke. " I could never forget such a wondrous sight! "

He raised his hands to Heaven and fell to his knees giving thanks to God for sending him to me. He began to blurt out his intent and I had to ask him to speak slowly, for I knew Greek, but it was not my natural tongue and he was talking much too fast.

He laughed and slowly began to explain. "I am commissioned by a very wealthy Greek – he is called Theophilus. - He has the authority to seek information of the life of Jesus. - God has anointed me to speak with those that were his witnesses. - The Prefect – Salvienus - has granted me privilege in this task."

He paused and drew a breath. I did not speak. This man, called Luke, took my silence to mean reluctance and his voice took on an air of pleading. "You see! – Jaacov – there is no one else that witnessed that night in the fields near Bethlehem – I have searched and the only ones that saw the great site were the shepherds – and you are the only one left – Oh! – Jaacov – the lion killer – you must tell me of that night!"

I looked into the face of this man and I saw the same fire of the Holy Spirit that shone in the face of Peter and John and my old friend Cornelius. I asked. "Tell me – Sire- does Mary still live?"

He lowered his head and replied. "I think not – for she was quite weak and feeble when I spoke with her. – That was years ago – it takes much time to travel and find these people that were witnesses to the life and works of Jesus. – Now! – Jaacov – Please! – Tell me of that night for there is no other that lives to tell of it!"

My story began at the oasis when I first met Mary, Joseph and my Roman friend, Cornelius. As I spoke, this man Luke wrote with his quill on the tablet of papyrus and frequently would ask for great detail. He was particularly interested in the exact words of the voice from heaven. His eyes would sparkle with joy as I told in great detail of that most glorious night.

I spoke late into the day and at his insistence, we took leisurely meals as he continued to write with great diligence.

As I unfurled my story he would frequently nod his head and murmur. "Yes! – That is what was told by John or Peter or another name, some of them I did not know. As the dark of night approached, I grew cold and asked Bridget to fetch my old cloak. She returned with my pack roll and I unrolled it on my lap. My old leather pouch rolled out and I heard the familiar clink of the stones and coins that were within. The sound took me back the many years to my youth and for a moment I fell silent. The thought entered my mind. "Should I tell this man, Luke, of my most private life? – Deep in my mind a small voice said:"NO THAT SHALL BE TOLD AT ANOTHER TIME.

Luke retired as our guest and I sat reminiscing on the years that had passed. I reflected on the words I had heard so many times. "You still have much to do!" Somehow the words did not plague me as before.

The night was dark and the stars sparkled in the heavens as they did that night so many years ago. I took the stones and coins from the bag and marveled at how they flashed and shined in the light of the twinkling stars. All these years had passed and this great wealth had never been called upon. I thought. "When you have Jesus – you have no need of wealth!"

Suddenly the Heavens flashed so bright I could hardly see. The clinking sounds of the falling stones and coins caught my attention as they scattered on the stone floor of the terrace. My body rose and began to float from the terrace out to the plains of the wilderness.

I looked back at the terrace to see Bridget picking up the stones and coins. She placed them in the old leather pouch and stepped to my chair where an old man reclined. The man was covered by my old cloak and his head lay as if he slumbered. Bridget placed the bag in the hands of the old man and then placed her hand to his forehead. She paused a moment then fell to her knees and buried her face in the bosom of the old man. I could barely hear her sobs as my face turned back to the brightness of the wilderness.

The fields were as green and lush as ever I had seen. A familiar figure waved at me from a low hill. I saw the crimson tunic of the Roman soldier and then the smiling face of my old friend Cornelius. Off to his side were the figures of a man and woman whose faces I could not remember, but instantly knew were my parents. The forms of the old shepherd, Baliue danced into sight and Malisch my friend of my youth waved to me. I was spellbound with wonder.

I seemed to move faster now as a flock of sheep came into view and there in the midst of the sheep on a beautiful patch of soft green grass sat my Rachel. Spread at her side was my pallet with a bowl of cool melon waiting. No words were spoken as I rushed to her side and lay upon my pallet.

Rachel pulled my head to her bosom and began to caress my cheek. The sky was bright with light and I looked to see a lion walking amongst the sheep. The sheep were unafraid as the lion lay down in their midst. As Rachel twinned my ringlets of hair in her fingers I heard a voice from Heaven. "IT IS FINISHED - JAACOV - WELL DONE MY GOOD AND FAITHFUL SERVANT!"

THE BEGINNING

www.ingramcontent.com/pod-product-compliance
Lightning Source LLC
La Vergne TN
LVHW051500080426
835509LV00017B/1848